Upgrading New Zealand's Competitive Advantage

The authors are keen to receive comments and suggestions on the ideas expressed in this book. These can be sent to Graham Crocombe through Oxford University Press, PO Box 11-149, Auckland, New Zealand.

All royalties from this book will be given to a Trust to fund further research, by New Zealand researchers, into aspects of New Zealand's international competitiveness. Enquiries should be sent to Graham Crocombe at the address above, or to the Chief Executive of the New Zealand Trade Development Board, PO Box 10-341, The Terrace, Wellington, New Zealand.

Upgrading New Zealand's Competitive Advantage

Graham T. Crocombe
Michael J. Enright
Michael E. Porter

with
Tony Caughey, Richard Hoddinott, Terry O'Boyle,
Scott Rockafellow, Bettina Schaer, Marie Sheppard,
Jonathan West

*Published in association with
the New Zealand Trade Development Board*

OXFORD UNIVERSITY PRESS
Auckland   Melbourne   Oxford   New York

Oxford University Press

Oxford University Press, Walton Street, Oxford OX2 6DP

OXFORD   NEW YORK   TORONTO
DELHI   BOMBAY   CALCUTTA   MADRAS   KARACHI
PETALING JAYA   SINGAPORE   HONG KONG   TOKYO
NAIROBI   DAR ES SALAAM   CAPE TOWN
MELBOURNE   AUCKLAND
and associated companies in
BERLIN and IBADAN

Oxford is a trade mark of Oxford University Press

First published 1991
© Graham T. Crocombe, Michael J. Enright, Michael E. Porter 1991

ISBN 0 19 558224 1

Cover designed by Chris O'Brien
Photoset in Times by Chromaset
and printed in New Zealand
Published by Oxford University Press
1A Matai Road, Greenlane, Auckland 5, New Zealand

Contents

Foreword

Two years ago, my knowledge of New Zealand was like that of most Americans. It seemed a far away place and evoked images of a rugged but beautiful terrain and a fiercely independent people.

Since then, I have come to know New Zealand much better. Working with my colleague, Michael Enright, and a group of talented and dedicated New Zealanders under Graham Crocombe, I have led an effort to take a deep and fundamental look at the New Zealand economy and the history, national attitudes and institutions that have shaped it. This study reveals many strengths of which New Zealanders can be proud. It also reveals, however, an economy that has fallen out of alignment with the mandates of modern international competition.

This book describes how and why the New Zealand economy is faltering in delivering a high and rising standard of living. It shows how New Zealand's industry has failed to broaden and upgrade its competitive advantages to cope with increasing international competition. It highlights how New Zealands' institutions and policies have retarded the progress of the economy. It also suggests that this decline is not inevitable, but is largely within New Zealander's hands to arrest.

The purpose of this book is to bring a fresh and independent analytical perspective to bear on problems that New Zealanders have been debating for decades and to provide the outline of a blueprint for change. While our recommendations leave many specifics to be worked out, it is New Zealanders themselves who must craft the specific policies that will best match the unique New Zealand context.

The time has come for New Zealanders to develop a consensus for change. Past government policies have failed, and company strategies still cling to past modes of behaviour. There will be some in New Zealand who will take issue with parts of our analysis or some of our conclusions. We welcome constructive debate and even criticism, as long as the result is change. We hope that this book will challenge New Zealanders to do so.

Michael Porter
Harvard Business School
Boston USA
March 1991

It is well known that New Zealand some 40 years ago had one of the highest standards of living in the world and that our economic success was driven by our comparative advantage mainly in agricultural production. What is not well known is how we as a nation can move from our present base to building competitive advantage in a wider range of industries. Our failure to develop and upgrade the competitive advantage of our foreign-exchange earners is well demonstrated by our steady fall down the world's per-capita income table. We have been weak in developing our skill base. We cannot rely solely on our domestic base to increase our standard of living.

The cornerstone of our economic recovery must be foreign-exchange earnings, and the Trade Development Board's mission is to enhance these earnings. As part of developing a strategic direction for the Board's activities, we took the initiative to fund the extensive, independent research programme on which this book is based.

We have been fortunate in having Professor Michael Porter's framework and intellectual stimulus for this study. A work of this size, scope and complexity is not the product of one person, but represents the collective effort of a team and the willingness of hundreds of companies in New Zealand to share their experiences of the past and their hopes for the future.

The rigorous analysis of our economy presented here uses a bottom-up approach, with the research focused primarily at the company and industry levels. From this extensive information-base this book has been prepared. A wide range of issues have been raised. Some need to be addressed by the nation as a whole, others by government. The Trade Development Board, for its part, will continue to focus its efforts on the company and industry level and will advance the key issues in these areas. It has joint-action groups established with our foreign-exchange earning sectors and through these it is already addressing many of these matters, including the upgrading of the infrastructure supporting our industries.

New Zealand's economic problems cannot easily be corrected. The report the Trade Development Board published last year, *A Goal for New Zealand: Ten by 2010*, identified the magnitude of our difficulties and started to map a route forward. The way forward has now been defined much more clearly in this book. All New Zealanders concerned about the future of our economy should read this book. Some of its findings will be hotly debated; however, there is much depth in the work, and I look forward to leading the Trade Development Board, as part of a team with other government agencies and institutions, in tackling the export-related issues involved in upgrading our economy and enhancing our wealth-creation capability.

Barrie Downey
Chairman
NZ Trade Development Board
Wellington
March 1991

Preface

Like many New Zealanders, I have long had a sense that our economy was not performing to its full potential and was therefore unable to deliver the standard of living we aspire to. The ongoing debate on exchange rates, inflation and wage rates always seemed to address only part of the issue. The failure of heavy government intervention in the economy was obvious, yet the early results of a rapid transition to a market economy appeared to hold little promise. I had a gnawing sense that we had not framed the debate in a way which would lead to prosperity.

The seeds of this project were planted when I was in the MBA Programme at the Harvard Business School in the United States. I had the good fortune to study under Professor Michael Porter, whose landmark books *Competitive Strategy* and *Competitive Advantage* had established him as one of the world's leading business economists. At that time, Porter was midway through a five-year research project on the sources of advantage in international competition based on the study of ten leading trading nations. Porter has since published this work in *The Competitive Advantage of Nations*. An exposure to Porter's early findings convinced me that he had developed a different and powerful framework for thinking about New Zealand's economic options.

Professor Porter, who had turned down requests from several other nations, and his Harvard colleague Professor Michael Enright, agreed to donate their time to an independent study of the New Zealand economy. The "Upgrading New Zealand's Competitive Advantage" project, that became more commonly known as the "Porter Project", was born. The project's methodology and intellectual capital have been drawn from Porter's works, and he himself has been an unflagging source of encouragement and insights into the project. Enright, the project co-ordinator for the ten-nation study, provided skills and experience that have been central to this work. Cheng Ong played an important role in getting the project established in New Zealand.

Early in 1990, a project team of New Zealanders, all motivated to make a positive contribution to the economic debate, was assembled with the ambitious objective of completing a study to the standard reached elsewhere in the world in half the time. The core research team that worked full-time on the project throughout 1990 included Tony Caughey, Terry O'Boyle and Bettina Schaer. We were joined in June by Marie Sheppard and Scott Rockafellow. This group all made important contributions to this book. Chris Courtney, Richard Hoddinott,

Linus Kent, Peter Robins, Lisa Sheffield, Anne Vitali, Jonathan West and Nicola Wheeler worked for shorter periods of time over the course of the study.

The public interest nature of the project led us to seek public funding to ensure independence from interest groups and to allow for the widest possible dissemination of our work. The Trade Development Board provided the bulk of the project's funding, without which the scope of our research would have been considerably curtailed. The Trade Development Board also co-ordinated contributions from other government agencies, including the Department of Scientific and Industrial Research, the Ministry of Agriculture and Fisheries, the Ministry of Commerce, the Ministry of External Relations and Trade, the Ministry of Forestry, the Reserve Bank and the Treasury.

This financial support was supplemented with contributions from other organizations. Professors Brian Henshall and Wayne Cartwright of the Graduate School of Business at Auckland University were instrumental in the establishment phase of the project. Professor Cartwright also participated in the industry study process. Ernst and Young provided the project team with office facilities for several months and computer equipment for the project's duration. Megan Jamieson of Ernst and Young undertook the study of the cut-flower industry. Denis Lee of the Ministry of Forestry contributed to the analysis of the forest-products industry. Alan Mettrick, Sandra Young and Nicola Downes of the Department of Statistics provided the project's statistical requirements. Val Pedersen of the Ministry of Commerce provided the project's information requirements during the initial stages. Air New Zealand provided considerable support with domestic and international travel.

Over 400 senior corporate executives and government officials generously gave of their time and insights in extended interviews and industry-related workshops. Over 2,000 executives participated in workshops that reviewed our preliminary findings and provided valuable comments and suggestions, as did many in the media. We experienced time and time again a widespread enthusiasm for the project, and a willingness by a wide cross-section of the community to further its objectives. Of all the things that we learned in the course of the project, this gave us the greatest hope for New Zealand's future.

The project has been the result of the goodwill and hard work of a large number of people, all motivated by a desire to make a positive contribution to New Zealand. Whatever value has been created by the project is a reflection of these diverse contributions.

Graham Crocombe
Project Director
Auckland
March 1991

Introduction

Why has New Zealand's economy underperformed over the last three decades? Why has our relative standard of living fallen from one of the highest in the world in the early fifties to around twenty-third? How did we end up as one of the most indebted peoples on earth? Why, despite one of the most rapid and far-reaching economic liberalizations ever, does our economy continue to languish and unemployment soar? How did New Zealand, which once prospered as a result of international trade, end up unable to pay its way in the world? Why do we appear unable to compete successfully in the global economy?

These questions have been the basis for much debate. However, this debate appears to have generated much heat and very little light. It has produced even fewer results. Not being a people for half measures, we have enthusiastically embraced bold economic strategies based alternately on heavy government intervention (Muldoonism) and unfettered market forces (Rogernomics). The bottom line is that our economic circumstances continue to deteriorate at an alarming rate.

Similar debates have raged around the world. The increasing integration of the global economy, along with rapid advances in technology, have rendered standard paradigms of trade and economic success obsolete. The world is changing but our understanding in New Zealand of these changes and their implications for government economic policy and corporate strategy appears not to have kept pace.

While our economy was once well equipped for economic success and produced a high and rising standard of living, this is no longer the case. In a real sense, the world seems to have passed us by. Improvements in our living standards have not kept pace with other small advanced nations, such as Sweden, Switzerland or Denmark. Some developing nations, like Singapore, now enjoy a higher standard of living, while others are improving more rapidly.

This book sets out the findings of the "Upgrading New Zealand's Competitive Advantage" project, which became known as the "Porter Project". It aims to bring a new perspective, new data and fresh ideas to the debate over New Zealand's economic options and hopefully to serve as a basis for positive action by individuals, companies, unions and government.

The project grew out of, and has become part of, an international study of the sources of national economic success overseen by Professor Michael Porter of the Harvard Business School. The theoretical framework and findings from the study of ten leading trading nations are described in Porter's book *The Competitive Advantage of Nations*. Porter's work, which takes a microeconomic approach that builds on an understanding of competition in actual industries, contrasts with more traditional macroeconomic approaches to the issue.

Using the same methodology as employed elsewhere in the world, a team of New Zealanders, including several graduates of the Harvard Business School, spent over a year studying the competitive advantage of New Zealand and how it might be improved. The first phase in the project was a detailed study of New Zealand's economic statistics. These statistics were used to understand New Zealand's economic performance and its patterns of success and failure in international competition.

Twenty industries in which New Zealand has a disproportionate share of world trade were identified for detailed study. These twenty industries account for over 85% of New Zealand's export earnings. Published data and extensive interviews of senior executives were used to analyse the history and the sources of competitive advantage in each industry. The results of the analysis were presented for comment and verification to each industry in a workshop for the industry chief executives. Over four hundred senior executives participated in this process.

A detailed audit of New Zealand's institutional environment was undertaken to assess its impact on the competitiveness of New Zealand firms and its influence on the ability of the New Zealand economy to grow and prosper. This audit was combined with information from the industry studies where the impact of specific institutions on specific industries was identified.

The different phases of the project were pulled together in a synthesis process, which attempted to integrate our observations of the New Zealand economy in the light of our knowledge of the other nations studied in the original Harvard research.[1] The preliminary results of our work have been presented to over two thousand executives, politicians and officials.

In order to develop a new perspective on our economic options, we have set about building an understanding of the New Zealand economy from the ground up with particular emphasis on our export industries. Why does the supermarket in Munich buy New Zealand kiwifruit and not Chilean? Why does the American farmer buy a New Zealand electric fence and not one made in the United States? Why does a Japanese tourist decide to visit New Zealand and not a range of other destinations? Most importantly, we set out to understand how New Zealand's competitive position has been achieved, and why in some cases it has faltered. An analysis of the patterns of competitive advantage in our export industries allows us to identify the key leverage points and constraints in the economy. Improving our ability to compete successfully in the global economy offers the greatest prospect of improving our standard of living and the quality of New Zealand life.

This book focuses on the New Zealand economy with sufficient foreign examples to place New Zealand in an international context. However, it has also

---

[1] A more detailed description of the methodology is provided in Porter, *The Competitive Advantage of Nations* (1990).

been designed as a compendium to *The Competitive Advantage of Nations*. Those interested in a more detailed account of the theoretical framework or additional information about the economies of other nations should consult that publication.

This volume is organized into seven chapters. The first sets forth an economic goal for the nation and assesses New Zealand's economic performance. The second provides a summary of Porter's framework. The third describes New Zealand's position in international trade. The fourth contains abstracts of four industry studies which are used to highlight particular issues for New Zealand. The fifth describes the determinants of national advantage for New Zealand industry in general. The sixth summarizes our analysis of the economy and provides a brief interpretation of how the present situation evolved. The seventh and last chapter draws a series of implications for New Zealand corporate strategy and public policy.

Our aim in this book is to provide a departure point for a constructive debate on New Zealand's economy and its options. It is not an end, but rather a beginning. We sincerely hope that it will be a contribution to the development of a positive momentum to turn around New Zealand's economic fortunes.

1

Setting the Context

Before beginning a discussion of the New Zealand economy, it is important to place this discussion in its proper context. We must have a notion of the appropriate economic goal for the nation and what determines whether or not this goal is achieved. We must also discuss a means of looking into the economy that provides us with the insights we require.

National Goals

The principal economic goal of a nation is to produce a high and rising standard of living for its citizens. The ability to do so depends on the productivity with which a nation's resources (including labour and capital) are employed. Productivity is measured as the value of output produced by a unit of labour or capital. It depends both on the quality and features of products (which determine the prices they can command) and the efficiency with which they are produced.

Productivity is the prime determinant in the long run of a nation's standard of living. The productivity of human resources determines their wages (or whether they are employed at all), while the productivity with which capital is employed determines the return it earns for its holders. High levels of productivity generate high levels of national income. High levels of national income allow the nation's citizens to improve their physical and material well-being, to trade off work against leisure, and to pay taxes to provide for infrastructure, services, and for the less fortunate.

A rising standard of living, then, depends on the capacity of a nation's firms to achieve high levels of productivity and to increase productivity over time. Sustained productivity growth requires that an economy continually **upgrade** itself. A nation's firms must relentlessly improve productivity in existing industries by raising product quality, adding desirable features, improving product technology, or boosting production efficiency. A nation's firms must also develop the capabilities required to compete in more sophisticated industry segments, where productivity is generally higher. At the same time, the upgrading economy is one which has the capability of competing in entirely new industries. Doing so absorbs the human resources freed up in the process of improving productivity in existing industries. The goal is not to have cheap labour or a "favourable" exchange rate, but rather to support high wages and to command premium prices for the nation's products in international markets.

The Traded Sector

International trade and foreign investment provide both opportunities and threats to boosting the level of national productivity. International trade allows a nation to improve productivity by allowing it to specialize in industries and segments in which its firms are relatively more productive than firms in other nations and to import in industries where they are relatively less productive. Imports, then, as well as exports, are integral in productivity growth induced by trade. Foreign direct investment can raise national productivity provided it involves shifting activities that are less productive in the nation abroad. Foreign investment that supports greater penetration of foreign markets or that frees up resources that can be put to more productive use at home will tend to increase national productivity.

Exposure to international competition creates for each industry an absolute productivity standard necessary to meet foreign rivals, not only a relative standard compared to other industries within its national economy. Even if an industry is relatively more productive than others in the economy, it will be unable to export unless it is also competitive with foreign rivals. If a nation loses its position in high-productivity industries, its ability to sustain productivity growth is threatened. The same is true when activities involving high levels of productivity are transferred abroad because domestic productivity is low. Understanding why a nation can or cannot compete in industries and activities involving high productivity, then, becomes central to understanding economic prosperity.

This book focuses mainly on the traded sector for a number of reasons. The traded sector is a large and increasingly important portion of the economies of all developed nations. The traded sector can provide particular leverage for economic growth. This is especially true for small nations, where international trade can unshackle domestic industries from the constraints of small local markets. International competition has had an increasing impact on the national income of most nations. As a result, international competitiveness has become an important issue in virtually every nation. In addition, the traded sector is where firms from many nations compete. It is in the traded sector where direct comparisons can be made between productivity levels of firms from different nations. It is in the traded sector that one can best see how the economic structures of different nations provide their firms with advantages or disadvantages. The traded sector thus provides a window into the relative performance of national economies.

National productivity is the weighted average of productivity in the traded and non-traded sectors. The non-traded sector is important in its own right and in its links with the traded sector. Efficiency or inefficiency in the non-traded sector can lead to advantages or disadvantages in international competition in the traded sector. Examination of the non-traded sector, however, does not provide the same opportunity for assessing the performance of a nation's firms and institutions in direct competition with those of other nations.

Unit of Analysis

To understand the determinants of productivity and the rate of productivity growth, we must focus not on the economy as a whole, but on **specific industries and industry segments**. While efforts to explain aggregate productivity growth in entire economies have illuminated the importance of the quality of a nation's human resources and the need for improving technology, any examination exclusively at this level must by necessity focus on very broad and general determinants that are not sufficiently complete and operational to guide company strategy or public policy. It cannot address the central issue for our purposes, which is **why and how** commercially valuable skills and technology are created. This can only be fully understood at the level of particular industries.

One finding of Porter's study is that there is no such thing as a competitive nation. Nations and firms succeed or fail in particular industries or industry segments. Each nation has its own pattern of success, and of failure, in international competition. The particular mix of industries that are exporting is more important than a nation's average export share. Only by understanding the patterns of a nation's success and failure in international competition, and then by understanding the sources of advantage and disadvantage of a nation's firms in a series of specific industries, can we determine which of the many features of a nation's economic environment are the most important for productivity growth.

Summary

The principal economic goal of a nation is to produce a high and rising standard of living for its citizens. This goal can only be achieved through high and rising levels of productivity. The performance of a nation's firms in international competition provides insights into a nation's ability to obtain high levels of productivity. The ability of a nation's firms to improve in existing industries and to compete in more advanced industries and segments determines the economy's ability to upgrade over time. A nation's firms succeed and fail in particular industries and industry segments. Aggregate measures provide a useful score-card of overall economic performance, but to understand why and how commercially valuable skills and technology are developed we must go to the level of specific industries.

These concepts provide us with several key questions we must ask in looking at the New Zealand economy. Has the New Zealand economy been able to provide a high and rising standard of living for its citizens? Have we achieved high and rising levels of productivity? What are New Zealand's patterns of success and failure in international competition? Is there evidence that the economy is upgrading? Have we widened and deepened our international position in existing industries? Are we evolving our product mix to industries and segments in which resources are used more productively?

New Zealand's Economic Performance

New Zealand's recent economic performance has been relatively poor. Over the last three decades, New Zealand has experienced a deteriorating relative standard of living, low economic growth, relatively poor productivity, a deteriorating balance of payments, rapidly rising external debt and, until recently, high inflation. More recently, we have seen rapid escalations in unemployment and corporate insolvencies. The discussion of these features here is not meant to be exhaustive; the figures and trends are well known to many New Zealanders. Rather the aim is to provide the setting for the more detailed look at the economy that follows.

Declining Relative Standard of Living. New Zealand's relative standard of living, as measured by per capita GDP, has fallen from the third highest in the world in 1950 to eighth in 1955 to twenty-third in 1987. In contrast, from 1955 to 1987, Switzerland moved from fourth to first, while Sweden moved from tenth to sixth. Singapore and Hong Kong have both passed New Zealand in terms of per capita GDP.[1] While per capita GDP is only one measure of economic performance, others tell a similar story. New Zealand has not been able to generate national income sufficient to maintain its standard of living relative to the rest of the OECD, to other small OECD nations, or to many non-OECD nations (see figure 1).

Poor Productivity. Underlying the relative decline in New Zealand's ability to generate national income has been poor productivity. New Zealand has one of the lowest output per employee ratios in the OECD (along with Turkey, Greece and Portugal). Even more troubling is that we are the worst in the OECD in terms of employee productivity trends. In other words, not only are we one of the least productive work-forces in the advanced nations, our improvement, as measured by labour productivity growth, is also the lowest. We are behind and are falling further behind. There is little evidence of economy wide upgrading of industry (see figure 2).

Increasing Unemployment. New Zealand's unemployment figures indicate that the economy is unable to employ many of our people productively. Over recent decades, government has had a commitment to full employment as a central social and economic goal. As a result, New Zealand's rate of unemployment has been historically low. The government sector has been used to keep unemployment low,

---

[1] A Goal for N.Z.: Ten by 2010, pp. 95 6, NZTDB.

Falling Relative Living Standards

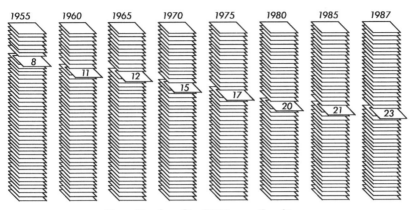

New Zealand's GDP per Capita
Relative to Other Countries

Source : BERL

Figure 1

Poor Productivity Trends

Average rates of change

	1967-74	1974-84	1984-86
GDP per capita			
OECD average	3.2	1.8	2.3
New Zealand	3.0	0.2	-0.3
Labour productivity in business			
OECD average	3.5	1.7	1.7
New Zealand	3.1	-0.7	0.1
Total factor productivity in business			
OECD average	2.2	1.0	1.1
New Zealand	1.9	-1.7	-0.7

Source: OECD, Economic Outlook, Historical Statistics and OECD estimates

Figure 2

and many of those employed in government have not been employed productively. Recent developments suggest that underemployment has been used to postpone unemployment. Failures to improve productivity have meant that unemployment has been put off rather than alleviated. Full-employment policies have masked the problem, but have not addressed its root cause — poor productivity.

Unemployment began to rise in the 1970s. The removal of protection in the mid 1980s resulted in the largest growth in unemployment New Zealand had seen since the Great Depression. Unemployment reached unprecedented levels, with more than 162,000 registered unemployed and over 14,000 on partially subsidized employment assistance schemes.[2] New Zealand's unemployment rate in 1990 was 7.4% compared to the OECD average of 5.9%[3] (see figure 3).

Rising Unemployment

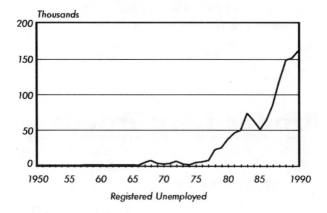

Source: Monthly Abstract of Stats 1954-90
(Latest = October 1990)

Figure 3

Low Compensation Levels. For those with jobs, in the long run, compensation levels reflect labour productivity. Given the relative productivity figures, it is not surprising that compensation levels in New Zealand rank nineteenth in the OECD. New Zealand is falling behind the rest of the world in terms of labour productivity and we are paying the price in terms of high unemployment and lower wages (see figure 4). The deterioration in our relative standard of living reflects this trend.

High Inflation. New Zealand had relatively low inflation rates until the early 1970s. The oil shocks of the early 1970s resulted in high inflation levels in many

---

[2] Department of Statistics, October 1990.

[3] Quarterly Labour Force Statistics, No. 3, OECD, 1990.

Productivity and Compensation Levels

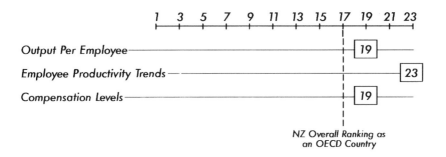

Sources: World Competitiveness Report 1990: IMD

Figure 4

nations. New Zealand's inflation rate, however, peaked at 18%, around five percentage points higher than the world average, and remained higher than most of the industrialized world. Labour market rigidities, a continued commitment to full employment, government deficits and a "cost plus" mentality of a protected business sector all contributed to New Zealand's inflationary difficulties.

In the mid 1980s, reducing inflation became a central economic objective of government. While previous governments had used direct wage and price controls to fight inflation, the Labour government increasingly used monetary policy. The Governor of the Reserve Bank had inflation targets written into his contract. Inflation began to fall in the latter portion of the 1980s largely as the result of an appreciating New Zealand dollar, reduced protectionism and weaker domestic demand (see figure 5).

Many Bankruptcies, Few New Businesses. The rate of bankruptcies and corporate insolvencies rose steadily during the 1980s, with a dramatic increase following the share market collapse. The level has remained high and roughly constant since 1988 (see figure 6). In addition, the rate of new business formation in New Zealand has tended to be relatively low. One study found that New Zealand's rate of new business formation was only 4% (4 new businesses formed per 100 businesses) compared to 5% in Norway, 6% in Ireland and 7% in the United States.[4] While upgrading the economy requires that some industries be left behind and some companies go out of business, we are losing companies at an

---

[4] Bollard, A. (1988), *Small Business in New Zealand.*

Persistent Inflation

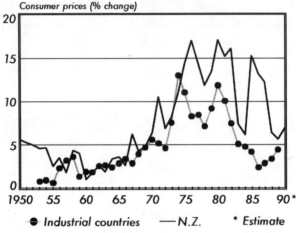

Figure 5

Increasing Bankruptcies and Company Insolvencies

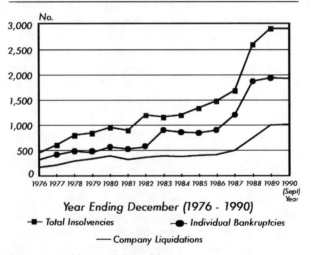

Figure 6

unprecedented rate and are comparatively slow to form new ones. Again, these are not indications of an economy that is upgrading its advantages.

Balance of Payments Problems. New Zealand's position in the international economy has also been deteriorating. The nation's terms of trade have deteriorated over the last forty years (see figure 7). In the 1970s, New Zealand began to encounter severe balance of payments problems. By 1990 New Zealand had been unable to pay its way in the world for fourteen consecutive years. These annual deficits can no longer be seen as a short-term problem. They have become a structural feature of the New Zealand economy and are forecast to continue for several years at high and increasing levels, even by the most optimistic of economic forecasters (see figure 8).

Steadily Declining Terms of Trade

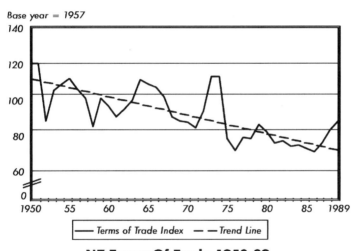

NZ Terms Of Trade 1950-89

Source: Dept of Stats

Figure 7

Huge Foreign Debts. Overseas borrowing has been used to fund the balance of payments deficits, resulting in a rapidly rising external debt. Gross total overseas debt rose from 12.9% of GDP in 1971 to 70.1% in 1990 (see figure 9). Private debt makes up 59% of this debt, and public debt accounts for the remaining 41%. By the late 1980s, New Zealand had become one of the most highly indebted small industrialized countries in the world.[5] The severity of the problem is reflected in

---

[5] IMF Government Financial Statistics 1989: In 1987, New Zealand's gross external central government debt was 29.12% of GDP, ahead of most other small industrial countries except Ireland (only 1982 figures available for Ireland). New Zealand's nearest rival was Belgium, with a gross external central government debt of 19% of GDP.

NZ is not paying its way in the world

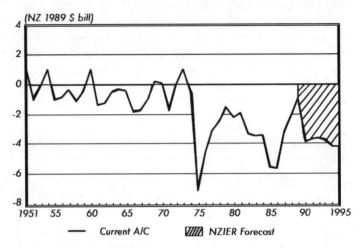

NZ Balance of Payments (1989 $)

Source: Dept of Stats; NZIER

Figure 8

There Is An Accumulated Debt Burden

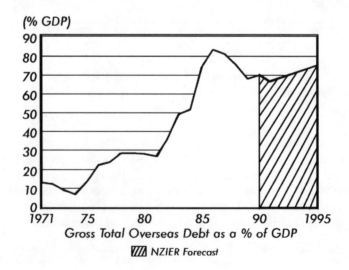

Gross Total Overseas Debt as a % of GDP

Source: NZ Planning Council & NZIER

Figure 9

New Zealand's declining credit rating in international credit markets and high real interest rates.[6]

New Zealand has historically been an importer of capital. However, this has traditionally been applied to building the productive capacity of the economy rather than supporting consumption at levels not supported by our productivity. Recent international borrowing by government has largely been used to fund our social welfare system and poor investments such as "Think Big", while the activities of private sector "investment companies" have also been relatively unproductive. The result has been an explosion in our debt to the rest of the world without the requisite expansion in our productive capacity to service these borrowings, let alone repay them.

Summary

New Zealand's economy has delivered a very poor performance. The economy has failed to generate the income necessary to maintain the nation's relative standard of living. Productivity is relatively low by OECD, standards and the trends are not promising. The economy has failed to generate enough jobs to keep all those wishing to work productively employed. The jobs it has generated pay low wages by OECD standards. Many companies are failing and relatively few are being created. Extensive overseas borrowing has failed to reverse the trend. Instead it has saddled us with a huge foreign debt which will burden the economy for decades to come. The indicators are not of an economy that has upgraded, but of one that has deteriorated. Our efforts have not resulted in high levels of productivity and national income. As a result it is becoming more and more difficult to achieve the standard of living to which we aspire.

---

[6] OECD Historical Tables: Between 1983 and 1988, New Zealand's real short-term interest rate was on average 7.4%, second highest in the OECD. Only Finland had higher real interest rates at 7.9%

2

Determinants of National Competitive Advantage

The Changing Character of World Trade

Over the last 100 years, the structure of world trade has fundamentally changed. In 1888, 76% of world trade was in agricultural products. By 1988 this had declined to 9% (see figure 10). The major growth has taken place in manufactured goods and, in more recent decades, in services. In the 1980s, growth rates in manufactured exports continued to outstrip growth rates in agricultural exports.[1]

Changes in the composition of world trade have resulted in changes in the fundamental dynamics of trade. In today's global economy, success is a function of a nation's ability to develop competitive advantage in advanced industries and industry segments rather than its ability to exploit comparative advantage of inherited endowments of factors of production. In the post-World War II era, resource-poor nations like Japan, Korea, and Switzerland have achieved rapidly rising living standards. In contrast, the economies of resource-rich nations like New Zealand and Australia have experienced difficulty in sustaining strong growth in living standards.

The industries that support a high and rising standard of living today are knowledge intensive. As the global economy has become more integrated, possessing cheap land, labour, or even capital has become less of an advantage. Success in international trade has become more a function of the ability to develop and deploy technology and skills than of proximity to low-cost inputs. Innovation, in the broadest sense of the term, has become vital to success in international competition.

Traditional comparative advantage arguments are no longer sufficient to

---

[1] *GATT: International Trade 1989 90*, vol. 1: Between 1980 and 1989 world agricultural exports grew at an annual average rate of 3.5%, while manufactured exports grew at an annual average rate of 8.0% and trade in services grew at a rate of 7.5% a year.

World Trade is Fundamentally Changing

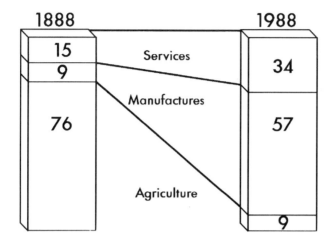

Source : GATT annual reports

Figure 10

explain patterns of trade in the modern world. Most of world trade now takes place among advanced nations with broadly similar factor endowments. Many nations now possess the basic infrastructure and skills necessary to engage in international industrial competition. Competition has globalized in many manufacturing and service industries. Globalization decouples the firm from the factor endowment of a single nation. Raw materials, components, machinery and many services are available to firms in all nations on increasingly comparable terms.

Much traditional thinking has embodied an essentially static view of competition focusing on cost efficiency due to factor or scale advantages. In contrast, the essential character and source of competitive advantage is innovation and change. In order to sustain competitive advantage, nations and firms must continually create and recreate new advantages rather than rely on existing advantages, no matter how favourable in the short term.

Towards a New Theory of International Trade

In his ten-nation study, Porter found that companies gain and sustain competitive advantage in international competition through improvement, innovation and upgrading. These are ongoing dynamic processes, not single once-and-for-all events, which demand continuing commitment and investment both to perceive and act upon opportunities. Porter identified four broad determinants of national competitive advantage that shape the industrial environment to the benefit or hindrance of a nation's firms. The determinants — factor conditions; demand conditions; related and supporting industries; and firm strategy, structure and domestic rivalry — are the forces within a nation that provide firms with the pressures, incentives and capabilities to undertake such improvement and innovation.

Factor Conditions

Factor conditions are the inputs necessary to compete in an industry, such as labour, arable land, natural resources, capital and infrastructure. Factors can be divided into basic factors and advanced factors. Basic factors are those which are passively inherited or created through moderate investment, including natural resources, climate, and unskilled or semi-skilled labour. Advanced factors are those developed through sustained investment in both human and physical capital, such as a modern digital data communications infrastructure or leading university research institutes.

Factors can also be divided into generalized and specialized. Generalized factors are those that can be employed in a range of industries, including a highway system, a pool of debt capital, or a pool of university graduates. Specialized factors are those that are relevant to a limited range or a single industry. Examples would include an optics research institute or a port specialized to handle newsprint.

The most significant and sustainable competitive advantage results when a nation possesses factors needed to compete in a particular industry that are both advanced and specialized. In contrast, competitive advantage based on basic and/or generalized factors tends to be easier to replicate, making them less stable sources of advantage.

The factors most important to modern industrial competition are not inherited, but created. Thus, a nation's stock of factors at any particular time is less important than the rate at which they are created, upgraded, and made more specialized for particular industries. Nations that continually invest in the creation of advanced and specialized factors often translate these investments into industrial success.

Selective disadvantages in basic factors can contribute to sustained competitive success, by prodding firms to overcome the disadvantage through innovation. More surprising, perhaps, is that an abundance of basic factors may undermine rather than enhance competitive advantage. Those with limited resources often use them efficiently, while those with abundant resources are often wasteful.

Demand Conditions

Home *demand conditions* play an important role in the creation of a nation's competitive industries. Even in a rapidly globalizing world economy, the nature of home demand has a disproportionate effect on how companies perceive and respond to buyers' needs. The most important features of domestic demand are the composition of demand, its size and pattern of growth, and the internationalization of domestic demand.

The composition of demand refers to the segment structure of demand, its sophistication and whether or not it anticipates foreign demand. A nation's firms are likely to gain competitive advantage in global segments that represent a large or highly visible portion of home demand, but account for a less significant share in other nations. Firms often succeed in industries where the presence of particularly sophisticated and demanding customers forces them to sharpen their performance at home. A nation's firms often gain competitive advantage in industries where the home demand anticipates foreign demand and therefore gives local companies a clearer or earlier picture of emerging buyer needs. It is the quality of demand in particular industry segments that is critical to success, rather than its size.

National passions are often the basis of successful international businesses, particularly in developing demanding and sophisticated consumers in the home market. A nation's firms are often leaders in industries that are related to some national passion. Americans have an unusually high interest in entertainment (sports, movies, television, records), contributing to American world leadership in these industries. The British passion for gardening plays out in leadership in the gardening-tools industry. Italian appreciation for excellence and flair in design is critical to their competitive success in industries from clothes and shoes to ceramic tiles and fast cars.

Of lesser importance than the composition of home demand is its size and pattern of growth. A large home demand may allow firms to achieve economies of scale in the domestic market. On the other hand, small domestic demand may force companies to explore foreign markets at an earlier stage in their development. Gradually rising home demand may keep companies focused on the domestic market, while a rapidly saturating home demand often pushes them to seek export markets.

A nation's domestic demand can internationalize and pull a nation's products and services abroad. The foreign operations of locally based multinationals are often excellent customers for a nation's firms. In addition, domestic-buyer needs and desires can be transmitted to foreign markets. The United States has "exported" demand for a number of American products, such as fast foods, entertainment and medical equipment.

Firms can selectively tap into foreign pockets of leading-edge demand by using a global strategy. However, tapping superior demand conditions in another country provides no unique advantage and is more often aimed at overcoming a deficiency in local demand conditions.

Related and Supporting Industries

The third broad determinant of national advantage is the presence in the nation of world-class *related and supporting industries*. Related industries are those that share common technologies, inputs, distribution channels, customers or activities, or provide products that are complementary. World-class related industries can provide a nation's firms with sources of technology, ideas, individuals and potential competitors that can be advantages in international competition.

World-class local supporting industries often deliver the most cost-effective or highest-quality input in an efficient and sometimes preferential way. More important is the advantage created by close working relationships. Suppliers and end-users located near each other can take advantage of short lines of communication, a quick and constant flow of information, and an a continuing exchange of ideas and innovations.

Nations typically are competitive in "clusters" of related and supporting industries. The complex web of interactions within these clusters can provide a major source of competitive advantage throughout the entire economic system. Often such clusters are geographically concentrated, making the interactions closer and more dynamic.

It is difficult to obtain the same level of interaction with foreign companies in related and supporting industries as with domestic companies. The upgrading, innovation and spawning of new firms and industries that one sees in clusters of local industries is less likely to occur if a nation relies heavily on foreign-supplier and related industries.

Firm Strategy, Structure and Rivalry

The final broad determinant is *firm strategy, structure and rivalry*, which encompasses the conditions in the nation governing how companies are created, organized, and managed, and the nature of domestic rivalry. Many aspects of a nation influence ways in which firms are organized and managed. Some of these include social norms and attitudes towards business, which are often reflected in government policy. These in turn grow out of the educational system, social and religious history, family structures and other unique national conditions. The socio-political environment structure and context tends to have a distinct impact on the kinds of industries in which a nation achieves international pre-eminence.

Goals, typical strategies and ways of organizing firms vary widely among nations. Although no nation exhibits uniformity across all firms, distinct national patterns are observable. No one strategy, structure or managerial system is universally appropriate. No nation is competitive in every industry. Instead, nations tend to succeed in industries where the strategies, structures and practices favoured by the national environment are well suited to competition in the industry.

The nature of competition and domestic rivalry has a fundamental impact on the international competitiveness of a nation's firms. The presence of local rivals is a powerful stimulus to the creation and persistence of competitive advantage. This is true of small countries, like Switzerland, and of larger countries, such as the United States and Japan. Domestic rivalry provides the essential motivation for firms to make the investments and take the risks to create new competitive advantages. Competition with foreign firms is a powerful stimulant to improvement, but it is rarely an effective substitute for domestic rivalry. The presence of domestic competitors automatically cancels the types of advantages that come from simply being in a particular nation. Companies are forced to move beyond basic advantages to create more sustainable advantages.

Two additional variables can influence the national environment in important ways. *Chance* events are developments outside the control of firms (and usually the nation's government). These events include pure inventions, breakthroughs in basic technologies, wars, and external political developments. *Government* at all levels can improve or impede the national advantage. Both chance and government are best understood through their influence on the four determinants. Chance and government policy can influence each determinant for better or worse.

Chance events are important because they create discontinuities that allow shifts in competitive position. They can nullify the advantages of previously established competitors and create the potential for firms from another nation with a "diamond" more suitable for new and different conditions to supplant them.

Government's proper role is as a catalyst and challenger; it is to encourage — or even push — companies to raise their aspirations and move to higher levels of competitive performance, even though this process may be inherently unpleasant and difficult. Government plays a role that is partial, that succeeds only when working in tandem with favourable underlying conditions in the diamond. Government policies that succeed are those that create an environment in which companies can gain competitive advantage rather than those that involve government directly in the process. It is an indirect, rather than direct, role.

The Determinants as a System

Individually and as a system, the four determinants create the context in which a nation's firms are created and compete (see figure 11). The determinants are mutually dependent and reinforcing. The state of one influences the state of the others as well as their effect as a dynamic system. Favourable demand conditions, for example, will not lead to competitive advantage unless there is sufficient rivalry to cause firms to respond. Domestic rivalry stimulates efforts to upgrade the factor base, helps make domestic demand more sophisticated, and stimulates the formation of new supplier industries.

Advantages in the entire diamond are not always necessary for competitive advantage in simple or resource-intensive industries and in the standardized, lower-technology segments of more advanced industries. In these industries, factor costs are frequently decisive. Competitive advantage in more sophisticated

"The Complete System"

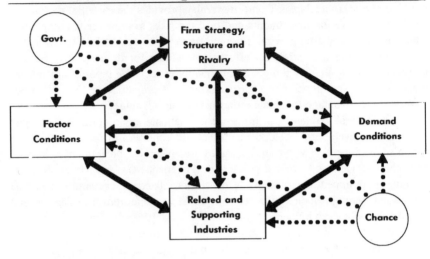

Source: *The Competitive Advantage of Nations, 1990*

Figure 11

industries and industry segments, however, rarely results only from a single determinant. Usually, advantages in several combine to create self-reinforcing conditions in which a nation's firms succeed internationally. This is because competitive advantage in sophisticated industries depends on the rate of improvement and innovation. The co-location of a critical mass of favourable conditions among the determinants is necessary to achieve and sustain competitive success in advanced industries.

Foreign competitors can sometimes duplicate one advantage or another. Moreover, a nation's position vis-à-vis some determinants may not be unique. However, national advantage arises when the system is unique. The entire system is difficult and time consuming to duplicate. The mutual dependence and reinforcement of the determinants are essential to upgrading, and the system is hard to penetrate from another home base. The process of building the system in the nation is also often protracted. Once in place, it allows the entire national industry to progress faster than foreign rivals can.

While the determinants can positively interact to sustain continual upgrading, they can also reinforce each other negatively. Poor investments in human resources combined with a high cost of capital can lead to firms with short-term investment horizons that tend not to invest in building more sophisticated advantages. This can stunt the development of related and supporting industries as well as local demand conditions, all of which can serve to reinforce the negative momentum in the system.

Ultimately, nations succeed in **particular** industries because the home environment is the most dynamic and challenging in that industry. The microeconomic environment stimulates and prods firms to upgrade and widen the advantages critical to success in that industry. No nation's environment has the requirements for success in every industry. The question for New Zealand firms is to identify those industries where they can build and sustain broad based competitive advantage in international competition.

An Illustration

As an illustration of the complete system at work we will use these tools to explain New Zealand's sustained international success in rugby. Why, for over a century, have the All Blacks been the team to beat in international competition? This example underscores how small countries can achieve competitive advantage if the system of determinants acts to stimulate innovation and improvement (see figure 12).

New Zealand has advantages in basic factors. New Zealand's mild winters allow rugby to be played throughout the year, unlike in some countries. The country has thousands of rugby fields, from Eden Park to the local primary-school field. New Zealand men tend to be larger than the average, which can be a definite advantage in a contact sport. These factor advantages do provide a level of advantage for New Zealand in international competition, but they are not decisive. They may be necessary but are not sufficient for sustained international success.

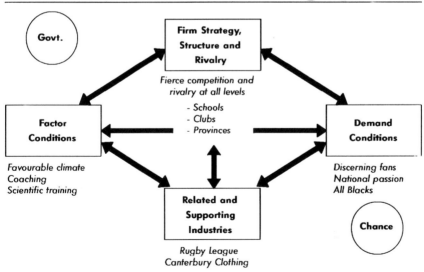

Figure 12

Far more important are New Zealand's advantages in advanced factors. The level of knowledge of rugby in New Zealand is unparalleled. Many New Zealand coaches and players are keenly sought by teams in other nations. "Grizz" Wylie and John Hart simply know more about coaching rugby than their foreign counterparts. New Zealand is a leader in specialist sports medicine and training. Many All Blacks attribute Jim Blair's physiotherapy and training advice as a national competitive advantage for New Zealand. As a result, New Zealand has been the source of many of the game's innovations on the field, such as the rolling maul, and off the field in terms of specialist coaching and training techniques. All in all, New Zealand is very favourably positioned in terms of all the inputs required for success in rugby.

While New Zealand is a small country, rugby is the national sport and, indeed, a passion, unlike in other nations, where it is typically a minor sport. The passion for the sport leads to there being a very knowledgeable spectator base that can be a harsh judge of performance and warm rewarder of excellence. New Zealand's demand conditions are among the most favourable in the world in terms of acting as a stimulant to the development of rugby.

Rugby's pre-eminence in New Zealand has led to the development of a series of related and supporting industries. Radio, newspaper and television coverage is unparalleled. Relatively large markets for rugby videos, books and specialist magazines have developed. The best selling New Zealand books, both at home and abroad, are often related to rugby. International matches and coaching clinics bring tourists to New Zealand. Several New Zealand suppliers of rugby equipment, such as Canterbury International, export internationally. Other sports, particularly rugby league, provide a source of new ideas.

The fact that rugby is a national passion helps it attract and motivate some of the country's most talented sportsmen. Making the All Blacks, particularly a test side, is seen as an outstanding achievement, while the leading All Blacks are national heroes. The great national interest focused on the sport, and particularly the All Blacks, creates additional pressures to perform. There are clear incentives to excel in rugby for both individuals and teams in New Zealand.

The intensity of the rivalry in New Zealand rugby is unparalleled anywhere in the world. The standard of our provincial rugby is on a par with most second-tier international rugby sides, and our better provincial sides can and do beat the top-tier international sides. This strong rivalry is a feature of the sport at all levels — schools, clubs, provincial and international. The fact that we have a single national team is not an advantage. The fact that we have the fiercest local rivalry is.

The Rugby System
The determinants work together as a system in New Zealand rugby. The sport is a national passion that attracts many of the nation's most talented sportsmen. Coaches and players have honed their expertise over decades of tough local competition, under the scrutiny of knowledgeable and demanding fans. A series of related and supporting industries have developed that assist in promoting the sport and developing its competitive advantage. The resulting system is tailored to this

particular endeavour. It is this specialized, interdependent system that is most difficult for other nations to replicate and therefore provides the basis for sustained international success. It is this system that has made the All Blacks the team to beat for over a century.

Stages of Development

National economies exhibit a number of stages of competitive development reflecting the characteristic sources of advantage of a nation's firms in international competition and the nature and extent of internationally successful industries and clusters. The stages address a nation's position in those industries subject to international competition, though they also capture the state of competition in many purely domestic industries. Each stage involves different industries and industry segments as well as different competitive strategies. The stages also differ substantially in the appropriate array of government policies concerning industry. It is **not** inevitable that nations pass through all the stages.

The four stages are: **factor-driven, investment-driven, innovation-driven and wealth-driven** (see figure 13). The first three stages involve the successive upgrading of a nation's competitive advantages. The fourth stage is one of drift and ultimately decline.

Stages of National Competitive Development

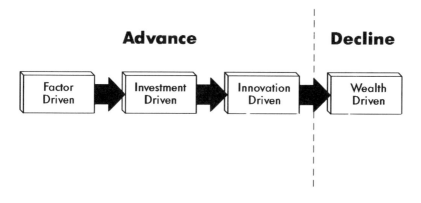

Source: The Competitive Advantage of Nations, 1990

Figure 13

Factor-driven Stage. In the factor-driven stage, virtually all internationally successful industries draw their advantage almost solely from basic factors of production. In the diamond only factor conditions are an advantage. Indigenous technology development is low. Very few of the nation's firms have direct contact with end users. Domestic demand for exported goods may be modest or even non-existent. The economy is sensitive to economic fluctuations and exchange rates.

Virtually all nations have had factor-driven economies at some time. In fact, relatively few nations have moved beyond the factor-driven stage. While abundant natural resources may allow a factor-driven economy to sustain a high per capita income for a time, it will tend to have poor foundations for sustained productivity growth.

Investment-driven Stage. In the investment driven stage, national competitive advantage is based on the willingness and ability of a nation and its firms to invest aggressively. They invest in modern facilities and in complex foreign product and process technology. In this stage, however, foreign technology and methods are not just applied, but improved upon.

Competitive advantages are drawn from improving factor conditions as well as firm strategy, structure and rivalry. Home demand is still generally unsophisticated. Related and supporting industries are still largely undeveloped. This stage is often characterized by rapid increases in employment and the bidding up of wages rates and input prices.

Innovation-driven Stage. In the innovation-driven stage, all the determinants in the diamond are in place in a wide range of industries. The mix of industries in which a nation's firms can successfully compete broadens and upgrades. Consumer demand becomes more sophisticated due to rising personal incomes, higher levels of education, increasing desire for convenience, and the invigorating role of domestic rivalry. The growing competitive strength of the nation's firms also leads to the emergence of sophisticated industrial customers. Clusters begin to form as world-class related and supporting industries develop.

Firms in an innovation-driven economy create new technologies and methods. They compete internationally in more differentiated industry segments. They compete on low cost due to high productivity rather than on low factor costs.

As the economy becomes more advanced, its clusters of competitive industries deepen and widen. It becomes less vulnerable to economic fluctuations and exogenous events. Industries are less vulnerable to cost shocks and exchange-rate movements because they compete on technology and differentiation. The proliferation of successful industries reduces dependence on any one sector.

Wealth-driven Stage. The wealth-driven stage is one that ultimately leads to decline. The economy becomes driven by the past accumulation of wealth and becomes less able to generate new wealth as the motivations of investors, managers and individuals shift in ways that undermine sustained investment and innovation.

Firms begin to lose competitive advantage in several ways. Rivalry ebbs.

Administrators replace entrepreneurs and company builders as senior managers. Firms take fewer risks and innovate less. Employees begin to lose the motivation to succeed. Government policies often focus on redistribution of wealth rather than its creation. The emphasis becomes gaining a share of the existing pie rather than making the pie larger. Rewards are often unrelated to performance. As a result, the nation's firms begin to lose competitive advantage to foreign firms.

3

New Zealand's Position in International Competition

An examination of changes in world trading patterns, and New Zealand's place within them, provides important insights into the deteriorating trends which have emerged in New Zealand's economic indicators. The international competitiveness of New Zealand's export sector provides a window into the strengths and weaknesses of our entire economy.

Patterns of New Zealand Competitiveness

No nation is competitive in every industry. Nations show clear patterns of success and failure in international competition; they succeed in some types of industries and they fail in others. These patterns are the function of a complex web of interrelationships between the social and economic structures within a nation that facilitate success in different industries and make it difficult for that nation to achieve success in other industries. These patterns show the state of development of a nation's economy. They can show if the nation's firms are successful in industries that provide the promise of future profits and growth. They can show if the nation's firms are widening and deepening their sources of advantage. They can show whether or not the nation's economy has upgraded over time.

Improving the international competitiveness of the private sector is fundamental to New Zealand's future. Trade is important to the New Zealand economy because it provides a channel to break the constraints of its small size. New Zealand cannot rely solely on the domestic base to increase its standard of living. New Zealand's traded sector already accounts for a significant portion of the economy (26% of GDP), though this portion is lower than that of several other small advanced nations (see figure 14).[1]

---

[1] The Netherlands figure (exports equal to 52% of GDP) includes significant entrepôt trade.

Potential for Growth in Trade

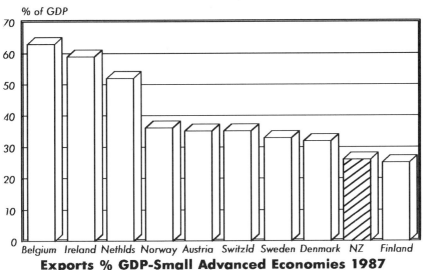

Exports % GDP-Small Advanced Economies 1987

Source: World Development Report 1989

Figure 14

New Zealand's long-term adjustment to the new global economic order has been poor. Our exports are still predominately resource-based commodities. In 1987, New Zealand earned 69% of export revenues from primary commodities. This compared to an OECD average of only 12%. Although manufactured exports have grown, making up 25% of New Zealand's exports in 1987, the OECD average of 80% remains substantially higher.[2]

The Structure of New Zealand's Trade

The structure of New Zealand's trade indicates that the country still relies on the exploitation of favourable natural conditions, rather than on the creation of new, ever more sophisticated advantages. The charts in Appendices 1 and 6 illustrate the patterns of national advantage in New Zealand and the ways in which they have changed.[3]

Narrow Range of Leading Products. The types of industries in which a nation does best in international competition provide insights into the national economy. New Zealand had very large shares of world exports in certain industries in 1987 (see figure 15). In kiwifruit, New Zealand's share of world exports was estimated at

[2] *World Development Report 1989*, World Bank.

[3] Appendices are located after the Statistics section at the end of the book.

Top 25 NZ Export Industries by World Export Share

1. Kiwifruit
2. Sheepmeat
3. Wool, scoured
4. Chemical wood pulp
5. Sheep pelts
6. Offal, inedible
7. Whole milk powder
8. Beef, boneless
9. Wool, greasy
10. Butter
11. Sausage casings
12. Casein
13. Offal, edible
14. Skimmed milk powder
15. Tallow
16. Fish fillets
17. Apples
18. Mechanical wood pulp
19. Racehorses
20. Wood
21. Aluminium
22. Woollen yarn
23. Fish, frozen
24. Venison
25. Cheese

Source: NZ Dept of Statistics, 1987

Figure 15

60%; our share of world sheepmeat exports was 55%; our share of world scoured wool exports was approximately 38%. New Zealand had more than 10% of world exports in certain dairy and meat products. Our top twenty-five industries by world export share were dominated by fruit, meat and animal products, wool, dairy products, fish and forest products. The industries in which we do best in international competition are related to primary production in agriculture and forestry.

This is in sharp contrast with the pattern observed in another small country, Switzerland (see figure 16). Switzerland excels in a number of industries related to international trading, including diamond and precious-metal trading. It succeeds in a wide range of machinery products, including textile machinery, heavy engineering equipment, machine tools and a variety of processing machines. The Swiss are leaders in pharmaceuticals, specialty chemicals and medical equipment, as well as in watches and instruments. Whereas the industries in which New Zealand has large export shares are relatively narrow, Switzerland has achieved substantial international success in a wide range of advanced, sophisticated manufacturing and service industries.

Another small nation, Sweden, provides an intermediate case (see figure 17). Sweden has large shares of world exports in forest products, iron and steel, paper and mineral processing machinery, telecommunications and transportation products. The top twenty-five are narrower in scope than those of Switzerland, but wider than those of New Zealand. The major difference between the Swedish and

Top 25 Swiss Industries by World Export Share

1. Diamonds
2. Coins
3. Weaving machines
4. Printing presses
5. Watches
6. Vegetable alkaloids
7. Amide compounds
8. Textured yarns
9. Dyestuffs
10. Knitting looms
11. Jewelry
12. Vitamins
13. Herbicides
14. Fans
15. Electromechanical hand tools
16. Clocks
17. Perfumes
18. Surveying equipment
19. Textile processing equipment
20. Hearing aids
21. Metal cutting machine tools
22. Precious stones
23. Paper manufacturing machines
24. Heterocyclic compounds
25. Textile extruding machines

Source: *The Competitive Advantage of Nations, 1990*

Figure 16

Top 25 Swedish Industries by World Export Share

1. Kraft paper
2. Kraft liner
3. Lumber
4. Iron powders
5. High carbon steel
6. Unmilled cereals
7. Power handtools
8. Wood pulp
9. Centrifuges
10. Plastic coated paper
11. Power hand tool parts
12. Light aircraft
13. Iron wire
14. Prefabricated woodwork
15. High carbon steel plate
16. Marine engines
17. Coppers
18. Motor vehicle chassis
19. Iron rod
20. Dairy machinery
21. Zinc concentrates
22. Tool blades
23. Pulp and Waste paper
24. Line telephone equipment
25. Rubber articles

Source: *The Competitive Advantage of Nations, 1990*

Figure 17

New Zealand lists is the prevalence in the former of advanced manufactured goods and machinery. Sweden succeeds in certain primary products, but also in a range of other industries.

The profile of leading export industries in New Zealand shows sharp differences from those of Switzerland and Sweden. Our top twenty-five list looks far more like Australia's (without the mineral wealth) and Chile's than Switzerland's or Sweden's (see Appendices 2, 3, 4 and 5).

Industry Clusters

Food Cluster Dominates. The cluster chart provides a more complete breakdown of a nation's export industries. The basic objective of the cluster chart is to provide a detailed picture of the sectors in which the nation has a disproportionate share of world trade and investment in narrowly defined industries. Porter found that each nation had its own distinct pattern of success in international competition that could be understood by examining its cluster charts. All of the industries in which New Zealand's share of world exports exceeds its average share (0.3% of world exports in 1985) were arrayed in categories based on end use. The chart was then supplemented with data on foreign investment, services and information from a number of sources to try to develop as comprehensive a list of industries as possible in which there was some indication that New Zealand firms had succeeded in international competition.[4]

New Zealand's cluster charts for 1985 and 1987 clearly illustrate the continued importance of temperate climate commodities to the country's export profile. The industries represented in the charts are dominated by those in the food and beverage sector, particularly in the primary goods part of the production process. This reflects New Zealand's traditional reliance on the export of dairy products, sheepmeat, wool and beef. Emerging industries found in the charts, such as fishing, kiwifruit, apples and venison have tended to be diversifications from within this cluster.

In addition, the charts show that New Zealand has a number of medium-sized positions in other clusters. Wool exports are found under textiles and apparel. New Zealand's exports of timber, pulp and paper are found under forest products. A range of aluminium products from the Comalco smelter are found under materials and metals. Some additional positions in a range of service industries appear under multiple business. These industries, including construction, investment management and engineering consulting, represent a small percentage of New Zealand's exports, but a significant portion of overseas investment.

The cluster charts tell a story of an economy that competes successfully in primary production in a relatively narrow set of commodities. This point is further illustrated by the lack of machinery, specialty input or service industries found in

---

4 The methodology for preparing the cluster charts is described fully in Porter, M.E. (1990), *The Competitive Advantage of Nations*, Free Press.

New Zealand's cluster charts. New Zealand shows competitive strength in a small number of industries. Within these industries we tend to be concentrated in the primary production parts of each business rather than the more sophisticated segments. In addition, New Zealand has been unable to widen significantly its position by expanding into machinery, specialty inputs and services related to its areas of strength. This failure, which we will return to later, has placed limits on the economy's ability to develop further and grow.

Swiss Breadth. Switzerland, a nation with few natural resources, has achieved strong international positions in an enormous range of industries for such a small nation. In direct contrast to New Zealand, few Swiss industries are dependent for their competitive success on favourable natural conditions. Important clusters of successful Swiss industries are found in health care, textiles and apparel, internationally oriented business services, machinery and equipment for a wide range of industries, specialty chemicals, processed food products, mechanical and optical instruments, and heavy electrical goods. Swiss firms have strong positions in all levels of the cluster charts. They are represented in upstream industries, industrial and supporting functions and final-consumption goods and services. They are represented in primary goods, machinery, specialty inputs and services (see Appendix 4).

The Swiss economy has clearly adapted to compete successfully in many sophisticated industries. The breadth of the Swiss economy has helped to maintain a very high and stable standard of living. The country's position in each industry tends to be highly specialized and focused on the most sophisticated segments, which are often the most profitable. The Swiss economy has shown the capacity to develop advantage in a wide range of high-productivity industries that continue to generate high levels of national income.

Swedish Depth. Sweden has fewer clusters of successful industries than Switzerland, but its positions tend to be somewhat more broadly based. Important clusters of successful Swedish industries are found in transportation and logistics, forest-related industries, ferrous metals and fabricated metal products, health-related products and telecommunications. Sweden's internationally competitive industries are largely in upstream and industrial sectors. It has a weak position in consumer goods of most kinds.

Sweden's historical advantages were based on natural resources, much like New Zealand's. Sweden has continued to be successful in a number of resource-based industries. What is more important, however, has been the ability of Swedish firms to build upon the nation's natural advantages to become more sophisticated participants in the industries in which it competes and to create strong positions in ever more advanced industries and segments. The Swedish forest-products cluster provides a good example. Swedish firms are not only exporters of wood, pulp and paper, they also have major positions in several related products as well as in associated machinery, chemicals and services. Examples include power hand-tools (chainsaws), motor-vehicle chassis (logging trucks), and prefabricated woodwork (kitchen cabinets, wooden flooring) (see

Appendix 5). The net result has been an upgrading of the Swedish industrial base that continues to support a high standard of living.

Other small nations have shown a similar ability to build upon resource-based advantages in order to compete successfully in related industries. Danish firms, for example, have built upon Denmark's agricultural heritage to compete successfully in food-processing equipment, pharmaceuticals, industrial enzymes and a range of biotechnology industries.

Limits to Productivity Growth. Overall, New Zealand's export sector is characterized by a heavy reliance on resource-based commodities. In contrast to other advanced nations, we see little evidence of developing advantages in more sophisticated segments and industries. New Zealand does not appear to be substantially upgrading the composition of its exports. This in turn has placed limits on our export and productivity growth. The New Zealand situation is in stark contrast with a number of other small countries. The small size of New Zealand is not a sufficient explanation for the country's difficulty in adjusting to the modern global economy. Other small countries, such as Switzerland and Sweden, have been very successful in the post-war era and have continued to rank among the countries with the highest standards of living in the world.

Reliance on these types of products and industries stems partly from New Zealand's historical relationship with Britain as "Britain's farm". As a British settler state, New Zealand historically exported coarse wool, yellow butter and fatty meat to the "mother country" in return for manufactures and capital (see figure 18). Despite a substantial diversification of markets in recent decades (at

Export Growth And Market Diversification

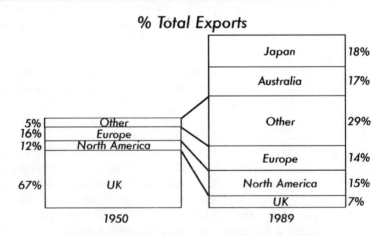

% Total Exports

Destination of Exports 1950 and 1989

Source : Dept of Statistics

Figure 18

present around 7% of our exports go to Britain and our traditional exports of butter, lamb and wool make up less than half our exports), the basic structure of New Zealand trade has remained essentially unchanged. We export simply processed, temperate climate commodities and import sophisticated goods and capital (see figure 19).

The general pattern of New Zealand's trade appears to be consolidating around this traditional focus. Appendix 6 illustrates the changes in the pattern of trade between 1979 and 1987. Exports of meat, dairy products, and wool remain important. In addition, New Zealand is increasing its share of world trade in the primary production of final-consumption goods (particularly food) and upstream industries (such as aluminium). For example, between 1979 and 1987, twenty-six of the food and beverage industries in which New Zealand competes showed substantial gains in world export share, compared with only seven industries that lost world export share.

The Structure of New Zealand's Export Industries

New Zealand's reliance on resource-based commodities would not be a problem if the industries concerned were able to generate the high and increasing levels of income necessary to achieve a high and rising standard of living. This, however,

New Zealand's Exports Are Still Primarily Resource Based Commodities

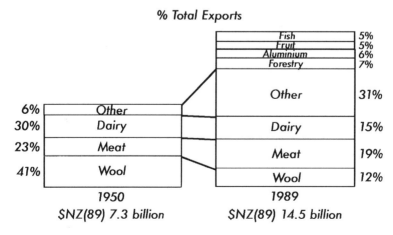

% Total Exports

1950		1989	
		Fish	5%
		Fruit	5%
		Aluminium	6%
		Forestry	7%
6%	Other	Other	31%
30%	Dairy	Dairy	15%
23%	Meat	Meat	19%
41%	Wool	Wool	12%
$NZ(89) 7.3 billion		$NZ(89) 14.5 billion	

Source : Dept of Statistics

Figure 19

has not been the case. New Zealand generally competes in structurally unattractive industries where the profit potential is low and where it is difficult for firms to shape the environment in their favour. This is one reason why increasing effort and investment in New Zealand's traditional industries has not resulted in a corresponding increase in the wealth generated by these industries.

Failure to Avert Declining Farm Incomes. In the post-war era, impressive increases in production volumes in the traditional industries have only managed to counteract steadily declining real prices for agricultural commodities (see figure 20). Improvements in production (measured in volume) that do not result in improvements in productivity (measured in value) do not increase national income, they merely keep it from falling. Thus we have been forced to run faster and faster, and work harder and harder. In fact, the fall in farm income (real farm incomes dropped 55% between 1980 and 1990) indicates that running faster has not allowed us to stay in place (see figure 21).[5] This has important implications for New Zealand's future prosperity.

Assessing the Profit Potential of Industries

While superior positioning within an industry can allow a firm to earn returns in excess of its competitors', industry conditions place limits on the returns available

Declining Prices Offset Increasing Volumes of Major Agricultural Exports

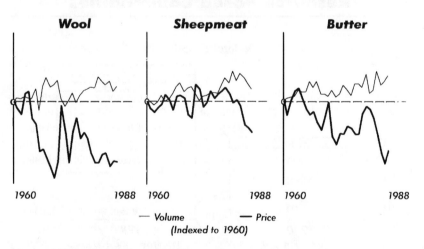

Source: IMF International Financial Statistics

Figure 20

5 NZ Meat and Wool Board Economic Service (1991).

Declining Farm Profitability

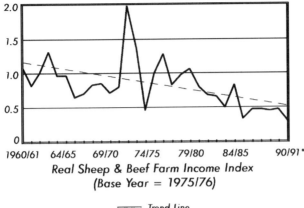

Real Sheep & Beef Farm Income Index
(Base Year = 1975/76)

——— Trend Line

Source: N.Z. Meat & Wool Board Economic Service
(* = estimate only)

Figure 21

to any competitor. The state of competition in an industry depends on five basic competitive forces, which are shown in figure 22. The collective strength of these forces determines the ultimate profit potential (or income-generating capacity) in the industry, where profit potential is measured in terms of long-run return on invested capital. Potential entrants and substitute products place a cap on the prices, and therefore the returns, that can be obtained in an industry. Powerful suppliers or buyers can often appropriate the value created by an industry. Rivalry among existing competitors can cause returns to be competed away.

Not all industries have the same profit potential. They differ fundamentally with the strength of the forces, which range from relatively unfavourable in industries like apples (where only a few participants earn spectacular returns), to relatively favourable in industries like software (where high returns are quite common). The five forces combine to create a relatively inhospitable environment in many of New Zealand's export industries.

Potential Entrants. Many of the industries in which New Zealand competes have limited barriers to entry. Often this is simply the nature of the industry. Many New Zealand exports possess little or no proprietary technology. Investments required to enter, at least at the production stage, are often low. The required managerial expertise can often be developed or acquired. This allows new entrants, or potential new entrants, to place continual downward pressure on prices and margins. This is particularly true in industries where New Zealand firms do not or cannot upgrade their competitive positions to keep ahead of new entrants.

Forces Driving Industry Competition

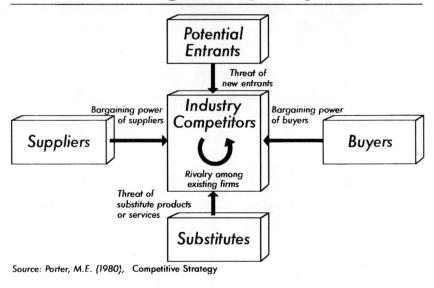

Source: Porter, M.E. (1980), Competitive Strategy

Figure 22

New Zealand's horticulture and forestry industries face increasing competition from Europe and Chile. The collapse of prices in the kiwifruit industry provides a classic demonstration of low barriers to entry leading to relatively low long run returns. While the kiwifruit industry was first developed in New Zealand, the barriers to establishing kiwifruit orchards elsewhere are relatively low. Consequently, growers in Italy and Chile rushed to plant kiwifruit. The result was the supply of kiwifruit greatly outstripping demand and a collapse in prices on international markets.

New Zealand's advantage in climatic conditions is further threatened by the development of large areas of land in Eastern Europe and the Third World which possess similar attributes. The forestry industry faces growing competition from Third World nations. Eastern Europe's unrealized potential in deer and dairy farming represents additional threats to important New Zealand industries. Eastern European and temperate Third World countries will find it easier to enter the kinds of industries in which we compete rather than sophisticated manufactures or services. This will continue to place pressure on the prices and profits of New Zealand producers.

Low barriers to entry make it difficult to sustain high levels of growth and profits. Relatively low levels of technology and differentiation in our export industries mean that even relatively underdeveloped nations can rapidly replicate New Zealand's export successes. The probability of the Eastern Europeans and others entering New Zealand's major export industries further heightens the pressure.

Substitute Products. It is relatively easy to substitute for many of the products and services that New Zealand provides. This is often because they are commodities that are difficult to differentiate, or because we have not made the investments in building differentiated products and services. New Zealand apples compete with a broad range of substitutes. The German housewife could decide to buy pears, oranges or bananas. This reduces her willingness to pay premium prices for apples in general, and New Zealand apples in particular.

Demand has stagnated or fallen in some of New Zealand's key export industries as substitution has increased. Increasing shifts to margarine have limited demand for butter. Demand for New Zealand lamb has been similarly affected by changes in consumer perceptions of fatty meats and increased substitution of white meats for red meats. Increased penetration of synthetic carpet fibres has had a major impact on the demand for New Zealand wool and, therefore, the prices New Zealand wool producers can obtain.

Supplier Power. New Zealand producers often have weak bargaining positions relative to overseas suppliers of critical inputs such as machinery, capital and transportation services. New Zealand imports a large portion of its industrial inputs and the country is often only a small customer in the global business of many suppliers. It is difficult to substitute for many of these inputs (agricultural equipment, transportation equipment and aircraft, for example).

The fact that we need these inputs more than the suppliers need our business gives us a poor negotiating position. Since most of our exports are transported to distant markets by sea, for example, our industries are vulnerable to international shipping companies. Similarly, we have a relatively poor bargaining position with foreign producers of machinery, supplies and components. This is true in our agricultural and forest-products industries (for instance, dairy processing plants and paper mills) as well as manufacturing industries (components for yachts, for example) and service industries (computers for software development).

Buyer Power. Even though New Zealand has diversified its range of trading partners, many New Zealand exports are sold in a small number of markets. In addition, in most of the industries in which New Zealand competes, we sell to powerful buyers who are in strong negotiating positions and able to bargain down our prices and margins. For example, a large portion of New Zealand's newsprint sales are made to two companies — Oji Paper in Japan and News Corporation in Australia. Clearly, these two powerful buyers are critical to our newsprint industry. The imbalance in power in the relationship provides these buyers with the leverage to drive down prices and margins. Because a large portion of New Zealand newsprint is sold to these buyers, our options are constrained.

The same pattern is repeated in a number of our industries. The ten largest wool buyers purchase almost three-quarters of the world wool clip. Two thirds of New Zealand's beef exports go to the United States. Almost half of New Zealand's fish exports go to Japan with another third to the United States. In each case, the bulk of our exports is sold to a small number of relatively powerful buyers. In several agricultural and horticultural industries, such as dairy products, meat, apples, kiwifruit and even wine, large supermarket chains handle an increasing share of our exports and have become more powerful in their negotiating position as a result.

The problem of powerful buyers is intensified by the fact that a number of these buyers are in low-margin businesses themselves (such as retailing) and are determined to reduce purchasing costs. This tends to put severe downward pressure on the prices obtained by New Zealand exporters.

New Zealand producers, on the other hand, have limited bargaining power with buyers. The lack of proprietary technology in most New Zealand products deprives us of leverage. In addition, New Zealand exporters are often the swing producers in global markets. In several industries, our exporters account for a small fraction of world production, even though they may account for a high percentage of world exports. As a result, our exports are used to "top up" domestic supply. In the dairy industry, for example, New Zealand accounts for approximately 25% of all internationally traded dairy products, but only 1.5% of total world production. Similar patterns are apparent in the meat, apple and forest-products industries. Our ability to influence prices in our favour in these industries is consequently constrained, and our vulnerability to market fluctuations is increased.

Industry Competitors. In many of New Zealand's export industries, we face fierce competition from overseas competitors. High levels of international competition make it difficult to charge high prices. New Zealand apples face competition from other exporters, such as Chile, as well as domestic producers in the major European and North American markets. New Zealand kiwifruit now faces significant competition from Chile and Italy. In construction services, New Zealand firms must compete with a multitude of local and international firms, many of whom are willing to accept low margins to gain or maintain market share. New Zealand's position in this industry is being challenged by competitors from Third World nations such as China, Korea and India.

In addition, slow growth and substantial exit barriers in many of New Zealand's export industries result in even fiercer competition than would otherwise occur. This tends to make firms compete even more vigorously on price, further lowering margins and returns.

Several industries in which New Zealand competes, primarily the agricultural industries (though wine and yachts also fall into this category), involve lifestyles that competitors value even if returns are low. Subsidies and protectionism (in advanced nations) and development plans targeting specific sectors (in Third World nations) tend to keep producers in the industry, even if they are inefficient. As a result, it is difficult for New Zealand producers to take advantage of their superior cost position. This, in turn, makes it difficult for us to turn our advantages into increases in productivity (which is measured in value) and income.

In the dairy industry, for example, New Zealand's direct costs for producing 1 tonne of butter are estimated at $US1,239 compared to the US's cost of $US2,148, the Netherlands' $US2,829 and Japan's $US4,949. New Zealand has similar cost advantages in the production of cheddar cheese, skim- and whole-milk powders and casein. However, major markets, including the EC, the US, and Japan, are protected from international competition by a variety of subsidies, tariffs and non-price barriers, nullifying New Zealand's cost advantage. Furthermore, New Zealand must compete with subsidized exports from the US and the EC in other markets.

Part of the rapid increase in Italian kiwifruit production stems from the willingness of the Italian government to finance growers to replace grape vines with kiwifruit vines in an attempt to reduce Europe's "wine lake". It would not be unreasonable to expect such government support to continue in the light of declining kiwifruit prices internationally. This example also underscores another aspect of these industries. Frequently there are few opportunities for developing other industries among our competitors, thereby reinforcing their commitment to these same industries despite their obvious difficulties.

Pressures on our Export Industries. These kinds of pressures are working to reduce the profitability of the industries that make up over 85% of our export earnings (see figure 23). This calls for careful, long-term positioning in each of the industries that we compete in, if we are to be successful. Even within difficult industries there are more attractive parts of the industry.

However, when we look behind the fact that we tend to compete in industries with low profit potential, we find that we also tend to have the weakest competitive position within the industry. This can be illustrated using an example from the kiwifruit industry. We need to keep in mind that this is designed to

NZ exports are generally in structurally unattractive businesses

		Buyer Power	Supplier Power	Substi- tutes	Barriers to entry	Compe- tition
Agriculture	Apples	HI	MED	HI	LO	HI
	Cut flowers	HI	MED	HI	LO	HI
	Dairy	HI	MED	HI	LO	HI
	Deer	HI	MED	HI	LO	HI
	Fish	HI	LO	HI	MED	MED
	Forestry	HI	MED	MED	MED	MED
	Goats	HI	MED	HI	LO	HI
	Kiwifruit	HI	MED	HI	LO	HI
	Meat	MED	MED	HI	LO	HI
	Wine	HI	LO	HI	LO	HI
	Wool	MED	MED	HI	LO	HI
Manufacturing	Electr. fencing	MED	LO	MED	LO	MED
	Methanol	MED	MED	MED	HI	HI
	Yachts	MED	LO	LO	MED	HI
Services	Construction	MED	LO	MED	MED	HI
	Education	MED	LO	HI	MED	HI
	Engineering con.	MED	LO	MED	MED	HI
	Software	MED	LO	LO	MED	HI
	Tourism	MED	LO	HI	MED	HI

Figure 23

illustrate a basic pattern of the competitive positions that is common to most of the industries in which New Zealand competes (see figure 24).

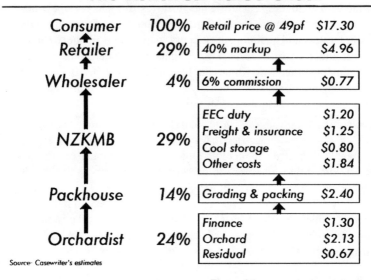

Orchard to Market
The Kiwifruit Value Chain

Consumer	100%	Retail price @ 49pf	$17.30
Retailer	29%	40% markup	$4.96
Wholesaler	4%	6% commission	$0.77
NZKMB	29%	EEC duty	$1.20
		Freight & insurance	$1.25
		Cool storage	$0.80
		Other costs	$1.84
Packhouse	14%	Grading & packing	$2.40
Orchardist	24%	Finance	$1.30
		Orchard	$2.13
		Residual	$0.67

Source: Casewriter's estimates

Figure 24

In a market with reasonable margins like the German market, roughly a third of the revenues accrue to the wholesaler and retailers while 43% of the revenues are expended getting the kiwifruit from the orchard to the market. On this calculation the New Zealand kiwifruit orchardist is left with sixty-seven cents should his kiwifruit fetch $17.30 a tray in Germany.

Far more important than who gets what share of the revenues is what investments they have made and what risks they have taken for the returns they receive. Although the kiwifruit growers receive a relatively large percentage of sales revenues, they also incur heavy costs, a large proportion of which are fixed, and bear substantial risk. They must make their investment in their orchards on a long-term basis, leaving them vulnerable to changes in consumer demand, new sources of supply or damage to their orchards from storms. Consequently, the New Zealand growers bear a high level of risk for relatively low returns.

The position of the German retailer contrasts with that of the grower. Retailing is a notoriously difficult business in most nations. Even so, the retailer is in a better position than the kiwifruit grower. Unlike the orchardist, the retailer need not make any investment in kiwifruit until shortly before sale. The time delay between the retailer making the investment in kiwifruit and receiving the revenue is a matter of days or perhaps weeks, rather than months as on the part of the kiwifruit grower. The retailer's costs associated with kiwifruit are variable. Should New Zealand kiwifruit not sell well, the retailer can switch to other suppliers or different fruits with a minimal amount of difficulty. The kiwifruit grower, in contrast, can only exit the industry with great difficulty.

This pattern is common among most New Zealand export industries, including the service industries. The pattern of distributor power in the market in tourism is strikingly similar to that of the retailer in kiwifruit. While it differs between markets, generally the best returns for the lowest investment and risk generally accrue to tour wholesalers and retailers in the source markets. Heavy competition for tourists from around the world leaves New Zealand tour operators in less than attractive negotiating positions with wholesalers from the source markets.

Summary

New Zealand exports in a range of structurally unattractive, and therefore low profit, industries. Low entry barriers and easy substitution limit the returns available in these industries. Powerful buyers and suppliers tend to further erode profitability. Fierce competition, driven in part by high exit barriers and non-economic considerations, compounds these difficulties. As a result, New Zealand producers are usually price takers rather than price makers for exports as well as for imports of machinery, industrial inputs, services and capital. This basic structural feature of many of the industries in which New Zealand competes, and our position within those industries, makes for an unfavourable long-term profit outlook.

The evidence suggests that New Zealand is consolidating its position as an exporter in structurally unattractive industries and segments. These industries will be hard pressed to generate the high and increasing levels of income necessary for New Zealand to repay its debts and dramatically improve its standard of living relative to other advanced countries.

Structural Features of New Zealand's Imports

The structural features of the industries in which New Zealand imports are fundamentally different from the ones in which we export. These differences have resulted in deteriorating terms of trade (the average prices we receive for our exports compared to the average prices we pay for our imports) and are a primary reason why we have been unable to pay our way in the world.

New Zealand's top twenty-five industries by export value and import value are shown in figures 25 and 26. The leading export industries show patterns similar to those of our top industries by export share. The top twenty-five industries by import value, on the other hand, show distinctly different patterns. We import

Top 25 New Zealand Export Industries by Value

1. Sheep meat
2. Wool, scoured
3. Beef
4. Wool, greasy
5. Aluminium
6. Butter
7. Kiwifruit
8. Sheep pelts
9. Whole milk powder
10. Cheese
11. Casein
12. Shellfish
13. Fish Fillets
14. Skimmed milk powder
15. Fish
16. Race horses
17. Mechanical wood pulp
18. Apples
19. Chemical wood pulp
20. Newsprint
21. Leather
22. Sausage casings
23. Woollen yarn
24. Onions, peas, corn
25. Hides

Source: NZ Dept of Statistics, 1987

Figure 25

Top 25 New Zealand Imports By Value

1. Motor cars
2. Petroleum
3. Medicaments
4. Telephone equipment
5. Trucks and vans
6. EDP peripheral units
7. Aluminium oxide
8. Gasoline
9. Computer parts
10. Steel sheets
11. Motor vehicle parts
12. Woven cotton
13. Ammunition
14. Aircraft
15. Electronic measuring devices
16. Books
17. Domestic appliances
18. Writing paper
19. Electronic circuits
20. Computers
21. Synthetic fibres
22. Printing machinery
23. Polyethylene
24. Chemical products
25. Racehorses

Source: NZ Dept of Statistics, 1987

Figure 26

automobiles, oil, communications equipment, computers, aircraft and a range of machinery.

It is often very difficult to substitute the kinds of products and services that we import. They are often high-productivity items in themselves, such as automobiles, aircraft or telecommunications equipment. Several involve high levels of technological sophistication and significant economies of scale in production. They require large investments in research and development, production facilities, marketing and distribution. As a result these industries have very high barriers to entry. Significant technological, managerial and capital resources would be required to enter the industries involved in making machinery for several important New Zealand industries such as pulp and paper, dairy processing, aluminium or methanol.

Many of the industries in which we import, including computers, aircraft and pharmaceuticals, are often differentiated products that command high margins. Several are structurally attractive industries that are experiencing rapid growth. New Zealand is often not an important market for what we need to import. As a result, international suppliers are less willing to accept lower prices in New Zealand than they would be in the world's major markets. For example, New Zealand has limited buyer power when purchasing defence supplies or telecommunications equipment.

Trade Patterns Reflect Poor Performance. New Zealand's mix of import and export industries is directly reflected in its relatively poor economic performance. The fundamental structure of New Zealand's trade as an exporter of resource-based commodities in low-profitability and low-productivity industries and an importer of sophisticated products in high-profitability industries has meant that our exports have earned less over time and our imports cost more (see figure 27). This has been directly reflected in the long-term downward trend, over forty years, in New Zealand's terms of trade. This deterioration has contributed to the balance of payments and foreign debt difficulties alluded to earlier.

The structure of New Zealand's exports and our sluggishness in adjusting to the rigours of competition in the post-war environment, have restricted our ability to participate in the post war boom in world trade. New Zealand's share of total world exports fell from around 1% in 1950 to less than 0.3% by 1987 (see figure 28). More fundamentally, this has taken place while the mix of simply processed commodity exports to sophisticated imports has steadily moved against New Zealand.

An Anomaly in the Global Economy. In the 1980s New Zealand remained an anomaly in the global economy (see figure 29). In essence, our living standards are those of an advanced, wealthy nation while our export pattern is remarkably similar to that of a low-income country. While almost all other advanced nations export in more sophisticated manufactures, New Zealand largely exported simply processed, resource-based commodities.

Structural Features of New Zealand's Import and Export Industries

Exports...

- Lower margin commodities
- Lower growth markets
- Limited economies of scale
- Slower technology change
- Slower productivity increases
- Lower barriers to entry
- Politically salient

- Poor industry structures
- Lower profit potential

...Earn Less Over Time

Imports...

- Higher margin complex products
- Higher growth markets
- Significant economies of scale
- Rapid technology change
- Rapid productivity increases
- Significant barriers to entry
- Less political

- Attractive industry structures
- Higher profit potential

...Cost More Over Time

Figure 27

Declining Position in World Trade

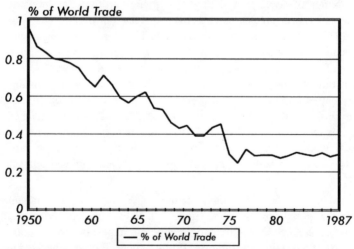

NZ's Percentage of World Trade 1950-87

Source: Yearbook of International Trade Statistics, UN, 1987

Figure 28

NZ is an anomaly in the global economy

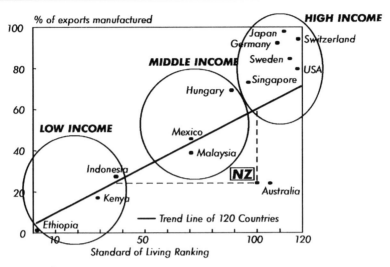

Source: **World Bank, 1987**

Figure 29

4

Industry Studies

In this chapter, issues that cut across New Zealand's export sector will be highlighted through abstracts of four of our industry studies. Space does not allow us to include the entire industry study, which was considerably more detailed. These four have each been chosen and summarized to highlight different issues facing New Zealand.

The dairy industry has arguably moved further than any of New Zealand's major traditional industries in upgrading its competitive position and reducing its exposure to commodity markets. The issue is whether the industry's "single-seller" structure has dampened the momentum for further upgrading and the role that domestic competition could play in accelerating the upgrading process.

The forest-products industry is an increasingly important export earner where New Zealand's primary source of competitive advantage is favourable growing conditions. The issue is whether New Zealand's limited position in processing, and the tendency to pursue short-term profitability through selling commodity products such as logs and pulp, will allow the nation to obtain the maximum benefits from its natural advantages and investments in the industry.

The electric-fencing industry is one of few New Zealand industries that obtains advantages from the interaction of several of the determinants of national advantage. Its success results not from natural resources, but from innovative products and the capacity to improve. While a small industry, its international leadership illustrates that competitive advantage has little to do with size. The issue is how a business environment can be developed in New Zealand that facilitates the emergence of industries that build upon unique features of our present industrial base.

The software industry is one of New Zealand's newest and fastest-growing industries. It illustrates that New Zealand firms can compete in rapidly changing, technology intensive industries, despite relatively unfavourable conditions. The software industry highlights the need for pools of skilled human resources and specialist financing mechanisms. The issue is how to develop education and financial systems that facilitate efforts to upgrade competitive advantage by New Zealand firms.

The New Zealand Dairy Industry

The dairy industry is important to the New Zealand economy. In 1989 it provided slightly over 15% ($NZ2.4 billion) of New Zealand's total exports and made up almost five per cent of GDP.[1] The bulk of New Zealand dairy production is exported. While New Zealand produces less than 1.5% of the world's total milk supply, it is a significant exporter of dairy products, with an estimated 25% share of world trade in 1989.[2] On the basis of data adjusted to exclude trade between EC countries, New Zealand's share of world exports was 27% in butter, 20% in whole milk powders, 49% in casein, 14% in skim-milk powder and 15% in cheese.

New Zealand is one of the world's lowest-cost producers of milk, with a cost advantage of 50% over its nearest rival. Despite continuing efforts to reduce the industry's exposure to the vicissitudes of commodity markets, commodities still make up the vast bulk of New Zealand dairy exports (see figure 30).

Dairy product mix has begun to move away from low-margin, high sensitivity categories

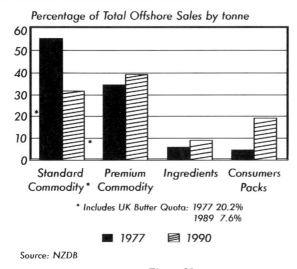

Figure 30

New Zealand producers have not been able to benefit fully from their cost advantages. Major dairy markets are partially or wholly protected from competition by subsidies, price-support schemes, tariffs and non-price barriers. In addition, the New Zealand producers compete with European exporters who receive subsidies of up to 50% of product cost. As a result of government

---

[1] New Zealand Department of Statistics, 1989 data.

[2] Estimate by New Zealand Dairy Board executives.

dismantling of agricultural subsidies in the mid-eighties, the New Zealand industry is currently the world's only major unsubsidized dairy-products exporter.

The dairy industry example illustrates features common to a number of New Zealand's export industries. The New Zealand industry focuses on primary production of commodity products. It has not built broad-based advantages in the development and marketing of branded and specialized products. Foreign multinationals, which have advanced marketing skills and distribution networks, have been able to extract profits and place tremendous pressure on producer prices. New Zealand's domestic demand is not sophisticated by world standards and therefore does not provide New Zealand with an advantage.

Government legislation has given "single-desk" selling rights (control over all New Zealand dairy exports) to the New Zealand Dairy Board. Single-desk control has not prevented declines in producer prices, nor has it allowed the New Zealand Dairy Board to grow at nearly the same pace as multinational food companies, such as Nestle (see figure 31).

The New Zealand dairy industry illustrates how factor advantages in commodity industries can be precarious. Real dairy prices have trended downwards for several decades, and have recently become more volatile (figure 32). It also illustrates that the upgrading of competitive advantage is limited without the interplay of the different parts of the diamond in the home base, particularly domestic rivalry.

Sales

(US $ billions)

Source: Financial Statements; Moodys Manual Of Investment

Figure 31

Real Dairy Export Prices have trended down between 1950-75 & have since been highly volatile

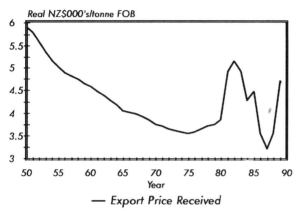

Export Price Received

Source: NZBD Annual Reports
Indexed CPI Base 100=1950

Figure 32

Products and Processes

Milk is the basis for a wide range of consumer and industrial products.[3] The manufacturing of other dairy products involves the disaggregation and transformation of the constituent parts of raw milk.

There are numerous production possibilities for raw milk that are not necessarily mutually exclusive. In simple terms, processing can either separate raw milk into cream and skim milk for further manufacturing, transform it into cheese or use the raw milk to make other milk products such as whole powder.[4] Each processing option produces different products which themselves can be further processed.

Industry History

The first dairy herd in New Zealand was established by a British missionary in 1814. English settlers soon found New Zealand well suited to the grazing of dairy cattle. The first recorded exports of dairy products from New Zealand were exports of butter to Australia in 1846. In 1882, refrigerated shipping made exports of butter and cheese from New Zealand to Britain and other distant markets possible. The New Zealand dairy industry soon produced far in excess of domestic

---

[3] Cow's milk accounts for 90% of world milk production, buffalo's for 7%, and sheep's and goat's for 3%. The New Zealand Industry only processes cow's milk.

[4] The composition of raw milk is approximately 4.8% fat, 9.1% solids non-fat, and 89.3% water on a weight-per-volume basis.

requirements. By 1915, New Zealand products were sold in Britain, Australia, South Africa and Canada.

British interests were extremely important in the New Zealand dairy industry's history. The first dairy factories had been owned by British merchants. British merchants controlled the distribution of New Zealand dairy products on and off until 1947. During the two world wars, there were forced sales of New Zealand dairy products to the United Kingdom.[5] The UK bulk-purchase agreements ended in 1954, but the New Zealand dairy industry remained heavily dependent on the UK market.

The threat of British entry into the EC prompted a move to find new markets for New Zealand's commodity dairy exports. By 1961, bulk sales had commenced to a number of foreign markets, including the West Indies and South-East Asia.[6] The entry of Britain into the EC in 1973, which excluded New Zealand from much of the UK dairy market, was a blow to the New Zealand dairy industry. New Zealand was granted special access to the U.K. for butter, the only non-EC country to be granted access. Although the quota has been negotiated downwards over the years, these sales (at prices far above world market prices) still accounted for more than a third of New Zealand's butter exports and about 10% of the New Zealand industry's export revenue in 1990.

The New Zealand dairy industry became concerned with issues of control and ownership at an early date. With thousands of fragmented New Zealand farmers supplying milk for sale to powerful international customers, the prevention of exploitation of local farmers became of paramount concern. The first farmer-owned co-operative factory was established in 1871. The co-operative structure was to develop as an integral feature of the New Zealand industry. The earliest dairy industry group was the National Dairy Association, which was formed in 1894 to lobby government.

The Dairy Produce Export Control Act was passed in 1923 to establish the Dairy Control Board to act as the central export seller to counteract the power of the British merchants. Over time, control of marketing passed back to the merchants and the Control Board's role became one of assisting in improving farm productivity. New Zealand farmers gained control of the marketing of dairy products in 1957, which was followed by the establishment of the New Zealand Dairy Board in 1961. The Board was given statutory powers to be the sole exporter of dairy products. It also plays a key role in improving farm efficiency.

The New Zealand government has played an active role in the industry's development because of the importance of the industry to the economy, and the political importance of the farm vote. The first Dairy Industry Act (1892) was passed to "regulate the manufacture of butter and cheese for export and to provide for the purity of the milk used in such manufacture".[7] Government controls were

---

[5] During both wars, New Zealand needed approval from the British government to sell any butter or cheese to third countries.

[6] Interview with Dairy Board executive.

[7] Dairy Industry Act, 1892.

soon extended to the domestic market. In 1935, producers were guaranteed a floor price for butter and cheese for the domestic market that was to be no less than the export price. Price guarantees were finally lifted for cheese in 1971 and for butter in 1982. The Dairy Board was required to bank with the Reserve Bank. Ministerial approval was required for overdrafts and reserve levels.[8] Government controls over milk pricing, banking and treasury were finally removed in 1988. Concurrently, the Dairy Board and co-operatives became liable for income tax for the first time.[9]

In 1990, the dairy industry in New Zealand was structured much as it had been since 1957. Farmers were members of co-operative dairy companies that were autonomous commercial entities, with independent powers to decide on investment, milk utilization and manufacturing operations. Only supplier-farmers could hold shares in the co-operatives.

The co-operatives were required to offer all export products to the Dairy Board, which was the statutory single seller of all New Zealand's dairy export products. The majority of Board directors are farmers elected by their colleagues, others are government appointees. Funding for the Board's activities came from borrowing and retained earnings after distributions to its seventeen member co-operatives. Following the removal of exchange controls in 1984, the NZDB began a major programme of overseas investments to build distribution systems in key markets.

International Competition in the Dairy Industry
Most dairy products are consumed in the nation where they are produced. Less than 5% of the world's dairy production is traded. The largest producers of milk are the European Community and the USSR, with annual production of over 100 million tonnes each. Production in the EC fell by about 5% each year in the 1980s. However, production in the USSR has been increasing at 2% per year, an amount equal to approximately one third of New Zealand's total exports.[10]

While total world demand for dairy products is mature, growth opportunities exist in some segments and markets. Different segments generate different margins and have different price sensitivities (see figure 33). As a general observation, the further the product is from a commodity item, the higher the margin and the lower the volatility in prices.

Most international trade in dairy products is in commodity products where price is the primary determinant. In many instances, there are a small number of large powerful buyers or, in some countries, single government purchasing agencies. The ability to assure quality and reliable delivery is important, but not sufficient to generate high premiums.

Milk production in most countries is influenced by direct government

---

[8] The Reserve Bank provided the industry with working capital at 1% annual interest, but required any surpluses to be deposited at the same time.

[9] Legislation was also passed to provide dividend imputation, which had the effect of stopping the double taxation of "dividend" income.

[10] Although New Zealand accounted for approximately 25% of world exports, New Zealand's production was about seventh in the world by volume.

As dairy products move down the value chain margins increase & price sensitivity declines

Stage in Value Chain	Margins	Price Sensitivity
Commodities	Low	High
Ingredients	Med-high	Med
Consumer - Standard - Specialty	Low-med High	Low Low

Figure 33

intervention to protect domestic farmers. Much of world trade comes from countries that export surplusses with substantial subsidies. The resulting price distortions affect all parts of the international dairy business, but are greatest at the commodity end, where prices tend to reflect the underlying subsidy schemes in the EC and US.[11] Commodity products prices can move by as much as 50% in a year.[12] GATT floor prices have had some stabilizing effect, but their effectiveness is limited because several large producers were not signatories to the accords.

Small changes in the proportion of the output of major producers redirected to the export sector dramatically influence New Zealand's export-dependent position. In early 1990, subsidy reductions in Eastern Europe forced the sale of stock on international markets. International commodity prices were expected to fall substantially as a result.

Branded consumer dairy products often involve the manufacturing and packaging of locally produced milk. The use of imported commodity inputs is influenced by subsidies and protectionist measures in major markets. In the developed nations, large multinational food companies have spent vast sums of money building brand recognition with the consumer and loyalty within the distribution channels. They have exploited economies of scope by supplying a

---

[11]International Dairy Markets, GATT (IDA), 1988.

[12]Some producers attempted to gain advantage by better defining specifications for industrial or large users.

wide range of food products. They have achieved significant consumer loyalty through strong branding and have been seen as preferred suppliers by large supermarket chains.

The manufacture of dairy commodities into food ingredients tends to take place close to final markets. The major buyers are food manufacturers with relatively sophisticated requirements. Protection often means that local milk has to be used in the manufacture of food ingredients. Competition is based on technical innovation to achieve superior functionality for the buyer. New product breakthroughs are quickly imitated. Continuous innovation for sophisticated customers is necessary to obtain and maintain leadership.

Production Cost Leadership
New Zealand is one of the lowest-cost producers of milk in the world (see figure 34). This is due to a combination of favourable growing conditions and an efficient farming sector that has constantly upgraded production efficiency. New Zealand dairy farms are pastoral farms characterized by cows being fed primarily through grazing high-growth pastures with minimal supplementary feeding. A combination of climate and soils have allowed New Zealand farmers to graze cows outside all year round. Cows in developing countries are often farmed on small, unsophisticated landholdings. In other developed countries, intensive farming, where cows are housed in barns or lots and fed rations that are brought to them, is more typical.[13]

New Zealand has substantially lower commodity costs...

Estimated direct costs to F.O.B.
at 200 km, 1989 (US$/Tonne)

	NZ	USA	Nethl'ds	Japan
Butter	1,239	2,148	2,829	4,949
Cheddar Cheese	1,687	2,762	3,568	6,077
SMP	1,283	2,074	2,668	4,515
Casein	3,359	5,666	7,397	12,782
WMP	1,579	2,473	3,203	5,474

... but these are countervailed by EEC & USA export subsidies

Source: Casewriter calculated from various sources

Figure 34

New Zealand's natural advantages are enhanced by a well-educated and innovative farming community. New Zealand farmers are among the most educated in the world. They tend to be more willing to adopt and adapt to new technology than most foreigners. It is estimated that at least 40% of New Zealand farmers have had some form of higher education related to farming, compared to 20% of Australia farmers.[14]

Significant advances have been made in enhancing milk quality and production efficiencies in New Zealand. The Dairy Research Institute was established in 1930. In 1939, national herd-testing was introduced. A network of agricutural research institutes has been founded to enhance cow productivity, farm-management techniques and soil-fertilizer programmes.

A Dairy Board livestock-improvement plan has been developed to measure the productive performance of more than 80% of the cows in the industry. The plan has led to New Zealand reinforcing its position as the world leader in sire selection for improved artificial insemination. Other New Zealand advances have included the breeding of specialized pasture species and genetic-improvement programmes. Information on new developments is quickly disseminated by the Dairy Board, Ministry of Agriculture extension officers and private farm consultants.

Unsophisticated Domestic Demand
New Zealand's per-capita consumption of dairy products is among the highest in the world. Consumption of raw milk and butter in New Zealand is 50% higher than in the EC, the US, Canada, the USSR and Eastern Europe. However, New Zealand's per-capita consumption of cheese is some 50% below that of the world's leading cheese-consuming countries, namely the US, Canada, the EC and Australia.[15]

Despite high per-capita consumption, New Zealand demand for dairy products lacks sophistication. New Zealand dairy buyers are not very discerning, except for their perception of the quality of salted butter, cheddar cheese and fresh milk. The quality of local demand has improved since the 1970s, when larger numbers of New Zealanders began to travel and many new products were introduced on the local market. The New Zealand market, however, still provides little stimulus for development of new consumer and industrial products.

The NZDB has located product-development centres offshore to take advantage of more favourable demand conditions. By 1990 the NZDB had established centres in Europe (fats), the US (proteins) and Asia (milk recombining).

A Small Cluster
The New Zealand dairy industry has benefited from the presence of several related and supporting industries. New Zealand is successful in a range of pastorally

---

[13]This is generally as a result of severe climatic conditions requiring animals to be housed. The temperate climate of New Zealand does not require this.

[14]Industry sources.

[15]See Harvard Business School Case-study N9-590-020.

based industries, including wool and meat. Technological improvements in one industry, such as electric fencing or superior pasture management, became available to all these industries. An environment of innovative farmers, research stations and farm-advisory services has further stimulated innovation and upgrading of pastoral farming in New Zealand.

Several industries have grown up in New Zealand to supply the dairy and related industries.A number have become successful international competitors in their own right, including electric fences, animal identification systems, genetic improvement of livestock through artificial insemination, milking equipment and milking meters. Despite the presence of successful firms in these industries, New Zealand is still a net importer of dairy technology, particularly processing equipment.

Overall, the interactions between the related pastoral industries and the small supporting industries have provided a modest source of competitive advantage to the New Zealand dairy industry. It appears that New Zealand has not taken advantage of the potential to build a deeper cluster of competitive industries around the dairy industry. The fact that the dairy industry has probably spawned more supporting industries than any other in New Zealand highlights the generally poor state of supporting industries within New Zealand.

Vigorous Rivalry in Processing

New Zealand's dairy co-operatives compete fiercely to attract farmer suppliers and to achieve the highest pay-out. Pay-outs to farmers vary by as much as 15% between co-operatives, reflecting different product mixes, processing efficiencies and economies. This competition has been a spur to improving processing efficiencies at the level of the co-operatives.

Increasingly, the co-operatives have striven for scale economies in order to improve returns to their supplier-farmers. This has lead to consolidation in the industry. In 1935, there were more than 500 co-operatives; by 1983 there were 36; and in 1990 there were 17. The two largest co-operatives controlled nearly 50% of the total New Zealand milk supply.

The net effect of rivalry in processing has been the improvement of efficiencies at the processing plants. New Zealand's processing plants are on a par with the best plants around the world.

Pressures for Upgrading and the Dairy Board

Given continuing pressure from subsidized competitors and powerful multinationals in commodity markets, the New Zealand Dairy Board has been under pressure to upgrade and diversify its products and markets. The Dairy Board's mission, however, is to achieve long-term maximum returns for milk produced by New Zealand farmers. This has restricted its entry into non-dairy consumer-foods markets, and has limited its ability to exploit economies of scope. The Board's intent has been to restrict its scope to dairy products and not to compete in other products like those of Nestle or Kraft, firms that have many brands across a wide range of food products.

The Dairy Board began to trade dairy commodities in the late 1970s in an attempt to improve and stabilize prices. This included buying dairy products from other countries to ensure continuity of supply to key customers. By 1990, the New Zealand Dairy Board was one of the world's largest dairy-commodities traders.[16] It has used its position to mitigate the volatility of commodity prices, with some success.

The Board had also diversified its sales base by developing more secure positions in a range of markets throughout the US, South-East Asia, Latin America and Japan. During the 1980s, the Board achieved small price premiums for its commodity products versus average world prices.[17] It also decreased the proportion of commodity product sold on volatile spot markets by nearly half in 10 years. These activities have led to improved access for New Zealand commodity products and some improvements in prices, both of which have been positive for the New Zealand industry.

The Board's long-term strategy has been to upgrade its product mix and marketing approach. It has become a vertically integrated international supplier. It has attempted to increase the amount of New Zealand milk products processed by its offshore subsidiaries to meet better the needs of buyers in those countries and to secure market access.

The Dairy Board invested some $US62 million in offshore subsidiaries and joint ventures ($US44 million in 1990) that undertook marketing, processing, and research and development activities. It launched a range of consumer products in several countries in the 1980s. The main successes so far have been Anchor aerosol cream in the UK, the importation and distribution of cheeses in the US, and the Anchor and Fernleaf brands of whole-milk powder in South East Asia. These activities have been important in building more secure and profitable markets for New Zealand dairy production.

Despite the improvement in product and market mix the Dairy Board achieved in the 1980s, some questioned whether it had moved far enough in this direction. In 1989, some 67% of New Zealands dairy exports were still basic commodities that could be sourced from many countries, particularly those with large export subsidies. Though this was a significant improvement from 80% in 1977, 40% of exports were in commodity butter (and its derivatives), a product line that faces declining demand and chronically depressed prices. While the move into more secure and profitable segments has made significant headway, the move has not been far or fast enough to arrest decline and increasing volatility in the prices received for New Zealand milk.

Other than the Anchor brand in Britain, the NZDB has no significant position in branded consumer goods in the industrialized world, i.e. one of the more profitable segments of the industry. The NZDB has been more successful in building brands in developing countries such as Sri Lanka, Malaysia and Singapore, which are generally smaller and less profitable markets for dairy products.[18]

---

[16]Interviews with New Zealand Dairy Board executives.

[17]*The World Markets for Dairy Products: GATT, 1981 1987* and *NZDB Annual Report 1988*, NZDB External Policy Division (adapted from Harvard Business Scool Case-study N9-590-020).

[18]The Fernleaf brand was established in parts of South-East Asia.

The New Zealand industry has made advances in product development and manufacture of milk proteins, milk powders and fat-based food ingredients. This has been achieved through work at the Dairy Research Institute in New Zealand and through development centres close to buyers in offshore markets.[19] Several of these products are market leaders that provided first-mover advantages, particularly in the food-ingredients business. Sophisticated manufactures, however, made up only 10% of the Boards' exports in 1989.

Issues for New Zealand

The issues facing the dairy industry are similar to those facing many of New Zealand's resource-based industries. Despite our cost advantages, which have been the result of favourable natural conditions and investments in production efficiency, our margins have fallen and our returns have become more volatile. This is due in part to the poor profitability of the industries we compete in, and in part to our positions in these industries. A significant upgrading of New Zealand's sources of competitive advantage will be necessary to obtain more secure and profitable positions.

This upgrading will demand sustained investments in building new advantages through developing sophisticated products and consumer brands, and reducing exposure to undifferentiated commodities. Indeed, of all New Zealand's resource-based industries, the dairy industry has moved the furthest and the most aggressively in differentiating its products, developing new products and building consumer brands in international markets. It provides an example to other New Zealand industries. These efforts, however, have still been insufficient either to arrest or stablize the declines in dairy prices (see figure 35) or to alter fundamentally New Zealand's position as a commodity exporter.

A key issue in the dairy industry, and in several other major New Zealand industries, is the role that more vigorous domestic rivalry could play in accelerating the shift from commodity to differentiated products. Vigorous domestic rivalry between seventeen processing co-operatives has contributed to the development of world-class processing efficiency in the New Zealand dairy industry. The current industry structure successfully focuses efforts in achieving cost leadership in milk production and processing. The same competitive dynamic needs to be unleashed in the quest for new product and market development.

Developing opportunities for New Zealand companies to compete in new segments of the dairy industry would require the creation of new enterprises and/or the expansion of some of the existing co-operatives in fiercely competitive offshore markets. Such an expansion, which at present is not permitted, would require New Zealand co-operatives to develop high levels of management, marketing and technical capabilities, capabilities that the present system has not developed. Development of the food-ingredients and consumer-products businesses would require sustained investment in management, marketing and technical skills to optimize these long-term investments. It would also provide exciting opportunities for talented New Zealanders.

---

[19]The Dairy Research Institute is funded 90% by industry and 10% by government. Prior to 1984, it was 50% funded by government.

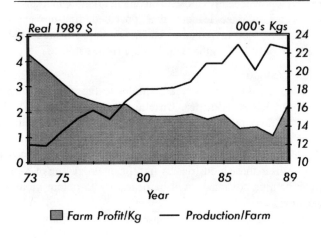

Rising Dairy Production
Falling Profitability

Year

◼ Farm Profit/Kg   —— Production/Farm

Source: NZDB

Figure 35

The point is not that the Dairy Board has made no attempts to develop new products and markets; however, New Zealand is more likely to overcome the challenges of upgrading beyond commodities with several local competitors each focused on a particular new idea, rather than a single entity trying to oversee an entire industry. New products and markets require skills that are best developed in a more entreprenuerial environment. Effective domestic rivalry, particularly in the non-commodity segments, could provide a powerful stimulus to upgrading in this and other New Zealand industries (see figure 36).

The New Zealand Forest-products Industry

The forest-products industry was New Zealand's fourth largest export earner in 1990, behind meat, dairy and wool. The industry is poised to play an even larger role in the New Zealand economy. Sufficient new timber supplies are likely to become available over the next two decades to more than double New Zealand's potential wood resource. In less than a decade, international expansion has built New Zealand's leading forest-products companies into significant global players.

There is little doubt that the industry will grow. Since New Zealand's domestic market is too small to absorb the additional timber, it will have to be exported (see figure 38). Timber resources can be exported in several forms that are processed to a greater or lesser extent: raw logs, debarked logs, wood chips, flitches (cut

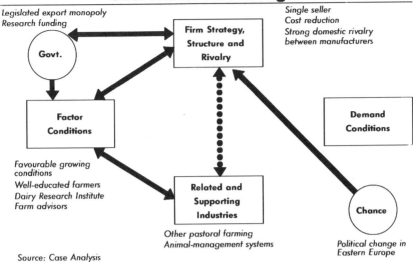

Figure 36

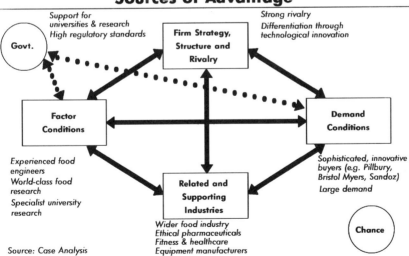

Figure 37

Growing Forest Products Export Potential

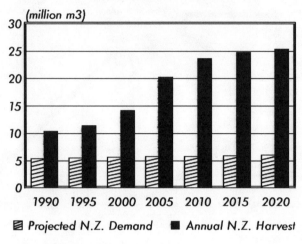

Projected N.Z. Demand   ■ **Annual N.Z. Harvest**

Source: Ministry of Forestry

Figure 38

lengths), various grades of sawn lumber, several types of wood-based panels or pulp and paper. Other possibilities include more sophisticated wood-based products such as furniture, flooring and pre-fabricated housing. Competing in each of these businesses requires different levels and types of investment, and offers different returns depending on one's time horizon.

The forest-products industry has some features that are similar to those of other New Zealand industries. It tends to rely on natural advantages such as rapid tree growth. Government has exercised significant control over the industry. There is limited domestic rivalry. Relatively few related and supporting industries have developed around the forest-products industry in New Zealand. New Zealand still focuses on commodity products such as logs, pulp and commodity paper products.

The industry is also unusual in several respects. Inbound and outbound foreign direct investment are important in the industry. Foreign investors, through direct ownership and joint ventures, play a larger role in the forest-product industry than in most New Zealand industries. Similarily, New Zealand forest-products companies are major investors overseas and are, in fact, among New Zealand's few multinationals.

During the 1980s, New Zealand firms became more sophisticated and important global competitors. However, they maintained a strong orientation toward factor-based cost competition in simpler commodities. Upgrading New Zealand's export mix to more sophisticated products and the development of a broad-based cluster of forest-products industries will require a different philosophy. Similarily, while international expansion is important, it does not compensate for a home base that lacks sophisticated demand, related and supporting industries, and active rivalry in the domestic market.

Wood Products

The forest-products industry provides a wide range of products. Most can be grouped under three main headings: raw materials (including logs and chips), reconstituted-fibre products (especially pulp, paper and fibreboard) and solid wood products (including timber, packaging timber, preserved timber, furniture, wood panels and other industrial products).

The main product of the forest-products industry in most countries is paper. Approximately two-thirds of world paper production consists of industrial paper and paperboard (used for packaging and wrapping). The other third is divided roughly evenly between newsprint and so-called "cultural" papers — for writing, printing and photocopying. In addition, many countries seek raw materials for their paper and timber industries. The international market for logs is strong and growing. Demand for many wood products, especially paper, is growing, and harvests from natural (non-plantation) forests are expected to decline markedly.

Pulp and paper dominate the New Zealand export industry. Pulp and waste papers accounted for 29.7% of forestry exports by value in 1988, while paper proper accounted for another 21.7%, making 51.4% of the total forest-products exports.[20] Sawn timber made up another 14.3%; unprocessed logs and woodchips 14.8%; fibreboard 7.8%; and assorted other products, including furniture and preserved timber 11.6%.[21] Each of these products is subject to different competitive forces and yields different margins.

The various products also provide very different returns to the wider New Zealand economy. For an average tonne of exported wood, processing to sawn timber and associated pulp and paper yields approximately two and a half times more sales dollars and about sixteen times as many jobs. Of course, these measures do not take into account the profitability of these choices. Profitability depends in the final analysis on the industry's international competitive position.

Industry History

As a lush, wooded, predominantly high-rainfall and temperate region, New Zealand provides an attractive environment for timber growing. The New Zealand forest-products industry began almost as soon as white settlers arrived in New Zealand. The enormous native kauri trees (which rivalled California's giant redwoods in size) proved to be ideal replacements for broken or damaged masts. Their gum was also used for varnish and paint.

Timber was also valuable for housing, cooking and heating. However, until the 1920s, only an estimated 10% of the forest felled in land-clearing operations in New Zealand was used for timber. Most was simply burned where it fell. In the

---

[20]Waste paper was an increasingly popular alternative to wood as a raw material for paper making.

[21]*Export of Forestry Products for the Year ended 31 December 1989 (Provisional)*, Ministry of Forestry, Statistics Section, SR 1, 1990.

late 1920s and 1930s, fearing depletion of wood resources, the New Zealand government initiated replanting programs and provided incentives to encourage private-sector planting. By 1938 the forerunner of New Zealand Forest Products, New Zealand Perpetual Trust, had plantations of over 170,000 acres. After some experimentation, one species, radiata pine, was found to be particularly suited to New Zealand's conditions.

Radiata pine grew naturally only in small areas of California. In its original habitat it had revealed few unusual features and grew only slowly and sparsely. In New Zealand's conditions, however, it thrived. Radiata pine grew up to seven times faster than indigenous species. It also grew faster in New Zealand than almost anywhere else in the world. Moreover, it could be harvested on a 30-year rotation cycle, compared to an average 60-100-year rotation for the main species available in Scandinavia and North America.

Before long, radiata pine was planted extensively across New Zealand. Since the 1960s, 1.2 million hectares have been planted and, in the 1990s, a large quantity is becoming available for logging. The forest-products industry was established in New Zealand in the 1950s and 1960s, with heavy government direct investment and incentives to encourage private investment, to utilize the radiata pine resource for export and import substitution.

The government encouraged the establishment of a pulp and paper industry. It provided some companies with generous grants and cheap logs, as well as subsidized infrastructure and inputs such as power, ports and railways. It also imposed heavy tariffs, mostly in excess of 40%, and in some cases total import bans to protect the industry from foreign rivals.

The government oversaw careful arrangements and agreements to ensure the industry's "orderly development". In essence, no competition was permitted, either domestic or foreign. The industry developed a cost-plus mentality. Not surprisingly, it also became inwardly focused. International competitiveness was not a problem; the industry was simply not allowed to face any effective challenge.

Deregulation and Competition in the 1980s
From its inception, the New Zealand forest-products industry has been heavily regulated and structured by direct government intervention. Approximately half of New Zealand's forests were planted by government agencies, and their end-uses deliberately oriented to maximize downstream processing in New Zealand.

In the mid 1980s, as part of its overall programme to deregulate the economy and expose New Zealand industry to market forces, the government made several key moves. First, it reduced or removed subsidies to tree growing. Most tax incentives for tree planting were abolished. In particular, a provision allowing the deduction of establishment costs was eliminated, and costs associated with the establishment of forest plantations were to be carried forward and deducted at the time of harvest.

Second, the government ceased below-market-price supply of logs to sawmills. In 1984, the government decided that log prices should reflect "replacement costs". While prices remained below market levels for a 5-year period as the new policy was phased in, they subsequently rose substantially. By 1990, sawmills had to bid in the open market for access to logs. However, two years into this period, the Forest Service was disestablished and its commercial activities taken over by the Forestry Corporation, which adopted a market-pricing policy.

Third, it scaled down tariffs and other protection against imports. Under the Closer Economic Relations treaty with Australia, which came into force in July 1990, Australian forest-products were allowed free entry to New Zealand, and vice-versa.

Fourth, and perhaps most importantly, the government decided to sell its own forest holdings, which amounted to about half of the total exotic forest estate. The resources would be sold to the highest bidder. Buyers would have exclusive logging rights, and would not necessarily be required to replant. Price maximization was the primary objective, and ensuring a competitive industry structure was not given any priority in the sales process.

The effect of these moves was to force the industry to fall back on its underlying competitive strengths. This was especially true for the growing proportion of New Zealand's production that would be exported.

By the beginning of 1991, the New Zealand forest-products industry was highly concentrated. Two firms held commanding positions:

- *Fletcher Challenge.* A widely diversified company and New Zealand's largest, Fletcher Challenge's global forest investments totalled $5.9 billion. About 25% of its forest-related assets are in Australia and New Zealand (about 20% were in New Zealand). In New Zealand, it controls 39% of paper production, 27% of market pulp production, 18% of sawn-timber production, and 45% of wood-panel output.

- *Carter Holt Harvey.* Another major diversified company with interests in fishing, building materials, office furniture, storage equipment, packaging, and milking and livestock equipment, Carter Holt controlled 40% of New Zealand's market pulp production (all of which was exported), 8% of paper and paperboard, and 17% of wood panels as well as sawn timber.

In June 1990, Carter Holt acquired Elders Resources NZFP, which had been the nation's leading forest-products company. This move reduced the number of large competitors in the sector to two. The new firm controlled 59% of New Zealand's market kraft pulp production, 61% of its paper and paperboard production, 38% of its sawn timber, and 62% of its wood panels. The Commerce Commission did not oppose the acquisition.

Competition in the Forest-products Industry

Competition in forest-products is driven by cost. Forest-products are commodities, in which suppliers with lower costs obtain higher margins. The international price of most forest-products is set by the interaction of supply and demand, with an increasing number of sellers and many buyers. The industry is subject to frequent cycles. Cost minimization is also critical to survival during downturns.

The major components of cost for forest products are logs, energy (electricity or fuel), processing (machinery and mills), labour, capital and transport. Most of these factors vary only within a relatively narrow band for producers in a particular country, but can diverge markedly from country to country. The costs of many of these components depend heavily on government policies.

The cost of logs depends on whether the logs come from plantation forests, where the costs of planting and tending are included, or virgin forests, where they are not. This — with other components of land costs — is reflected in wide variations in stumpage rates between countries. Other important costs are logging, transport and administration. There are substantial variations in log costs among nations.

Many countries are nearing the end of their readily accessible natural forest. In addition, pressures to preserve natural forests are increasing, especially in tropical and industrialized countries. In coming years, the industry will rely increasingly on plantations, so that favourable natural growing conditions and accumulated forestry expertise are likely to become more important. The costs of logs between countries is often affected by direct government interventions, such as subsidies in Chile, or indirectly, through artificially low exchange rates.

Energy costs also vary widely from country to country. Pulp and paper mills need large quantities of electricity. Electricity rates for pulp mills are frequently set by negotiations over bulk contracts. Governments often keep these rates artificially low in order to attract new investments.

Transport expenses are the most important variant for export sales. Transport costs for the large, bulky, and heavy raw materials and outputs are high and distance-dependent. Transport costs have made forest products a regional or "multi-domestic" industry. Competitors in Europe and North America have reduced their costs by locating plants near to both raw materials and final markets. This allows them to dominate their local and regional markets despite significant disadvantages in other cost components.

Processing costs vary widely between product types. However the industry is typically capital-intensive. For newsprint and other paper products, the major costs are, in order of importance, pulp inputs, energy, labour and overheads. Because many of these costs are lower per unit with larger output, scale is an important source of reduced costs. The minimum cost-efficient scale of pulp and paper mills has increased with technological advances.

To be successful in kraft pulp, for example, producers need large-scale plants and a ready and cheap source of wood fibre. The minimum efficient-scale kraft-pulp mill produces between 300,000 and 500,000 tonnes per year. At a capital cost of about $US2,000 per annual tonne of capacity, a greenfield mill could cost between $US500 million and $US1 billion. Kraft-pulp manufacturing requires relatively less electricity than other processed wood products and less labour per unit of output. Labour makes up only an estimated 8% of finished product-costs under current technology.

The largest cost component for medium-density fibreboard is wood; the second is power. Modern mills, such as the continuous-line process used at Nelson Pine Industries, have reduced the input of labour to only a few per cent of total expenses. Because the final product is so much more valuable and compact than the raw materials, transport costs are also relatively low.

In more sophisticated segments, such as fine papers for art, or related industries, such as paper-making machinery, competition is based more on differentation. Often competitive success in these industries requires superior technological and marketing skills.

Competitive Advantage and Disadvantage in the New Zealand Industry

The primary source of competitive advantage for the New Zealand forest-products industry is its fast-growing trees, which facilitate a reasonably low-cost position. However, New Zealand does not enjoy cost leadership (see figure 39). Research efforts through the Forest Research Institute into purpose-grown trees have improved upon New Zealand's cost position.

The New Zealand industry also benefits from the experience of harvesting several generations of its key planted forest types. New Zealand foresters know exactly how to extract optimum growth rates from their combination of natural factors. In addition, fast-growing trees have provided New Zealand management with a better understanding of forestry economics. This has been central to the international expansion of New Zealand forest-products multinationals.

There are pockets of sophisticated demand in the New Zealand market, such as

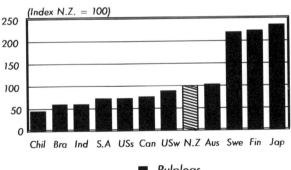

Comparative Costs
Softwood Pulplogs
(1988)

Source: Ministry of Forestry

Figure 39

panels, but these are not a major source of new products that can be sold in international markets. Limited competition in the domestic market means that consumers are offered a limited product range. The small size of the domestic market has focused management on international expansion.

New Zealand's electricity costs are not high compared to those of other industrialized nations in general. However, by comparison with other forest-product producers, including those in the OECD, New Zealand electricity costs are in the middle to upper range. While negotiation of bulk contracts with governments has often removed major cost disadvantages for New Zealand producers, they gain no advantage over international rivals in this element of cost.

Location has been an advantage for New Zealand firms in certain markets. Transport costs are higher in New Zealand than in other forest-product countries. However, New Zealand is closer to the Australian and East Asian markets than most of its competitors. Actual delivery costs are therefore often lower in these markets for New Zealand producers than for potential competitors. To Japan, New Zealand products are estimated to enjoy an average 36% lower delivery cost than Chile or Brazil. To Australia, New Zealand has a $US15 per tonne lower delivery rate than its closest rival.

Labour costs are relatively high in the New Zealand forest-products industry. While wages are modest by international standards, productivity is lower than in other countries. It has been estimated that it takes 5 person hours to produce a tonne of pulp in New Zealand, whereas in Canada it takes only 2.5 hours.

Low productivity, the natural result of years of protection, has hindered New Zealand's ability to compete in processed-wood products. In many instances, further processing of raw materials in New Zealand subtracts, rather than adds, value.

In summary, New Zealand producers enjoy an advantage at the level of tree growing and in their local markets due to prohibitive transport costs for competitors (see figure 40). However, New Zealand currently possesses few of the elements needed to compete effectively in most downstream processing on a world scale. New Zealand companies have responded to these realities by expanding overseas through acquisition. New Zealand companies have negligible positions in more sophisticated segments or related industries.

New Zealand's Options

There are several options for the export of the timber resources coming on stream in New Zealand. Compared to other nations, New Zealand grows a high percentage of high-quality logs. Much of New Zealand's forest resource has been intensively managed. Intensive management involves thinning, tending and careful monitoring. An intensive management regime that has produced a high-quality resource, with a high proportion of wood suitable for sawing. Raising timber of this quality has been far more expensive than raising timber solely for pulping.

The intensive managment programme has resulted in forests that can produce the clear, knot-free lumber that is preferred for furniture manufacturing,

NZ Forest Products
Strengths & Weaknesses

	Advantages	*Disadvantages*
Growing	• Favourable climate • Accumulated experience • Govt sunk costs	• Competition from virgin logging
Lumber	• Ease of sawing/treating	• High cost of capital • Low productivity • Outdated technology • Poor image of radiata pine
Pulp & Paper	• Availability of resource • Cheap transport to Asia	• Low productivity • High costs

Figure 40

woodturning and items such as kitchen woodware. New Zealand's forests are also well suited to producing structural and building timber, which has to be free of excessive knots, warping, rot, and twisting of the grain. New Zealand has not been able to compete successfully in these downstream segments due to inefficiencies in the processing stage. New opportunities and challenges will become available to the local industry as large amounts of quality clearwood timber become available over the next decade.

The quality of New Zealand's resource suggests another possible use — clearwood processing for decorative and display purposes. Globally, the supply of quality timber has been affected by severe overcutting and rising environmental concern. Meanwhile, the market for the product is expanding. Prices are expected to rise in the 1990s. New Zealand is potentially well placed to serve this market. Its industry is based on plantation forests, which are not subject to environmental controversy. Other countries with large plantation forests, such as Chile, have only recently begun to manage their forest resource for high-quality timber production.

However, whether New Zealand's industry can succeed in this segment is an open question. Clearwood production is relatively labour-intensive, and success hinges on the quality and reliability of supply. Productivity and efficiency in the industry will need to improve significantly for New Zealand to become internationally competitive in this segment.

Two types of processing, kraft pulp and medium-density fibreboard, are not seriously disadvantaged by New Zealand's position. Neither relies heavily on the elements in which New Zealand suffers high costs, and both draw strongly upon New Zealand's strength as a producer of fast-growing radiata pine. Indeed, the characteristics of radiata pine provide both with significant advantages.

In New Zealand, kraft-pulp mills use relatively cheap pulp logs and wood left over after sawmills and others take the prime cuts. The easiest way to guarantee the long-term and large markets necessary for investments in kraft pulp is to enter joint ventures with paper makers in other countries. Some New Zealand thermo-mechanical pulp producers have taken this road. Others have simply sought long-term contracts. Both make the pulp supplier heavily dependent on the importing partner and tend to hold down margins.

The raw materials for medium-density fibreboard, lower-grade offcuts and residues from sawmilling are also cheap in New Zealand. Disadvantages in New Zealand's power costs could be mitigated by negotiation of bulk contracts. New Zealand's disadvantages in processing have not seriously inhibited the development of medium-density fibreboard manufacturing.

New Zealand's capacity in medium-density fibreboard greatly exceeds domestic demand. As with pulp, one way to ensure markets overseas is to form joint ventures. Nelson Pine Industries, for example, is a 50-50 joint venture between New Zealand's Corporate Investments and Sumitomo, one of Japan's largest forest-products companies. Sumitomo agreed to take 36% of the plant's output for the Japanese market. With an estimated break-even point of 45% capacity utilization, the joint venture effectively eliminated risk for the plant.

Growing exports of clearwood, kraft pulp and fibreboard are not representative of the overall direction of New Zealand's forest-products industry. While kraft pulp and medium-density fibreboard are important exceptions, in general New Zealand has developed few advantages in wood processing. The consequence in the subsidy-reduced environment of the mid to late 1980s has been an accelerating tendency to export wood in a relatively less-processed, or even entirely unprocessed, form.

Exporting logs has several advantages for companies, particularly from a short-term viewpoint. It involves relatively little risk and investment outlay. In market downturns, trees can be left in the ground. The labour input is low and companies are less exposed to potentially belligerent unions which could shut down multi-million dollar plants. Large-scale processing mills require high rates of capacity utilization to be profitable and are very susceptible to cyclical downturns.

Issues for New Zealand

The principal issue for the New Zealand forest-products industry is the form in which its timber resources are exported. The question is whether the maximum value can be obtained from the resource.

In recent years, the percentage of logs in our exports has risen dramatically. This reflects New Zealand's underlying pattern of competitive advantage in forest products. In particular, it reflects the weaknesses of created advantages and the historic reliance of the industry on its natural-factor endowment and government support.

The government has paid for and/or actively encouraged the planting and tending of much of New Zealand's forests. There is no guarantee that the sale of cutting rights to large quantities of state-owned forests will ever cover these costs. Given the present state of our forest-products industry, it will not be surprising if large quantities of our high-quality resources are exported in unprocessed form. This would accentuate New Zealand's dependency on its advantages in growing trees and limit the value returned to the wider New Zealand economy.

Building a more secure and profitable industry that can make a major contribution to the New Zealand economy will require a different approach. If New Zealand is to build this type of industry, the dependence on commodity markets for simply processed products must be reduced and sources of advantage upgraded. Firms must make the large investments necessary to build world-class plants, rather than simply making profits off past investments by government. Sustained investment in upgrading the skill base in the workforce and management must take place. Labour productivity must be significantly improved. Research and investment must be deployed strategically to build new advantages in processing to augment New Zealand's advantages in growing trees. International expansion of our forest-products firms is necessary, but does not compensate for a weak home base (see figure 41).

New Zealand Forest Products Industry Sources of Advantage

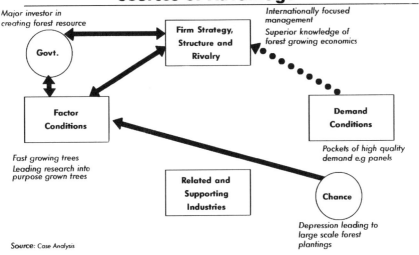

Source: *Case Analysis*

Figure 41

The New Zealand Electric-fencing Industry

New Zealand companies are by far the world leaders in the production and export of electric-fencing equipment, a $200 million industry in 1989. New Zealand producers accounted for about 20% of world production and in excess of 50% of world exports. In 1989, New Zealand firms exported $30 million in electric-fencing equipment.

New Zealand fencing equipment is known throughout the world for its superior performance. The success of New Zealand firms has been based primarily on continued innovation in upgrading and adapting basic technology to farmers' requirements rather than in advances in electronics technology.

The New Zealand electric-fence industry illustrates how the determinants of national competitive advantage interact. This is one of very few New Zealand industries we studied where leadership is based on exploiting created advantages rather than natural advantages. It is one of the few industries that takes advantage of sophisticated domestic demand. It is one of the few in which there are several local rivals. The way in which the individual determinants interact in electric fencing is rare within New Zealand industry.

There is a preoccupation in New Zealand business and government with the size of an industry rather than its competitiveness. Electric fencing is an example of how a very small industry can build a sustainable competitive position by tapping into unique features of the New Zealand environment.

Products

Electric fences are used to control animals, either by keeping them in a particular area or, in the case of predators, out of a given area. Electric fences are used primarily to control farm animals, mainly sheep and cattle, but are also used for a range of animals from snails to elephants. Electric fences give a short, sharp, but safe, shock, which is sufficiently memorable to ensure control.

Electric fences have been used both to replace and supplement stone walls and conventional fences made of wire and palings. There are significant cost savings in using electric fences. It has been estimated that a four-wire electric fence represents only 33% of the cost of a conventional eight-wire high-tensile wire fence. More importantly, electric fences are easily moved, giving farmers the ability to move animals from place to place within a paddock. This system of pasture management has resulted in production-efficiency gains of up to 20% in some types of farming.

Electric fences consist of three components: an energizer which produces an electric current; an insulated fence post; and the transmitting wire, which carries the electric current produced by the energizer. Electric fences are powered by either electrical mains or batteries. Mains-powered energizers are more reliable, and their use is recommended where possible.[22] Battery-operated systems are used in remote locations and in regions without a widespread electric-power supply, such as the Australian outback.

---

[22] *7th Gallagher Power Fencing Manual*, 1987.

Most New Zealand manufacturers purchase components for assembly within New Zealand. Others have their products manufactured under contract by other firms. Some of the New Zealand firms have licensed foreign companies in countries such as Argentina in order to lower labour and freight costs and overcome local content regulations.

Industry History
The electric fence was invented in the United States in the 1930s. The first fence systems employed a low-powered energy source and were easily shorted by grass and vegetative growth. These fences were used only for short-distance temporary fencing in the dairy industry. They were not considered suitable for permanent fencing, particularly in heavy-rainfall conditions.

Two pioneers of the New Zealand electric-fence industry, Bill Gallagher and Hubert Christie, introduced electro-mechanical battery-powered fences in the late 1930s. Bill Gallagher saw electric fences as a useful addition to the range of services he offered in conjunction with his farm-machinery repair business. Hubert Christie was an innovative dairy farmer who appreciated the benefits the system could offer.

Progress in the New Zealand fence industry was steady, but not spectacular, during the late 1940s and early 1950s. The development of the first solid-state energizer by Speedrite (Hubert Christie's company) in 1959 resulted in a significant improvement in reliability. The solid-state energizer had no moving parts that could wear out through mechanical action. This preceded other notable New Zealand advances, such as the first use by electric-fence manufacturers of the then novel transistor.

The next major technological breakthrough occurred in the 1960s. Ruakura, a government research facility, created the first unshortable fence which met international safety requirements. This breakthrough came about when it was demonstrated that fences that employed high-current pulses did not short. New Zealand manufacturers soon produced energizers of two to five orders of magnitude more energy per pulse than the original pulse models. This system made long-distance electric fencing practical.

Sophisticated Home Demand
New Zealand demand for electric fences in the 1960s and 1970s was fuelled by efforts on the part of New Zealand farmers to drive down costs and increase productivity. Prices for New Zealand's animal-derived products — meat, wool and dairy — had declined consistently in real terms since the 1950s. Even when prices moved against the trend (such as in the case of wool during the Korean war) it was only a temporary reprieve from the continual slide in prices.

The efforts to raise productivity centred on the two main costs of New Zealand farm-animals and land use. Continued upgrading of animals took place through breeding programmes that included the introduction of new and exotic breeds. On the land, productivity was improved through the use of new grass seeds, fertilizer programmes finely tuned to crop requirements, and electric fences for easy control of animals and pasture management.

The New Zealand fence manufactures have benefited from the advanced state of the nation's farming industries. New Zealand farmers are sophisticated in world terms. They are more likely to have tertiary qualifications than their overseas counterparts and are more willing to use new technology to improve productivity. The Ministry of Agriculture has also assisted in the dissemination of new technology through their extension programmes. The sophistication of the New Zealand farming community has a distinct impact on the electric-fence industry. New Zealand farmers were quicker to adopt electric fencing than farmers elsewhere. Similarly, the penetration of electric fencing in New Zealand is higher than elsewhere in the world.

While the United States is the world's largest market for electric fencing, American farmers tend to be less sophisticated than their New Zealand counterparts. As one industry source said, "To sell ashtrays you must first convince people to smoke — to sell electric fences you must first teach them to farm!" A major contributory factor to the relatively unsophisticated American demand is the nature of farming in many parts of the United States. American farmers tend to use housing and feed lotting, rather than grazing the animals on pasture. Pasture management and the electric fence have more limited potential under these conditions.

The relative sophistication of New Zealand farmers has allowed New Zealand firms to develop products for the local market that anticipate foreign demand. New Zealand farmers are discriminating, educated and sophisticated consumers of electric fencing systems. Their feedback provides the New Zealand industry with a continuing source of competitive advantage. In addition, the presence of several large pastoral industries in New Zealand provides fencing firms with opportunities to develop products that can be used to control a range of different animals.

Intense Rivalry
Growth in the market for electric fencing has encouraged the entry of new manufacturers into the industry. In the 1970s and early 1980s there were as many as eight New Zealand companies competing in an expanding, but still relatively small, market (in the order of $12 million). Several of the competitors were family firms, and rivalry was sometimes personal and intense.

Limited patent protection meant that innovations were quickly copied. To maintain market share, companies had continually to improve the quality of their products and service. Plastic Products provides an example of what happens to companies that do not keep up with rivals. It was the first firm to commercialize the energizer developed by Ruakura. The company believed that solid-state components would not fail and therefore did not set up a service organization. Their initial success (in the 1960s they sold 10,000 units in Ireland, for example) was quickly followed by their demise. Plastic Products had not appreciated that events beyond their control — such as lightning — could cause havoc with an electric-fence system. When this happened, their lack of a service-support organization rendered their products useless.

Other New Zealand competitors, although later into the game, innovated around this problem by using modular building blocks. When a problem occurred, the energizer was taken to a service agent who simply replaced the broken module. Plastic Products responded too late to this innovation and subsequently went out of business.

Intense rivalry among New Zealand firms makes it necessary to improve products continually or be forced to exit the business. Incremental innovations and product improvements by New Zealand firms had, by 1970, resulted in electric-fencing systems that were remarkably more advanced than the product offerings of foreign competitors. New Zealand firms continue to innovate. A recent example is the simple, but extremely useful, incorporation of a light into the energizer module. This has shortened the time it takes to track down a fault in the system by up to 50%.

Unlike many New Zealand industries in which there is more than one player, no industry association has been formed in electric fencing, no joint research has been undertaken and no attempts at co-operative marketing at either the national or international level have been attempted.

Internationalization
The small size of the New Zealand market for electric fences and the intense rivalry among local firms has made building an export business an imperative. Superior products allowed the New Zealand firms to gain foreign acceptance. Gallagher started exporting in the 1970s. Others soon followed suit. Government export incentives schemes, which were used by several firms, provided some of the stimulus. Overseas expansion was steady through the early 1980s, but by the late 1980s sales had fallen slightly from their 1986 peak.

In 1989, New Zealand firms' exports of electric fencing reached $30 million, accounting for over 60% of New Zealand electric-fence production. In 1990, some 75 precent of New Zealand production was exported. The major New Zealand firms, Gallaghers, Speedrite, Donaghys and PEL Industries, accounted for roughly 50% of world exports.

The major overseas markets for the New Zealand firms are Australia, the United States, Canada, the United Kingdom and the Netherlands. These nations have received the most attention from the New Zealand companies, since they follow modern farming practices which readily benefit from electric fences. Opportunities to sell electric fencing in developing countries, where farmers are usually poorly educated, are still limited.

The New Zealand companies have concentrated on building representation through local distributors of agricultural products in foreign markets, often through joint ventures. Marketing has focused on demonstrating the effectiveness of electric fencing directly to farmers at field days. This "value for money" approach has worked to the extent that in certain markets electric fences are called "the New Zealand fencing system".

The United States, while the largest market, is the home of the least sophisticated competitors. US technology has been described as not having moved since the mid-1950s. US energizers are viewed as "tin boxes" which are low priced and essentially disposable.

European competitors have concentrated on energizers. They have begun to supply complete fencing systems like the New Zealand companies only recently. Local suppliers are market leaders in Denmark and Germany. German firms were the leaders in France before being displaced by New Zealand companies.

Danish and German fence producers, such as Horizont Agratechnik GMBH, have strength in the traditional dairy markets in both Denmark and Germany, but were not a match for the New Zealand firms in new product areas such as fences for sheep, or in more "exotic" farming such as goats and deer. European suppliers had recently improved their position in energizers and had begun to supply accessories. Several competitors, particularly from Germany, were beginning to provide farmers with complete fencing systems.

Issues for New Zealand
The international pre-eminence of the New Zealand electric-fence industry illustrates how the determinants can interact to facilitate the development of competitive advantage. The interaction of sophisticated consumers and active local rivalry has provided the foundation for the sustained competitive advantage of the New Zealand industry.

New Zealand's competitive advantage depends on the continued change and innovation of companies competing furiously to satisfy demanding local customers who are often more sophisticated than overseas farmers. Strong positions in factor conditions, demand conditions, related industries and domestic rivalry have all reinforced the ability of New Zealand firms to compete successfully in international markets. New Zealand farmers have, in turn, been better able to capitalize on the invention and subsequent technological improvements of electric fences.

Small industries in highly focused segments where strong competitive positions can be developed have a vital role to play in the New Zealand economy. Such industries may facilitate diversification of our export base and upgrade productivity in related industries. New Zealand firms should seek out opportunities in industries, like electric fences, which are closely related to areas of New Zealand strength and where the determinants are favourable (see figure 42).

The New Zealand Software Industry

While New Zealand had the lowest percentage of technology intensive exports in the OECD, its software exporters developed a foothold in one of the world's most rapidly growing industries during the 1980s. New Zealand's software exports, negligible in 1980, had grown to an estimated $100 million by 1990 and continued to grow at a rate almost four times that of New Zealand exports as a whole (see figure 43). Software exports made up less than 1% of total New Zealand exports in 1990. However, the profitability of New Zealand's software exports was ten to twenty times that of New Zealand's resource-based industries. In terms of the profits generated for New Zealand, software was a significant contributor.

The New Zealand Electric Fencing Industry
Sources of Advantage

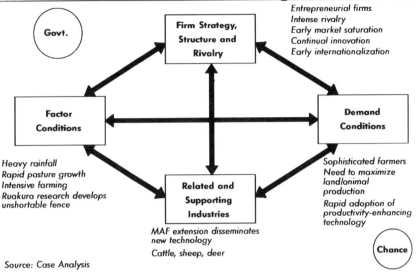

Figure 42

Rapid Growth in Software Exports

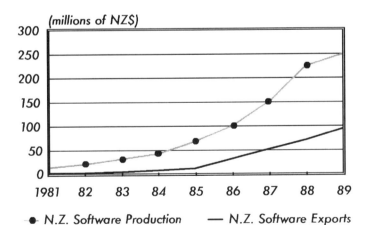

Source: Compass Hoby, Analysis

Figure 43

In contrast to the bulk of New Zealand's export industries, the software industry tends to be concentrated in some of the most sophisticated segments that serve the specialized needs of local and international customers. Entrepreneurship has played a critical role in developing and sustaining the position of New Zealand companies in this technology-intensive and rapidly changing industry.

The software industry illustrates that New Zealand companies can compete in one of the world's most rapidly growing and technology intensive industries. While "Kiwi ingenuity" and entrepreneurship have secured a foothold in this industry, a more favourable home environment must be built if the industry's opportunities are to be fully realized. The New Zealand software industry illustrates the need for sustained and well-directed investment by firms, industry associations and the education system in building the industry's business and skill base.

Products

Software is a set of coded instructions that direct the operations of a computer. At the broadest level, software is segmented into systems and applications software. Systems software manages the internal operations of the computer. Applications software is designed to perform specific tasks. Advances in computer technology continues to reduce the price-performance ratios of computers, which in turn accelerates demand for software of all types.

Industry History

The development of the New Zealand software industry, as that elsewhere, has closely tracked improvements in, and the availability of, computer-hardware technology. As computers have become cheaper and more accessible, demand for an ever-growing range of software products has emerged.

The New Zealand software industry had its start when an IBM mainframe was installed by the Treasury in 1960. Some software for this machine was developed in-house although much of it was imported with the hardware. The high cost of computers meant that only a small number of government departments and large firms in New Zealand used them until the introduction of the mini-computer in the early seventies. The wider application of computers in New Zealand that resulted from this created demand for locally developed software and stimulated the development of the local industry. Several of New Zealand's leading software exporters of today, such as FACT International and several of the companies that were acquired to form PAXUS, were founded around this time.

The combination of high import duties and New Zealand's isolation made computer hardware relatively more expensive in New Zealand than elsewhere. This resulted in tremendous pressures to develop software which would optimize the value of hardware investments and reduce the need for imported software. Local software developers that were able to improve the performance or capabilities of hardware met a ready local market. Many of these products had international sales potential.

The introduction of the personal computer in the early eighties vastly increased computer penetration in New Zealand as it did elsewhere in the world. It also stimulated demand for software written for the personal computer. This led to a second wave of new software businesses being formed in New Zealand. In 1981, the year that the IBM PC was introduced, over thirty new software firms were formed, more than twice the number of the previous year.

The introduction of new technologies continued to create opportunities for new products and stimulate growth. The possibilities of computer networking, artificial intelligence and the increasing integration of telecommunications and computer equipment provide a range of new possibilities.

While the first instances of exports of software from New Zealand occured in the early seventies, it wasn't until the mid-eighties that software exports exceeded $10 million. Australia (44%) and the United States (38%) were the major foreign markets, although there had also been sales of New Zealand software in many other parts of the world. The larger New Zealand firms operated sales and support offices in the major markets. Several, such as PAXUS, had research facilities offshore. By 1990, approximately a quarter of New Zealand's three hundred sofware companies were involved in exports, although thirty firms made up over 90% of exports. PAXUS, Linc and FACT were the largest exporters (see figure 44).

Pockets of Sophisticated Demand
New Zealand demand for software has not generally been at the leading edge. Many of New Zealand's successful software exporters, however, have developed products for pockets of sophisticated demand in New Zealand that were then sold internationally.

NZ Software Industry Structure

TIER 1	TIER 2
70% of Industry Revenue	30% of Industry Revenue
30 Firms	270 Firms
90% of Exports	10% of Exports
Average 33 Employees	Average 3 Employees
Average Turnover $5.8 million/firm	Average Turnover $280,000/firm
Average Exports $2.6 million/firm	No Exports
Alliance	No Alliance

Source: Industry Interviews

Figure 44

New Zealand's horticultural industries depend on their ability to export premium fruit to distant markets. The demand for improvements in fruit-grading systems technology is correspondingly intense. AWA New Zealand created a fruit-grading system, LYNX, to address this market. LYNX employs a sizing system to sort fruit into different grades for packing. A colour-recognition system is then used to reject fruit that fails to meet specifications. This information is simultaneously stored in a database for management and control. LYNX is available in modules so it can be adapted to specific customer requirements. Working with sophisticated customers in this particular segment within New Zealand has resulted in a product that is increasingly sold in international markets.

Small Domestic Market
The small size of the New Zealand market often means that there are close interactions between local customers and software companies, usually at senior-executive levels. Several New Zealand software companies find it easier to gain access to senior managers in New Zealand than overseas. The software companies are able to get rapid feedback on areas that require improvement and on new-product ideas which sometimes translate into first-mover advantages.

In addition, the small size of the New Zealand market means that a successful product quickly saturates the local market. Firms that seek significant growth have to expand into international markets.

"Kiwi Ingenuity"
Innovation in software is often dependent on the ability to conceive and develop new and/or improved applications. New Zealand lacks many of the benefits that are present in the United States and some other nations. New Zealand does not have a plethora of world-class university software programmes or research efforts, leading-edge computer-hardware companies, a large pool of trained software engineers or large and sophisticated software markets. In spite of these disadvantages, several New Zealand software companies are successful in particular segments. "Kiwi ingenuity" has been a major factor.

The Linc Development Centre, the leading supplier of programmer productivity tools for Unisys mainframes, provides one such example. In its area of expertise, Linc Development's innovative capacities exceed those of Unisys's own research laboratories. The company was founded in 1978 by Gil Simpson and Peter Hoskins. They had been frustrated by the difficulties in programming in Cobol, the traditional programming tool at that time. As a result, they developed Linc, which requires approximately a tenth of the amount of code as Cobol for a given application and increases programmer efficiency up to twenty times. Linc, which also has the capacity to be rapidly adapted to meet changing circumstances, eventually became the world leader in its segment.

Determined entreprenuers have played a central role in each New Zealand software success story. The companies, their products and strategies often clearly bear the mark of the central entreprenuer.

Capital Constraints

The development of software products is a risky endeavour. Many product-development programmes never result in saleable products. Markets are often overestimated. A successful mass-market product, like Lotus 1-2-3, however, can generate phenonmenal investment returns. Such an industry has special financing needs.

In the United States and Britain, sophisticated venture capitalists specialize in the financing of high-risk, high-return ventures and often participate in the management of the ventures they invest in. Many of the world's leading software companies have been backed by venture capitalists. New Zealand lacks a professionally organized venture capital market. Local software companies cannot draw on this source of capital and management expertise.

New Zealand's high interest rates means that bank finance can be prohibitively expensive, particularly as software ventures, like start-ups in many other industries, generally have long periods of negative cash flow before the first sales are secured. New Zealand banks lack experience with software companies and consequently are reluctant to lend to them. Best Knowledge Systems was a New Zealand company sold by a bank receiver to overseas interests. Shortly after its sale, its products achieved significant success in the United States.

Limits in New Zealand's equity and debt markets force New Zealand entrepreneurs to finance operations with personal savings or contract programming. It has also led many New Zealand firms to seek alliances with multi-national hardware vendors. These alliances provide access to finance and distribution channels but also reduce the potential profitability of the New Zealand companies.

Limited Human-resource Development

Skilled people are the key resource required by software companies. In New Zealand, however, linkages between the education system and the local software industry are limited. While the number and range of computer-related courses offered at New Zealand universities has grown, many local software companies refuse to hire these graduates on the grounds that they lack a practical business orientation. Many senior New Zealand software executives received their training in the industry while working for foreign multinational hardware vendors. These multinationals continue to be an important source of business and technological experience, since New Zealand firms or industry associations have only limited training programmes. On-the-job training tends to be the primary source of skills upgrading within the New Zealand firms.

Issues for New Zealand

"Kiwi ingenuity" and determined entrepreneurs have given New Zealand companies a foothold in this rapidly growing, global industry. These have not been sufficient to hold some succesful companies in New Zealand. Paxus, the largest software company to originate in New Zealand, is now owned by foreign interests. Most of its senior executives and research activities are located either in Australia or the United Kingdom. Pressures to remain close to the international

New Zealand Software Industry
Sources of Advantage

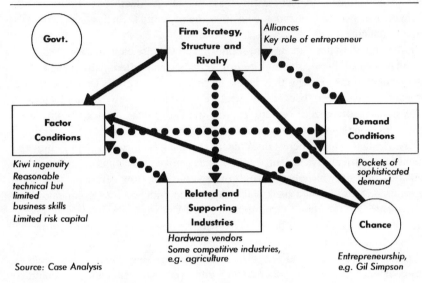

Figure 45

customer base, pools of skilled personnel and innovation in technology made being headquartered in New Zealand increasingly problematic.

New Zealand software companies face several disadvantages compared to their international competitiors. Foremost among these disadvantages are a lack of highly trained personnel and a poor climate for new business formation and growth. Both will have to be remedied before the industry can achieve more widespread and sustained success.

In order to achieve true international success, the industry needs to develop broader and deeper sources of advantage. Computer-science education needs to be more closely aligned with the skills needed by industry. Companies need to institute training programmes at all levels. Sustained investment by firms, industry associations and the education system are needed to raise software skills. A specialized financial infrastructure needs to be developed to support the requirements of high-risk, high-growth companies.

The software industry illustrates that New Zealand firms can compete in sophisticated segments of rapidly-growing, technology-intensive industries. However, it also highlights the need for continual upgrading of an industry's skills base and for finanical markets with the capacity to support new and growing businesses.

As the world economy becomes more integrated, firms will often move to those locations that are most favourable for their particular industries. This is where their odds of true success are greatest, and where they can capture the highest

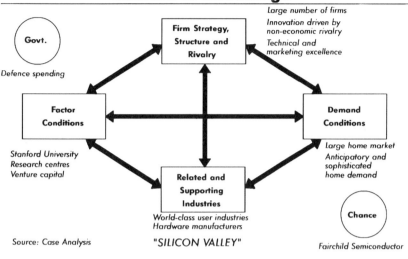

Californian Software Industry
Sources of Advantage

Figure 46

value for their ideas, talents and fledgling companies. Some of New Zealand's leading software companies have been sold to foreign interests willing to pay a price greater than the perceived value of staying independent and based in New Zealand, while others have moved to other countries. Building a more positive business environment in New Zealand is crucial to allow emerging industries, such as software, to form and to grow into international success stories.

Summary

The four industries discussed in this chapter illustrate important issues for the New Zealand economy. Each shows the need for continued upgrading of firm capabilities. Each provides examples of opportunities that New Zealand firms have yet to exploit fully. Several of the issues raised by these industries are systemic throughout the New Zealand economy. These issues are discussed more fully in the next chapter.

5

The Determinants of National Advantage in New Zealand

This section will analyse the sources of advantage of New Zealand firms with respect to the determinants of national advantage. The analytical framework outlined in Chapter 2 will be used to isolate the influences of the local environment on New Zealand firms' ability to compete in the international market-place. This chapter builds on detailed studies of twenty of New Zealand's export industries and our analysis of the institutional context within which New Zealand firms operate.

This "micro" approach involved understanding the nature of competition and the sources of advantage and disadvantage of New Zealand firms in each industry. It became readily apparent in the course of the study that each industry had a unique set of determinants that influenced its structure and presented it with challenges and opportunities. An understanding of each of the individual industries led to insights into the traded sector and the New Zealand economy as a whole. These insights are summarized in this chapter.

Industry Sample. We studied twenty industries in which New Zealand has a disproportionate share of world exports. In total, they accounted for some $NZ15.7 billion, or 85% of total export earnings in 1989 (see figure 47).

The industries were chosen to provide a comprehensive picture of New Zealand's traded sector. We studied New Zealand's traditional industries, including dairy, meat and wool, industries which have been important to the economy for decades and still make up the bulk of our exports. We studied other industries, such as forest products, apples, kiwifruit, fish, construction and tourism that have become important in the past two decades. We have also studied a group of emerging industries, such as deer, wine, yachts and software, which have only begun to make an impact in the last decade.

In some cases, industries were considered for their perceived potential rather than actual earnings. The Education Amendment Act of 1989, for example,

20 Export Industries Studied

NZ$ 15.7 billion - 85% of total exports

	Traditional	Growing	Emerging
Agriculture	Dairy Meat Wool	Forest Products Apples Fish Kiwifruit	Deer Goats Wine Cut Flowers
Manufacturing	Manufacturing		Electric Fences Yachts Methanol
Services	Tourism	Construction	Software Eng. Consulting Education
	$11.9b 76%	$3.4b 22%	$0.4b 2%

Source: Case Study Analysis

Figure 47

allowed state educational institutions to charge full fees to foreign students for the first time. This opened up the opportunity of earning foreign exchange from foreign students. In some cases, such as methanol, New Zealand's position in international trade appears to have been funded by the taxpayer rather than representing true competitive advantage.

Industry Study Overview. Space does not allow us to provide abstracts of all the industry studies in this document. Figure 48, however, provides a picture of the relative importance of the different determinants of national advantage in fostering competitive advantage in the industries studied. It is, of course, impossible to summarize months of work and hundreds of pages of industry studies in a single figure. The chart does, however, show several patterns:

(i) The primary source of competitive advantage for the majority of New Zealand's export industries that make up the vast bulk of our exports is our favourable natural-factor conditions complemented by efficient production. These industries compete mostly on the basis of low-cost primary production that relies on basic-factor advantages.

(ii) There is a very small group of New Zealand industries in which the uniqueness of some aspect of New Zealand demand conditions has led to the development of an internationally competitive position. These industries make up less than 5% of New Zealand's export earnings.

(iii) Government, through its historic role as central actor in the economy, has had

NZ's Sources of Competitive Advantage

Legend:
- ● Strong Influence
- ● Moderate Influence
- ○ Some Influence
- Blank - no influence

	Factor Conditions		Demand	Related and Supporting Industries	Strategy Structure & Rivalry	Govt.	Chance
	Availability	Creation					
Factor Driven							
Apples	●	○		○	○		●
Cut Flowers	●						
Dairy	●	●		○	○	○	●
Deer	●			●			●
Fishing	●				○	○	●
Forest Products	●	○			○	●	●
Goats	●	○		●			●
Kiwifruit	●	●		○	○	○	●
Meat	●	●		○	○	○	●
Methanol	●					●	●
Tourism	●	○	○	○	○	○	●
Wine	●				○		
Wool	●	●		○	○	○	
Demand Driven							
Construction	●	○	●	○	○	●	○
Electric Fences	●	○	●	●	●	●	●
Eng. Consulting	●	○	●	○	○	●	○
Software	●	○	●	○	○		●
Yachts	●	●	●	●	●		●

Figure 48

an impact on shaping the development of our export sector. While, on balance, government has impeded the development of broad-based competitive advantage in the New Zealand economy, there are some cases where government policy and action have contributed to the development of competitive advantage in New Zealand industry.

(iv) Favourable chance events have had a major impact on the development of our export base.

(v) Very few New Zealand industries have developed multiple sources of competitive advantage. The industries with more than one or two sources of competitive advantage, such as racing yachts and electric fencing, are very small.

These patterns, and others based on our study of New Zealand's export industries and institutional structure, will be the subject of the rest of this chapter.

Factor Conditions

Factors of production can be grouped into five broad categories: physical resources, infrastructure, human resources, knowledge and capital. The mix of factors employed differs widely among industries. A nation's firms can gain competitive advantage if they possess low-cost or high-quality factors that are significant to competition in a given industry.

Physical Resources

Favourable Land and Climate. New Zealand enjoys an abundance of favourable physical resources. Its temperate climate is ideal for pastoral farming, horticulture and forestry. There are few droughts; grass grows year round. New Zealand's farm land is among the most productive in the world. For example, the Bay of Plenty region, with its hot summer, gradually cooling autumn and relatively cold winter, provides favourable growing conditions for kiwifruit. Trees grow very quickly in New Zealand. Radiata pine, for example, grows faster in New Zealand than most places in the world.

New Zealand's "clean, green and unspoiled" image provides a basis of differentiation that New Zealand firms can use to market agricultural products. Since the Chernobyl nuclear disaster, European buyers have become more sensitive to the environmental conditions in which meat is grown. The New Zealand deer industry is attempting to differentiate its venison by capitalizing on New Zealand's appealing image.

New Zealand's topography with mountain peaks over 12,000 feet high less than 20 miles from the sea provides spectacular sights for tourists, as do the geothermal regions. These settings are enhanced by the nation's low population density and "clean, green" image. New Zealand's unique geographic position means that a range of very different environments from subtropical in the Bay Islands to the fjords of the South Island are in close proximity. The climate is ideal for a wide range of outdoor activities. Tourists can go skiing in the Southern Alps, sailing around Auckland harbour or hiking along the Milford Track.

Isolated Location. New Zealand's location in the southern hemisphere provides advantages to several of our agricultural industries. New Zealand's growing season is counter-cyclical to that of its northern hemisphere competitors. Local producers export certain products, including kiwifruit and apples, during the northern hemisphere's off season.

New Zealand's relative isolation, combined with strict quarantine regulations, have kept the nation free of debilitating diseases such as foot-and-mouth disease. New Zealand's location resulted in its obtaining the world's seventh largest exclusive economic zone at the Law of the Sea Conference. This has been the foundation of the development of the New Zealand fishing industry.

New Zealand's relative isolation has long been considered a disadvantage in that we are far from the markets of North America and Europe. It is not clear that this is as much of a disadvantage as it once was. The Pacific Rim economy is growing far more rapidly than that of North America or Europe. New Zealand is well situated geographically to take advantage of this trend. Many of our industries, such as dairy, wool, meat, tourism and construction, have been active in serving Asian markets.

Natural Resources. Natural resources figure prominently in several of New Zealand's export industries. As mentioned, the fishing industry harvests unique species of fish, such as orange roughy, that are found within our territorial waters. The aluminium smelter at Tiwai uses South Island hydroelectric power. New

Zealand's methanol industry, centered at New Plymouth, uses natural gas from the Maui gas field.

Infrastructure

Inefficient Ports and Shipping. Although New Zealand has invested heavily in infrastructure, the national infrastructure is not a source of advantage to most of our industries. Given that roughly 90% of our exports are transported by sea, it is difficult to overestimate the importance of New Zealand's ports to our economic prosperity. Relative inefficiency in our ports adds costs to virtually all of our exports, many of whose margins are already under pressure. New Zealand's ports and shipping facilities have not been competitive with those of other nations. While New Zealand's ports process an average of 25 containers per hour, Japan's process 40 and Singapore's process 64.[1]

The government has moved to improve efficiency in the ports. These improvements have led to significant savings, particularly for our agricultural exporters. The Dairy Board estimates that it will save $4-5 million a year, or 25-30% of local component costs due to improved productivity at the ports.[2] Federated Farmers estimates that the average New Zealand farmer has benefited by some $3,500 a year.[3] New Zealand's waterfront workforce was halved in twelve months, with first-year savings estimated at $58 million. The Port of Tauranga handled an average of 2,550 cargo tonnes per ship day in port in the first quarter of 1990, a 60% improvement over the previous year's 1,550.[4] While these improvements have reduced our disadvantage with regard to port services, port services have not improved to the point that they are a competitive advantage to New Zealand's exporters.

Singapore's efficient and low-cost port provides a range of local industries with a source of competitive advantage. Some Singaporean companies have used reliable delivery to win contracts from competitors that are closer to the client but cannot guarantee delivery. The efficiency of Singapore's port also aids the local ship-repair and trading industries, and helps make Singapore an excellent location for regional distribution centres and multinational companies. New Zealand's ports have not provided the nation, or its firms, with this sort of advantage.

New Zealand exporters are further disadvantaged by uncompetitive shipping. This is particularly true between New Zealand and Australia. Union contracts require ship operators to maintain two full-time crews on each ship. Union-imposed restrictions prohibit ships from other nations entering the trade. As a result, the trans-Tasman route is one of the most expensive in the world. One study found that New Zealand crew costs were 24% higher than the OECD average.[5] Dry bulk-freight rates for Australian or New Zealand flagged ships were

[1] *Ports and Shipping Reform in New Zealand*, New Zealand Business Roundtable, September 1989.

[2] Extract from MAF Discussion Paper on Shipping and Port Reform 1990.

[3] *Trans-Tasman Transportation: A Report on Progress*, Trebeck, D. (1990), ACIL Australia.

[4] *Management Magazine*, November 1990.

[5] Report on New Zealand Shipping Industry Reform Task Force, July 1990.

approximately twice those available from foreign flag operators in mid 1990. Some products are more economically shipped via Singapore or Japan than directly between Australia and New Zealand.[6] Shipping company and union initiatives have reduced the discrepancy, though shipping costs continue to disadvantage New Zealand exporters. The problem is that these uncompetitive shipping rates nullify a large portion of the gains we would expect from the Common Economic Relations with Australia and our close proximity to that country.

Adequate General Infrastructure. New Zealand's road, rail, airport, and telecommunications systems are generally regarded as adequate, yet provide no particular advantage to New Zealand firms. All of these systems have been deregulated to varying degrees in recent years. Restrictions on entry and prices were removed from road transportation. The rail system has been corporatized and deregulated. The telecommunications system has been privatized and deregulated, though is still a virtual monopoly. The airports and post have been corporatized, while the ports have been restructured.

Significant reductions in excess manning indicate that these moves have improved the efficiency of New Zealand's national infrastructure. At the time of corporatization of Telecom in 1987, the organization had 25,000 staff including 2,500 in the head office. By 1990, there were 14,000 staff and only 330 at the head office. During this time services were improved and extended. This is only one example of the type of improvement that is being made, and that could be made, in improving the efficiency and cost of New Zealand's infrastructure.

Limited Specialized Infrastructure. The instances in which New Zealand has invested in **specialized** infrastructure that provides a distinct advantage to its companies are isolated. Most of these examples are related to agriculture, such as the transportation of perishable produce. The Department of Scientific and Industrial Research, in conjunction with the New Zealand Apple and Pear Marketing Board, pioneered the incorporation of controlled atmosphere storage into shipping containers. This technology improved New Zealand's ability to deliver fresh produce to distant export markets and helps New Zealand fruit exporters compete with foreign fruit producers.

Summary. On balance, the national infrastructure in New Zealand provides few sources of competitive advantage. Improvements in recent years have been aimed at "catching up" with overseas competitors rather than building a competitive lead. New Zealand's distance from major markets is a natural disadvantage that might be overcome by world leadership in infrastructure.

Human Resources
New Zealand faces fundamental human-resource challenges. We have not invested aggressively in creating the pools of human-resource skills needed to be internationally competitive. The rate of participation in the workforce is low as are the levels of training and skills. Many economically active people have emigrated,

---

[6] Trebeck, D. (1990), op. cit.

particularly to Australia. The education system is not well designed to develop economically useful skills. Limited management training, convoluted and antagonistic labour relations, low skill levels, and the nature of the industries in which we compete have contributed to one of the lowest levels of labour productivity in the industrialized world.

Low Participation in Education. On average, young New Zealanders spend far less time in formal education than is common in most industrialized nations. Our school retention rates are lower than those of many other nations in the OECD (see figure 49). This pattern is evident in all age groups up to age 24. Combined with low retention is the fact that our school year of 190 days a year is shorter than Australia's 200, Germany's 220 and Japan's 240 days a year. Less than a third of the young New Zealanders who complete high school go onto to tertiary education while in Europe, North America and Asia the portion is typically in the order of two-thirds.

Education Participation Rates - % Of Age Group

	16 years	18 years	20 years	22 years
Australia (87)	85.8	46.4	31.6	20.1
Austria (85)	85.6	47.7	16.2	13.7
Belgium (86)	92.3	69.0	47.6	21.6
Canada (86)	94.7	53.1	34.1	18.6
Denmark (86)	89.6	66.6	36.6	23.7
Finland (86)	92.1	64.8		
France (86)	87.1	55.6	25.5	13.3
Germany (86)	100.0	83.8	34.8	26.9
Greece (85)	69.7	43.2		
Ireland (85)	80.3	39.6	15.4	5.5
Japan (80)	84.0			
Netherlands (86)	89.5	58.8	31.3	17.0
NEW ZEALAND (88)	78.0	34.6	26.5	16.5
Norway (86)	85.1	62.6	23.7	22.6
Sweden (80)	87.4	44.7		
Switzerland (86)	81.9	73.2	29.6	16.9
Turkey (86)	35.3	14.9		
U.K. (81)	68.0	36.3		
United States (86)	94.0	58.6	37.1	22.0
N.Z. RANKING	16th	18th	9th	10th

Source: Education Department

Figures in brackets next to each country is the year the latest data is available

Figure 49

Low retention rates in education are reflected in our workforce. Over 38% of the New Zealand workforce has no recognized educational qualifications[7] (see figure 50). This stands in sharp contrast to Japan's workforce, of which less than a third of the workforce lacks qualifications, and Germany's, of which less than a quarter lacks any qualifications. In 1984, 60% of New Zealand's school leavers

---

[7] *Household Labour Force Survey*, New Zealand Department of Statistics, March 1990.

Qualifications

Population aged 15 years and over

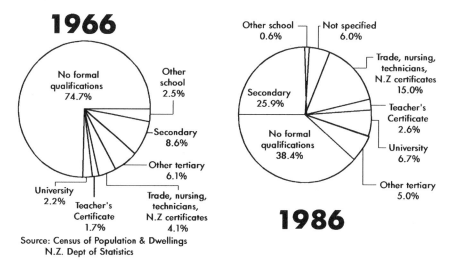

Source: Census of Population & Dwellings
N.Z. Dept of Statistics

Figure 50

entered the workforce with no formal qualifications. This compared to an average of under 10% in Switzerland, Denmark and Austria.[8] In a global economy where high living standards are increasingly a function of the levels of education and training in the workforce, these statistics provide cause for grave concern. The lack of educational qualifications of our young people, who represent our future, is particularly troubling.

Low Participation in the Private Sector. A relatively low percentage of New Zealanders have educational qualifications and are in the private sector. Figure 51 graphically illustrates the percentage of New Zealanders active in the workforce. The first bar shows that 66% of New Zealand's population is between 15 and 65 years of age and included in the pool of potential employees. The resulting proportion of natural dependents (i.e children and elderly people) is the third highest in the OECD.

The second bar divides the available labour pool into state beneficiaries, state employees, and people of working age that are not participating in the workforce. Once these segments are accounted for, 36% of the country's population remains. In other words, 36% of all New Zealanders are working in the private sector. These people are essentially responsible for generating the wealth to support the entire society.

---

[8] *Tomorrow's Skills*, NZPC, May 1989.

"One in Five"

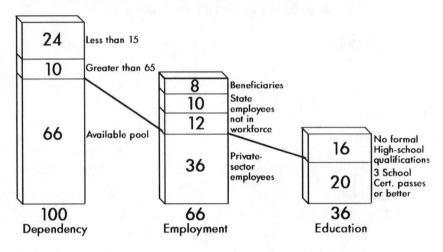

Source: Department of Statistics;   *National Bank Business Outlook*   ; *Household Labour Force Survey* , March 1989; *World Competitiveness Report 1990*   IMD.

Figure 51

If we look at the 36% of the population in the private sector workforce, we find that only 20% of our entire population is in the private sector workforce and has a high-school education. This can be seen in the third bar, which divides the 36% between those with 3 School Certificate passes (or better) and those with no formal high-school qualifications. The net result of this analysis is rather sobering. Only one out of five New Zealanders is likely to be in a position to make real contributions to upgrading our economic base.

Relevance of Curricula. It is not clear that even educated New Zealanders have the skills necessary to create the levels of national income we aspire to. The relevance of the education provided by our schools and their role in developing economically meaningful skills are important issues. New Zealand's education system has not adequately prepared many New Zealanders to contribute to their own and the nation's economic well-being.

New Zealand's education system has tended to focus on social objectives, rather than subjects with direct economic value such as sciences, engineering, mathematics and management. While the social objectives are laudable, there is a question of balance. A national education system that focuses on academic achievement rather than technical, scientific and managerial skills faces serious difficulties in preparing people to compete in an increasingly competitive world. Such a system is unlikely to help create the national income necessary to fund many of the nation's social goals.

Lack of Language Skills. Competing successfully in international markets will require greater fluency in the languages of our customers. Increasingly, they are not likely to be European, let alone English speaking. However, our commitment to foreign-language learning has been limited and not well matched to New Zealand's trading requirements. In 1988, for example, 19% of all secondary-school students were studying European languages compared to 3% studying Asian languages, particularly Japanese.[9] Yet Japan is already our largest trading partner, and significant further growth in New Zealand-Japan trade is widely anticipated. The most popular foreign language is French, even though France is of minor economic importance to New Zealand.

Lack of Technical Preparation. The focus of our curriculum at all levels appears to have been developed with little regard for skill bases that will be critical to success in an increasingly technological world. Participation and performance in such areas as mathematics and science is poor compared to other advanced nations. In a world in which competitive success is increasingly based on the mastery of new technology, a declining proportion of our high-school and university students are taking technology-related courses. Roughly three-quarters of secondary-school students have little or no experience with technology subjects.[10] An OECD study estimated that should these trends continue, by the turn of the century the number of New Zealand's technology-based graduates will decrease by over 20%.

Engineering skills have become increasingly important in modern international competition, yet New Zealand trains relatively few engineers. In 1986, fewer than 10% of third-level students were studying engineering. This was significantly behind Singapore, with over 43%, Sweden with 18%, and Germany and Japan with 17%. Both Denmark and Switzerland had a significantly higher percentage of students studying engineering than New Zealand. Canada and Australia, two other nations that tend to export primary products, had figures comparable to New Zealand (see figure 52).

Those institutions that do teach technical subjects are having difficulty in attracting students. Auckland University takes all the science and engineering students it can find, but according to university officials, the school system does not produce people with an interest in acquiring technical skills. Shortages of scientists in New Zealand are predicted for the next several years.[11]

Lack of Training for Industry. New Zealand's institutions of higher learning generally do not focus on skill areas critical to upgrading the economy. New Zealand graduates more lawyers each year than it graduates students in agriculture, forestry, horticulture and veterinary science combined (see figure 53). This latter group of industries makes up over 85% of New Zealand's exports and needs skilled individuals to improve their competitive position.

---

[9] Levett, A., and Lankshear, C. (1990), *Going for Gold: Priorities for Schooling in the Nineties*, p. 17, Daphne Brassell Associates Press.

[10] Levett, A., and Lankshear, C. (1990), op. cit., p. 16.

[11] Watt, L. (1991), "Big Chance for Eager Scientists", *Sunday Star*, January 1.

Low Numbers Studying Engineering in NZ

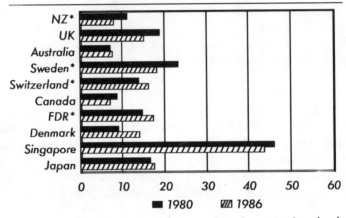

■ *1980*   ▨ *1986*

% of students studying engineering at tertiary levels

Source: Yearbook of International Trade Statistics, UN, 1987

(* 1987)

Figure 52

University Degrees Completed by Subject 1989

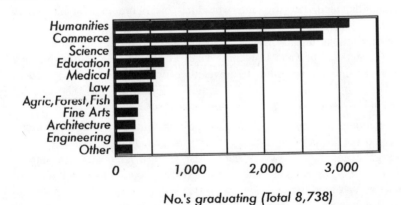

No.'s graduating (Total 8,738)

Source: Ministry of Education

Figure 53

The demand for commerce courses in New Zealand has outstripped supply. In 1985 there were 800 applicants for bachelor of commerce courses, but only half gained entry. In 1990, 867 were accepted from a pool of 1,551 applicants. Approximately one-third of all commerce students will graduate in accounting rather than management studies.

Lack of a Vocational Focus. Our education system has a distinct academic and theoretical bias. Many of our graduates in areas like engineering and computer science have a theoretical focus poorly suited to industry. The status of our theoretically inclined universities is far higher than that of our more vocationally oriented polytechnics. Teachers of vocational subjects are accorded lower status than their colleagues. While very few New Zealanders will actually require academic training for their working careers, our education system tends to focus on preparation for university. It tends not to provide a relevant and excellent preparation for work for the majority of students that do not go on to full-time tertiary education.

Industry Dissatisfaction with the Education System. As the full extent of New Zealand's economic difficulties have become apparent to even the most optimistic observer, the debate on the mix of objectives in our education system has become more intense. Our research has found a widespread and deep-seated dissatisfaction in industry with the contribution that our education system is making to New Zealand's economic development. There is a large body of opinion in industry that our education system is not equipping people with the skills necessary to compete successfully in the global economy.

Burgeoning unemployment provides ready evidence that tens of thousands of New Zealanders lack the skills to be able to support themselves in productive and rewarding work in the modern economy where skills are paramount. This dissatisfaction has yet to be channelled towards a consensus as to the objectives and processes that will be needed to build a world-class education system tailored to our economic needs and social aspirations.

Limited Management Education. Opportunities for management education, while improving rapidly in recent years, remain limited. Success in international competition will require a new breed of manager. International success will require a fundamentally different and more sophisticated orientation to competition than New Zealand management has been used to. It requires rapid assimilation of new consumer trends, competitor responses and technologies on an international scale. The pace of change in the international market is far more rapid than has been the case in the New Zealand market. Success in competition requires being essentially proactive in meeting the requirements of international customers against the best competitors in the world, rather than being reactive to local conditions. These are different performance standards than most of New Zealand management has been used to dealing with.

Accountancy training is often used as a surrogate for management training in New Zealand. Many of our business students study accounting rather than marketing, strategy, finance or international business. This training, however, tends to be better suited to administration than to the active creation of new products or marketing concepts. New Zealand tends not to be successful in industries, such as consumer goods, finance or technical products, that require skills in marketing, finance or management of new technologies. Experienced people with sophisticated marketing, financial and managerial skills, in fact, are in short supply throughout the New Zealand economy.

Many of our managers have no formal management training. One New Zealand study found that while 72.6% of the local workforce had no formal educational qualifications, some 65.5% of managers had no formal educational qualifications either. Many New Zealand managers felt that management education was essentially irrelevant to their careers.[12]

Private Training Programmes. In some countries, such as Germany and Switzerland, apprenticeship and private training programmes make significant contributions to the human-resource base. In Italy, several industry associations sponsor industry-specific training programmes.

New Zealand lacks strong private training programmes. Participation in New Zealand's apprenticeship schemes declined from 9,117 in 1986 to 5,611 in 1989. There is widespread dissatisfaction in New Zealand on the part of participants and employers about the current structure of New Zealand's apprenticeship programmes. Our apprenticeship programmes follow the British model and tend to be restricted to traditional trades, such as automobile mechanics and electricians. They have often not kept pace with the introduction of new technologies. The quality of the on-the-job instruction and supervision varies enormously. This is in sharp contrast to apprenticeship programmes in Switzerland and Germany, where participants often learn the most up-to-date technologies and skills. It would appear that there is much potential for our apprenticeship schemes to replicate the advantages of the German and Swiss programmes.

New Zealand firms tend not to make heavy investments in human-resource development. The exceptions are often our major companies, such as Fletcher Challenge, or the subsidiaries of foreign multinationals. Few companies in the twenty New Zealand industries we studied had organized training programmes or invested in developing the specialized skills required to be competitive in their industry. In other nations, industry associations often co-ordinate industry-specific training programmes. New Zealand's industry associations are often preoccupied with trying to lobby government rather than actively assisting to upgrade their industries human-resource base.

In the software industry, for example, most New Zealand firms source experienced staff from foreign-owned companies rather than developing them through company training programmes. This reliance on foreign companies for skilled human resources often constrains the potential of local software developers by limiting the number of skilled people available in the market. However unfavourable this situation might be for New Zealand-based software companies,

---

[12] *Management Magazine*, June 1990.

it is actually a far more favourable situation than that faced by firms in many other New Zealand industries, in which there are no large or foreign firms that undertake professionally organized human resource development.

Emigration. Emigration exacerbates New Zealand's shortage of economically productive people. Since 1979, there have been 574,370 long-term departures of New Zealanders. Taking into account immigration and returning New Zealanders, the net loss over this period has been 151,000 people. Although it is difficult to track the final destination of all those that emigrate, over 300,000 New Zealanders are permanently settled in Australia. A recent study conducted by the Australian Bureau of Immigration Research found that these New Zealand immigrants earn the highest weekly household incomes of all national groups in Australia, including native-born Australians. These New Zealanders have an average weekly household income 50% higher than that in New Zealand and are far less likely (by two and half times) to be on a government benefit than New Zealanders who stay at home.[13] In other words, the New Zealanders that emigrate tend to be among our most productive people.

Labour Relations. The quality of relationships between management, employees and firms is critical to upgrading skills and improving productivity and thereby competitiveness. These relationships in New Zealand have been commonly marked by deep seated antipathy between management and employees in the workplace. This kind of atmosphere works directly against the potential for creating new sources of advantage for all participants in the enterprise.

New Zealand has had one of the highest incidences of industrial disputes when compared to other advanced nations. In terms of working days lost, New Zealand ranked twenty-first out of the twenty-two countries in a recent international survey.[14] Many of New Zealand's labour disputes have occurred in industries critical to the export sector, such as the meat, transport and waterfront industries. New Zealand vessels continue to enforce rigid lines of demarcation between the four classes of seafarers (seamen, cooks and stewards, engineers and officers), which are each represented by a seperate union. Most maritime nations have instituted the practice of "general purpose manning" associated with multi-skilling. These demarcation issues partly explain why extra crew numbers are required on New Zealand vessels.[15]

Strained labour relations have resulted in limited investments in new technologies and limited investments in worker training. New Zealand ranked eighteenth out of the twenty-one countries surveyed in 1990 in terms of the willingness of the workforce to accept the introduction of new technology.[16] This

---

[13] New Zealanders in Australia had a weekly household income of $NZ1,084 versus $NZ708 for New Zealanders in New Zealand. 5.7% of New Zealanders in Australia were on government benefits, versus 14.1% of those in New Zealand. 10% of New Zealanders in Australia had university degrees compared to 8% of Australians. 22% of New Zealanders in Australia had trade certificates compared to 18% of Australians. Source: Australian Bureau of Immigration Research, 1987.

[14] *The World Competitiveness Report 1990*, p. 227, IMD.

[15] *Ports and Shipping Reform in New Zealand*, New Zealand Business Roundtable and Federated Farmers, September 1989.

[16] *The World Competitiveness Report 1990*, p. 112, IMD.

has resulted in inefficiencies that were sustainable in a protected economy, but cannot be sustained in a more open economy. These inefficiencies hinder a number of New Zealand's industries in international competition. Several New Zealand meat exporters have recently begun to cut their meat in Korea and Japan because labour productivity is so much higher there.

In recent years, there have been improvements in labour management relations, which has led to significant improvements in productivity. However, these improvements have not been of a magnitude such that they provide a competitive advantage to New Zealand industry in international competition.

Summary. New Zealand's private-sector participation rate is low by OECD standards. The educational attainment of the private-sector workforce is also low. Those who are educated often do not have the skills necessary for modern economic competition. A significant portion of the economically active have chosen to leave New Zealand. The heavy and well focused private and public investments that are a feature of Germany, Switzerland and Japan (not to mention emerging nations such as Korea and Singapore) are not a central feature of the New Zealand human-resource development system. In a world where the nation's productivity and standard of living are more and more dependent on the quality of its skill base, New Zealand has cause for grave concern.

Knowledge Resources

Research and Development. New Zealand also faces challenges regarding its base of knowledge resources. There are few examples of world-class, specialized knowledge bases in New Zealand. One reason is New Zealand's relatively low level of investment in research and development. Research and development accounted for less than 1% of New Zealand's GDP in 1987, well below the OECD average of 1.58%. New Zealand ranked seventeenth out of the twenty-three OECD countries on this measure (see figure 54). Sweden, Switzerland, Japan and Germany, all nations that have competed successfully in a wide range of industries, all invest at least 2.85% of GDP in R&D each year.

The institutional structure under which R&D is performed is usually more important than the quantity of research expenditure. The institutional structure often influences the extent to which research is focused on commercially valuable areas. Most of New Zealand's R&D expenditure is contributed by the government. In 1987, the private sector accounted for only 39% of New Zealand's R&D expenditure, far below the OECD average of 49% (see figure 55). In the OECD, only Greece, Iceland, Portugal and Australia had government supplying a larger percentage of R&D expenditures. The high proportion of government funding is due in part to the government's traditional importance in the nation's economy and in part to the mix of industries in our economy. Government tends to be more active in R&D in the agricultural sector than in other sectors.

Government R&D. In 1987, 53% of government R&D was invested in research related to our agricultural industries and only 10% at any form of manufacturing. The three government organizations most involved with R&D in New Zealand are the Department of Scientific and Industrial Research, the Ministry of Agriculture

R&D as a Percentage of GDP
1987

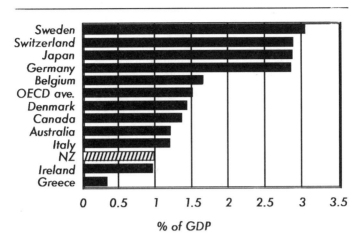

Source: OECD in Figures, 1990 edition

Figure 54

Percentage of R&D Financed
by Government
1987

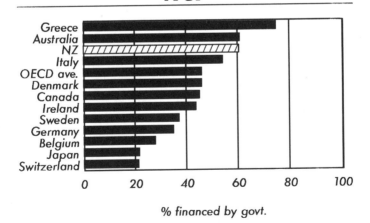

Source: OECD in Figures, 1990 edition

Figure 55

and Fisheries, and the Ministry of Forestry. Most of the research carried out by these agencies is targeted at productivity improvements at the grower or primary-producer level. While this work has enabled New Zealand to be a world leader in certain types of agricultural production, it generally does not foster innovation in downstream activities such as marketing and distribution. This reflects a focus on the production side in our industries that will be discussed later.

Industry R&D. There are several predominantly industry-funded institutes such as the Dairy Research Institute and the Wool Research Organization of New Zealand. These institutes are funded primarily through levies on producers by their respective producer boards. Their research programmes tend to focus on improvements in production, processing technologies and identifying opportunities for product development. The Wool Research Organization has also been active in the development of new technologies in related or supporting industries. It has made contributions in woollen carpet technology that have widened the uses for New Zealand wool. In addition, it has helped develop world-class scouring expertise now in use in New Zealand and sold internationally.

Few New Zealand exporters make heavy commitments to in-house research and development. As the majority of New Zealand's exports are commodities where we compete on price, much of the research that has taken place has been targeted at improving our cost position rather than developing new products or entering downstream or related industries. This has served to reinforce the focus on cost-based strategies rather than the development of differentiation strategies.

New Zealand firms spend only 0.45% of sales on R&D, one eighth of the US average. According to one study, only 30% of New Zealand manufacturers had a defined R&D policy and fewer had a separate R&D budget. In the last several years, New Zealand firms have cut R&D expenditure to improve short-term profits. In addition, New Zealand managers do not have backgrounds that lend themselves to a focus on R&D. Only 30% of large New Zealand manufacturers had a technically qualified person in general management. The equivalent figures for the European Community was 80%. Two-thirds of the senior managers in leading Japanese manufacturers had scientific or engineering degrees. Local managers felt that, in general, New Zealand's scientists were unaware of market requirements.[17]

There are a few exceptions to this general observation. The Yacht Research Unit at Auckland University has played a small, albeit important, role in upgrading the technological base in New Zealand's yacht-building industry. Several advanced technologies in yachting have been developed at the Unit, which has provided the local industry with another source of competitive advantage as well as trained engineers. Industry participants estimate the Unit to be two to three years ahead of similar institutions in other parts of the world.

The Linc Development Centre in Christchurch possesses the largest Unisys computer installation in the southern hemisphere. Aoraki Corporation uses this

---

[17] Pearson, M. (1989), "Why Treasury Opposes R&D Tax Breaks", *Management Magazine*, April.

facility to modify and upgrade their Linc productivity software, a highly sophisticated and differentiated product that has been sold around the world.

These examples show that investment in the creation of advanced knowledge bases that are directed at producing superior, differentiated products can be successful in New Zealand. However, they are exceptions to the general pattern of underinvestment by New Zealand's industries in the creation of world-class knowledge bases.

Even in our agricultural sector we have not gone as far as some nations. There are eleven agricultural universities in Denmark (a nation of five million people) in contrast to New Zealand's two. Furthermore, while our research efforts have been in improving productivity in agricultural production, Danish research has been much more broadly based. Denmark originally leveraged off an agricultural base in the brewing, meat and dairy industries. Sustained investments in specialist research at private and public research facilities has led to leadership in a number of bio-technology industries, such as industrial enzymes and pharmaceuticals (insulin). In addition, Denmark is an exporter of dairy processing and fermentation equipment.

Capital Resources

New Zealand businesses face capital constraints that limit their ability to develop sustainable competitive advantage. The level of household savings, government demands on national-capital resources, poor capital productivity and limited capital markets all influence the accessibility and cost of capital.

Low Household Savings. New Zealand's household savings rate, one of the lowest in the industrialized world, declined from around 6% of household incomes to just over 1% during the 1980s. There are several reasons for this low and declining rate. New Zealanders appear to have tried to maintain consumption levels despite falling real incomes. Government fiscal and monetary policies resulted in negative real interest rates for much of the seventies and early eighties, making it unwise to save.

The welfare state has unintentionally dampened incentives for individuals to save. Subsidized housing, unemployment benefits, non-contributory superannuation, and free health and education services all serve to reduce the incentives for individuals to save. Social-welfare payments, as a percentage of household incomes, rose from 13% in 1975 to 26% in 1989. This was primarily due to increases in the numbers receiving unemployment, domestic-purposes and sickness benefits and superannuation (see figure 56).[18] While other nations, such as Sweden, have been able to maintain a high household savings rate and a commitment to social-welfare policies, this does not appear to have been the case in New Zealand.

Large Government Deficits. Government spending has placed heavy demands on New Zealand's capital resources. Large government deficits appear to have become a structural feature of the New Zealand economy. A commitment to the

---

[18] Barry, P. (1990), *Do Household Savings Matter?*, The Treasury.

Social Transfers
Percent of Household Disposable Income

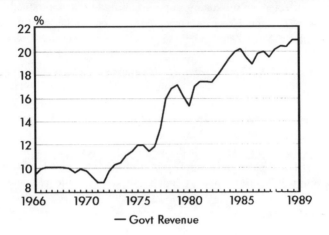

Source: Reserve Bank of New Zealand

Figure 56

Welfare State, which makes up the bulk of government spending (see figure 57), and large government investments in the 1970s and early 1980s that were written off at a cost of billions, have been key contributors to this problem. The government deficits have been funded by borrowing on domestic and international capital markets. Government borrowing has consumed a large portion of the nation's capital resources, "crowding out" private-sector investment. The accumulated public-debt burden amounted to 62% of New Zealand's GDP in 1989. The size of the national debt itself is now a major contributor to the growth in government spending. **Servicing** the accumulated government debt took up 16% of government expenditure in 1989. This made it the second largest government expenditure item after social welfare. The New Zealand government nows spends more taxpayer dollars each year on debt servicing than on education.

High Interest-rate Structure. Low levels of savings and heavy government demands on national capital resources have contributed to New Zealand's interest-rate structure, which is among the highest in the OECD (see figure 58). High interest rates raise the rate of return necessary for investments to be economically viable. High rates on "risk free" government investments discourage investment in the private sector, particularly in new endeavours. New Zealand's high interest rates effectively preclude many kinds of long-term investment and contribute to New Zealand's high rate of corporate failures. The increasing level of indebtedness (both private and government) has resulted in a

Government Expenditure & Revenue as a Percentage of GDP

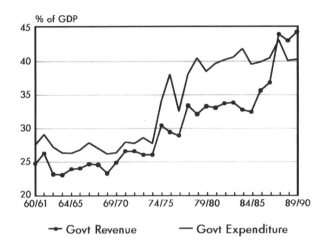

Source: NZPC, RBNZ, IMF

Figure 57

High Real Interest Rates

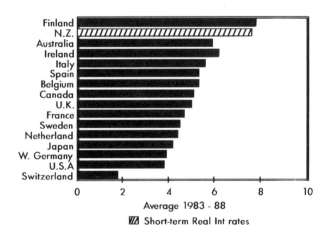

Source: OECD Historical Tables

Figure 58

decline in the perceived creditworthiness of New Zealand loans. Uncertainty surrounding the economy's ability to support the debt burden and the stability of the country's economic policy have led foreign investors to demand a high-risk premium on investments in New Zealand, placing further upward pressure on interest rates.

Limited capital availability in New Zealand constrains business development and economic growth. Lenders and investors have limited amounts of capital to invest. They become risk averse and concentrate their universe of investments in safe, conventional transactions, typically with New Zealand's larger enterprises or in government bonds. As a result, many small and medium-sized companies simply cannot obtain capital. This skew in New Zealand's capital markets away from small and medium sized businesses appears to constrain growth in exports from this sector and contribute to New Zealand's low level of new business formation.

Limited Corporate Funds. Low productivity, low margins and slow growth in much of New Zealand's industry make it increasingly difficult for New Zealand companies to generate capital internally. This is compounded by the poor investment track record of New Zealand management as reflected in its low capital-productivity performance. In addition, many New Zealand firms pursue short-term business strategies and don't invest in new productive capacity. These factors limit the potential of New Zealand firms to increase revenues and profits, which further limits the level of capital formation in the economy.

Many New Zealand firms and investors with funds have consciously reduced their exposure to New Zealand by expanding overseas or holding capital offshore. Capital is one of the most mobile of factors and should investors not feel confident about New Zealand's economic prospects, prudence would suggest holding capital offshore. While it is difficult to quantify this "capital flight", uncertainty over the future prospects for the New Zealand economy has undoubtedly caused large corporations and investors to hold substantial funds offshore.

Limited Specialized-capital Markets. New Zealand lacks much of the financial expertise and advanced specialized-capital markets that have helped industry in other nations. Holland's cut-flower industry is served by a banking system that has an intimate understanding of the industry and has developed specialized expertise in cut flower risk assessment. The industry co-operative bank, Rabobank, accepts flower bulbs as collateral. In contrast, New Zealand bankers have yet to develop such specialist risk assessment for the flower industry. New Zealand's cut-flower producers consequently suffer a competitive disadvantage relative to their Dutch counterparts.

The situation faced by New Zealand's software companies provides another example. Compared with banks in the United States or United Kingdom, New Zealand banks are less experienced in dealing with the risks associated with software development. As a result, they are uncomfortable lending to companies that lack tangible assets and a positive cash flow. Some New Zealand software managers have responded to financial constraints by purchasing tangible assets they don't need in order to provide banks with loan collateral. Others accept more risk in the form of personal guarantees than their foreign counterparts. Many compromise long-term strategies in favour of short term measures that generate near-term cash flow or forgo international growth opportunities. A number have found it necessary to enter alliances with overseas companies or to sell out to overseas interests.

The United States venture-capital industry has developed specialized skills for the equity financing of high-risk, high-growth enterprises. This is a key source of advantage for a range of industries such as software, bio-technology and medical products. The presence of a vibrant venture-capital market in the United States is an important part of American pre-eminence in these industries. The lack of a professionally organized venture-capital market in New Zealand is an important constraint on the development of New Zealand industries such as software and agricultural technology.

New Zealand's Capital Cycle. Figure 59 illustrates the complex set of interactions and constraints that influence the accessibility and cost of capital within New Zealand. The linkages described in this capital cycle are manifold and mutually reinforce a negative spiral that continuously exacerbates the capital constraints. Some of these constraints are basic, such as limited availability of capital and high interest rates. Others are more subtle, such as the limited availability of small-business finance tailored to the requirements of particular industries such as yacht building, engineering consulting or education services. Each serves to limit

New Zealand's Capital Constraints Limit Competitive Advantage

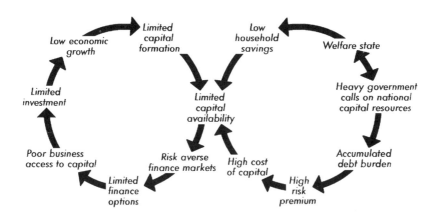

Figure 59

the productive investment we need to generate new wealth and create new capital. This negative spiral serves to impede rather than promote the development of competitive advantage throughout the economy.

Factor Conditions Summary

The New Zealand economy was built upon successful exploitation of favourable climate and growing conditions. This required massive investment, especially in the first half of this century, to turn native forest into farms and orchards and, in other areas, poor-quality land into man-made forests. This effort has resulted in New Zealand being one of the most efficient producers of primary products in the agricultural, horticultural and forest products industries. This in turn has provided us with much of the wealth we derive from exports. The combination of favourable growing conditions and an efficient primary-production sector made New Zealand prosperous. While this was once sufficient to generate one of the highest standards of living in the world, it appears unlikely that this base will be able to sustain high living standards into the next century.

In today's world, the quality and productivity of the human resource base has become more critical to sustaining competitive advantage than inherited-factor advantages. New Zealand has not adapted well to this shift. We have continued to invest in improved agricultural productivity, but the returns from this investment have been diminishing. We lead the world in few areas of knowledge and science. These areas tend to reinforce our reliance on basic factor advantages rather than create more sophisticated advantages.

As a nation we are not aggressively investing in the types of factors necessary for economic growth. Our education system is misaligned with the requirements for economic success. Upgrading our skill base does not appear to be a pressing priority of our firms. As a nation we underinvest in research and development; much of what is done has to be done by government. Our capital resources are being used, or overused, to maintain current consumption rather than to upgrade our economic base. The results are capital shortages and one of the highest interest rate structures in the world. While our infrastructure is adequate, it does not provide advantage to a nation dependent on trade with countries on the other side of the earth. In summary, ours is a nation that is not building the foundations for a more secure and prosperous future.

Demand Conditions

There are few pockets of world-class demand conditions in New Zealand. As a result, demand conditions, as a determinant of competitive advantage, provide little stimulus to New Zealand industry. New Zealand demand neither drives innovation nor anticipates international trends. Decades of protectionism have reduced consumer choice. We estimate that less than 5% of New Zealand's exports derive any major competitive advantage from local demand conditions.

Consumer Demand

Consumer demand in New Zealand is not sophisticated in world terms. A general unwillingness in New Zealand society to complain about poor products and services has limited the development of sophisticated consumer demand. This attitude appears to be derived from the British "stiff upper lip", where complaining about poor quality is seen as poor form, and more a reflection on the character of the person complaining than on the poor product or service. The result, however, is that local consumers do not push New Zealand companies to improve as fast as in other nations. This reduces the long-term competitiveness of New Zealand firms.

As New Zealand's relative living standards continue to fall, the average consumer is increasingly forced to purchase products that are inferior to those purchased in other advanced nations. New Zealand's domestic demand tends to steer firms to segments of the market that are more vulnerable to competition from developing — competition that is generally based on price rather than differentiation.

Resource-based Industries. New Zealand's per-capita consumption of several food products is high by world standards. However, this seems largely a function of local availability. Government subsidies, which ended in the 1970s, were aimed at encouraging consumption of basic foodstuffs such as meat, eggs, bread and milk. While these measures have raised per-capita consumption of these items they have done little to stimulate sophisticated demand in food products.

New Zealand has one of the highest per-capita consumption rates of dairy products in the world, but unsophisticated local demand has not forced our dairy industry to innovate and continue to introduce new products. Home demand is skewed towards basic products, such as cheddar cheese, whole milk and butter, rather than highly processed or differentiated products. This can be contrasted to French dairy consumption, which is also high but more discerning. This sophisticated domestic demand has enabled French cheese-makers to become world leaders in a range of high-margin, differentiated cheeses, markets in which New Zealand has made little headway.

Kiwifruit has traditionally been sold in New Zealand as a low-cost fruit (largely as a result of dumping non-export grade fruit on the domestic market), yet is positioned overseas as an exotic and expensive fruit. The New Zealand market cannot, therefore, be used as a test market for international markets. A recent initiative of the Kiwifruit Marketing Board, to improve the quality of kiwifruit on the local market and develop it as a microcosm of world kiwifruit demand, will hopefully remedy this situation.

The New Zealand cut-flower industry does not have a defined export standard, nor does it have standards for the domestic market. The quality of the products sold in New Zealand would, in many cases, be unacceptable to international buyers. Key export varieties are not readily available in the home market. Home demand does not force New Zealand flower growers to develop a wider and improved product range, even though the size of the home market exceeded the export market in 1989. In contrast, the Dutch cut-flower industry has one standard for all products — domestic quality is the same as export quality. Produce that does not meet acceptable standards is destroyed. In some cases, growers of substandard flowers are fined. Demanding home consumers have been important in building the leading position the Dutch enjoy in the cut-flower industry. In New Zealand, local-demand conditions have not provided New Zealand exporters with any competitive advantage.

Concentrated Suppliers and Distribution. In some cases, it appears that concentration of suppliers or distributors in New Zealand may have slowed the development of new products and services. The New Zealand Apple and Pear Marketing Board has a legislated monopoly on the local market as well as exports. Retailers, in a government review of the apple industry, complained that controls over retail supply by the New Zealand Apple and Pear Marketing Board led to a sameness in price and presentation. This makes it very difficult for market signals in New Zealand to be used to anticipate new customer requirements elsewhere in the world.

Consumer-demand Advantages. There are some areas in which New Zealand's consumer demand has been an advantage.

Sport is a national passion in New Zealand. The country has led the world at different times in rugby, middle-distant athletics and several other sports. Not surprisingly, New Zealanders are discerning consumers of outdoor, sporting and recreational products. This has assisted several New Zealand companies to produce world-class products, such as Canterbury in rugby jerseys and Line 7 in fashion wet-weather gear for sailing.

New Zealand's yacht-building industry derives advantage from high per-capita ownership of yachts and very sophisticated and demanding local yacht owners. New Zealand sailors are among the best in the world. Extensive and intensive local racing has also facilitated the emergence of top-flight designers and boat-builders. New Zealanders want, and demand, high-performance yachts and strive for the very highest of performance standards. The presence of demanding and sophisticated domestic customers has been a source of international competitive advantage enjoyed by the New Zealand racing-yacht building industry.

Industrial Demand

A general lack of leading-edge industrial demand at home has made it more difficult for New Zealand firms to be at the forefront of world trends. New Zealand businesses face little pressure to innovate or target the high-quality end of product lines. A primary production orientation often means that New Zealand producers have little interaction with the ultimate consumer. In some industries, goat fibres for example, there is no further processing in New Zealand. In such situations, market signals are difficult, if not impossible, to incorporate into strategy. The opportunity to learn from sophisticated local consumers rarely exists.

The New Zealand Dairy Board taps into a pocket of leading-edge demand through its North American Regional Development Centre at Petaluma. The Centre concentrates on the development of protein-based and cheese-based systems for the food-ingredients market. It is positioned to take advantage of the world's leading demand conditions for this segment of the global food-ingredients industry. While an appropriate employment of global strategy, this does not provide the Dairy Board with a unique advantage. Instead, it compensates for the lack of sophisticated demand at home.

Industrial Demand Advantages. There are, in New Zealand, small isolated pockets of sophisticated industrial demand. In agricultural inputs, progress in electric-fencing and animal-identification systems has been enhanced by relatively well-educated farmers who have forced New Zealand manufacturers continually to innovate. The New Zealand farmers' willingness to incorporate new technology that improves on-farm productivity has provided a fertile ground for the development of farm-management technology. Indeed, electric fencing is commonly known around the world as "the New Zealand fencing system". The New Zealand market provides a window through which local manufacturers can anticipate trends in world demand for electric-fencing and animal-identification systems. This home demand has been a part of the reason why these manufacturers are world leaders in their industries.

The demanding geographic conditions in New Zealand, and her location on a seismic belt, has forced local construction companies to develop expertise that has been translated into international success. The diversity of geological and topographical features found in New Zealand creates a range of technical challenges for the construction and engineering consulting industries. Tough government building standards have provided additional impetus for New Zealand firms to develop their capabilities.

Demand Conditions Summary

Local-demand conditions provide little competitive advantage to New Zealand industry except in a few small pockets related to agricultural technology and sports. In contrast to other nations where sophisticated local demand can be used to anticipate international trends, New Zealand exporters often do not take the local market seriously. Some New Zealand firms have attempted to overcome poor local-demand conditions by tapping into pockets of sophisticated demand elsewhere in the world. However, this does not provide the unique advantages that could flow from actively investing in building the local market so that it can be used as a test market for world trends in particular industry segments.

Related and Supporting Industries

Relatively few of New Zealand's export industries have benefited from dynamic interaction with world-class related and supporting industries. The cluster charts and our industry studies reveal that there are few clusters of competitive industries in New Zealand. The only major clusters are in pastoral farming and horticulture.

Foreign Examples

A Danish Cluster. New Zealand has not been able to deepen and widen its clusters of competitive industries to the same extent as some other nations. Figure 60

Relating and Supporting Industries - Denmark

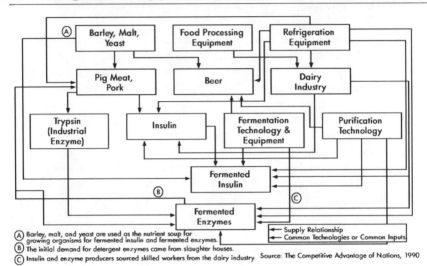

Figure 60

shows the inter-relationships between just some of the industries in which Denmark is internationally competitive. Although insulin was not discovered in Denmark, the presence and development of clusters of related and supporting industries enabled Danish firms to attain and maintain a leading position in the industry.

The pork-meat industry supplies the pancreas from which insulin has traditionally been extracted. Fermentation technology and equipment were initially developed for the brewing industry. Barley, malt and yeast are used as inputs to the brewing industry and as nutrients for the organisms that produce fermented enzymes. Purification equipment for insulin was initially based on dairy equipment. Refrigeration equipment is used as a supply input to the beer, dairy and fermented-enzyme industries. Fermented insulin (introduced in the 1980s) makes use of production technology similar to that of fermented enzymes and purification techniques similar to those of porcine insulin. Two of the world's leading hospitals for the treatment of diabetes are located in Denmark. The system feeds on itself as so many industries are connected and share common sources of innovation and avenues to upgrade.

Swedish Forest Products. Another example, also relevant to New Zealand, is the Swedish forest-products cluster(see figures 61 and 62). Sweden is a leading competitor, not only in pulp and paper, but also in wood-handling machinery, sulphur boilers, conveyer systems, pulp-making machinery, control instruments and paper-making machinery. While it is generally uncompetitive in chemicals,

The Swedish Forest Clusters

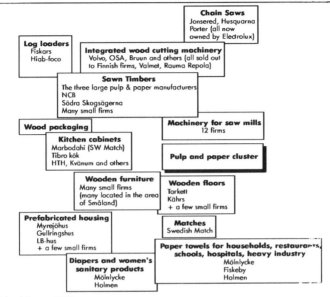

Source: Michael Porter, 1990

Figure 61

The Swedish Pulp and Paper Cluster

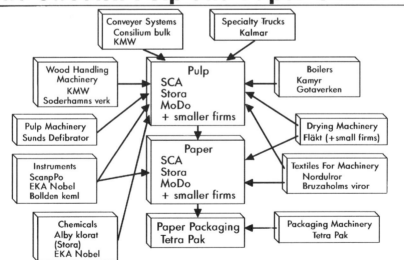

Source: Michael Porter, 1990

Figure 62

Sweden is internationally successful in chemicals used in pulp and paper-making machinery.

In contrast, the forest-products industries in New Zealand are small, and restricted to primary goods, pulp and paper and prefabricated housing (see New Zealand's cluster charts in Appendices 1 and 6). New Zealand has no internationally successful machinery, specialty transportation, instruments or specialty chemical industries related to the forest-products cluster. In recent times, New Zealand's percentage of forest-products exports that are made up of logs has actually increased. This indicates that New Zealand's position in wood processing and other related industries may be deteriorating rather than improving.

Supplier Industries

We found few instances of New Zealand industries that benefited from world-class supporting industries. The few world class supporting industries we did find were concentrated in agriculture and horticulture. In agriculture, these were related to farming and more particularity to supplying inputs for on-farm production. Similarly, the few New Zealand world-class supporting industries in horticulture are focused on production.

Examples of such supporting industries include ear tags for animals, electric fencing and agricultural consulting. Several of these have developed in conjunction with New Zealand's dairy industry. A number of companies are prominent exporters in their field: Gallagher, a manufacturer of electric fencing equipment; Allflex, which makes animal-identification systems; Tru-test, making milk-production meters; and AHI, making milking equipment. Despite the success of these companies, New Zealand remains a net importer of most agriculture and farm maintenance equipment. Virtually all processing equipment is imported, often from other small agricultural nations such as Denmark and Sweden.

Related Industries

There are also some cases of related industries providing the stimulus to create new industries in New Zealand. Most of these industries are relatively small within the agricultural production cluster. The goat and deer industries have evolved from the farming of cows, cattle and sheep. These industries share common inputs (fencing and animal-husbandry techniques) and certain production processes (slaughtering) and transportation technologies. The skills developed to farm successfully various types of livestock have been the basis for the development of these related industries. The industries tend to be related through on-farm production and processing technology, but not through common marketing and distribution channels. In horticulture, for example, apples, grapes, flowers and kiwifruit are related industries that share common supply inputs (fertilizers and cool stores) but do not employ common distribution channels.

Related and Supporting Industries Summary

Related and supporting industries rarely provide a significant source of competitive advantage to New Zealand firms. The few cases identified are not clustered in close geographic proximity (a feature which often improves their interaction). While there are successful firms in industries that support the dairy industry, these are single companies rather than company or industry clusters.

The lack of related and supporting industries in New Zealand is a symptom of the fairly minimal investment that industry has made in creating advanced and specialized inputs. This has led to the reliance on imported inputs. Various government policies (such as agricultural subsidies and protection of inefficient import-substitution industries) have tended to distort market signals and relieve the pressure to seek new sources of advantage by diversifying into related and supporting industries.

New Zealand industries tend not to grow outwards from the original base into a cluster of related and supporting industries. Our industrial clusters lack both breadth and depth, making it difficult to develop new industries. This eventually weakens the competitive position of the base industries. The development of related and supporting industries is one way that sources of expertise and advantage ripple through the economy and move it forward. The absence of significant related and supporting industries in New Zealand has meant that so far this avenue for further growth and prosperity has not played a major role.

Our economy lacks the momentum that dynamic clusters of related and supporting industries can provide. The lack of related and supporting industries in New Zealand minimizes the potential to build, broaden and widen the basis of sustainable advantage. It limits the potential to move away from a focus on agricultural production and the likelihood of developing new industries. This stunts the development of new sources of advantage as well as new industries. One avenue to upgrading the economy is to invest heavily in the development of dynamic clusters related to our existing competitive strengths.

Firm Strategy, Structure and Rivalry

Overall, there are several shared characteristics in the way that New Zealand firms tend to compete. These are determined in part by the goals of New Zealand managers, employees and companies, including considerations of lifestyle, security and ownership structures. The strategies and structures adopted by New Zealand firms in the face of such considerations have contributed to New Zealand's economic difficulties.

Most New Zealand industries do not contend with vigorous rivalry. Some of the nation's leading export industries are legislated monopolies, while others are relatively tight-knit oligopolies. New Zealand industry in general has not taken advantage of the invigorating stimulus of domestic rivalry.

Goals
Sharp differences exist among and within nations in the goals that firms seek to achieve, as well as the motivations of their employees and managers. Nations tend to succeed where goals stimulate unusual effort, the upgrading of individual skills

and a sustained commitment tailored to the requirements of particular industries and industry segments.

The Goals of New Zealand Managers and Employees. The motivations of the individuals who manage and work in firms can enhance or detract from success in particular industries. The central concern is whether managers and workers are motivated to develop their skills as well as to expend the effort necessary for creating and sustaining competitive advantage. In New Zealand, the prevailing goals of individuals do not appear to lend themselves well to the upgrading of the economy.

Kiwi Lifestyle. The ideal "Kiwi lifestyle" involves a relaxed approach to life with plenty of time for family and recreational pursuits. This lifestyle was originally influenced by New Zealand's natural beauty, temperate climate and prosperity. Images of Japanese managers and workers hard at work for long hours and devoted to their companies' success have little appeal.

Lifestyle considerations limit the success of some of our companies. One software entrepreneur, for example, when asked why his company had not attempted to export a product that was highly successful in New Zealand, said that he earned an acceptable living and would rather spend his weekends sailing than adapting his products for overseas markets. Such choices, though personal and understandable, constrain a company's potential to grow and develop world-class competitive advantage. It also limits the jobs and income such operations can generate for New Zealand.

Low Status of Business. Business achievement, particularly as reflected in the accumulation of wealth, is often not seen as socially positive in New Zealand. Profits are commonly seen as being "made from other people" rather than as a reward for hard work. In addition, business is accorded a low status by New Zealand society, much as it is in the United Kingdom. This combination dampens the commitment New Zealanders are prepared to make to business endeavours.

Search for Security. As a result of two world wars, the Great Depression and a deep-seated sense of isolation, New Zealanders have long placed a heavy emphasis on security. Security has become an overriding theme in social, political and business affairs. New Zealand was one of the first nations to develop a comprehensive, government-funded social-welfare system. Comprehensive health care, free education, generous unemployment support and non-contributory retirement benefits were all seen as central responsibilities of the state.

The pursuit of security is also reflected in business attitudes. Managers often seek government protection from "excessive" local competition and "unfair" foreign competition. Job stability is often seen as fundamentally more important than moving upwards or growing the company. The result of these conditions is a preoccupation with seeking government protection and a failure to pursue aggressive company strategies.

Limited Incentives for Individuals to Upgrade their Skills. The shortcomings of New Zealand's education and training systems described earlier are amplified by a system that does not encourage individuals to seek training opportunities or upgrade their skills. Until recently, government income-support programmes, strong unions and protected markets have insulated the average Kiwi from many of the adverse consequences of low skill levels. A persistent government commitment to full employment has unwittingly dampened the pressure on individuals to invest personally the time, effort and money in improving their own skills. As a result, education has often not been seen as the path to a more prosperous future. Until recently, easy access for 16 year olds to the unemployment benefit provided a financial incentive not to pursue further education. High marginal tax rates (recently reduced), have served to reduce incentives at the individual level to improve skills, productivity and contribution to the nation's economic well-being.

Reward systems within companies and nationally tend to reflect New Zealand's values. Pay tends not to be as heavily based on individual performance as in many other nations. Rapid promotion of outstanding employees has only recently begun to gain acceptance. This has reduced the incentives for people to work hard and make individual contributions to improving their companies.

Non-Economic National Priorities. National prestige and priorities also strongly influence where a country develops competitive advantage. Nations tend to be competitive in activities that are admired or depended upon; that is, where the heroes come from. Outstanding talent is a scarce resource in any nation. The allocation of this resource can be affected by prestige or national priority. A nation's success is influenced by the type of education this talent chooses to obtain and where it chooses to work.

In New Zealand, national prestige tends to be accorded to sporting heroes. Of those attracted to a career in business, the best and brightest tend to pursue careers in law and accounting. This has resulted in New Zealand having more qualified accountants per capita than almost any other nation in the world; we have more than sixty times the number of accountants that Japan has on a per-capita basis.[19] The focus on the legal and accounting professions leaves New Zealand with managers better trained for administration than creating new products, services and strategies.

Goals of New Zealand Companies

Company goals are most strongly determined by ownership structure, the motivation of equity and debt holders, the nature of corporate governance and the incentive processes that shape the motivation of senior managers. The goals of New Zealand companies do not generally provide the impetus for innovation and upgrading.

Ownership Structures. Almost two-thirds of New Zealand's exports are either controlled or influenced by producer boards. Producer boards were established by government over the years at the request of New Zealand's primary producers. The goals and strategies of producer boards are strongly influenced by their statutory obligations. The producers, as the shareholders and majority directors,

---

[19] Hooley, G., and Franko, G. (1990), *The Making of New Zealand Managers*, Otago Business School.

have charged producer boards with selling all production that meets certain quality standards, with the objective of maximizing returns to the producer. The producer boards' statutory obligations provide little stimulus for diversification into potentially more profitable upstream, downstream or related industries. The result tends to be incremental strategies that focus on existing products and markets, rather than attempting to develop new ones.

The leading New Zealand corporations, such as Fletcher Challenge and Carter Holt Harvey, are substantial exporters who also have extensive international operations. They are all publicly listed companies with strong connections to New Zealand. They are largely managed by New Zealanders, despite their substantial international activities and significant foreign-share ownership. These companies are involved largely in commodity industries in New Zealand and have invested in similar industries abroad. They have taken action to develop international markets and operations, though their investments tend not to upgrade the product mix of New Zealand industry.

Smaller private companies are important in many of our smaller, emerging export industries such as agricultural technology and software. The goals of these firms tend to be complex, with personal pride and a commitment to continuity of employment for staff figuring prominently among them. The managers of these companies often develop strategy with very long time horizons and frequently are personally committed to their products, firms and industries. Profitability is often not the key objective, but rather an important objective among many others. Many of these firms have been innovators in developing new products and industries. Frequently, these firms are closely identified with their original founders, such as Bill Gallagher of Gallaghers, a world leader in electric-fencing systems, and Gil Simpson of Linc, which leads the world in productivity tools for Unisys systems.

Impact of Capital Markets. While the activities of many small firms are encouraging, finance for small and medium-sized firms in New Zealand is quite restricted, particularly for new product development and expansion. Specialist financing instruments tailored to the requirements of particular industries have not been available in New Zealand. Several engineering consulting firms, for example, have not been able to bid on large contracts offered by the World Bank, for which they are qualified, because they cannot raise the requisite finance.

The New Zealand capital market points management towards low-risk investments that provide short-term returns. Unfortunately, many of the investments critical to building and sustaining competitive advantage are not of this nature. Our capital markets tend to dampen the incentives for business to make the heavy and sustained investments needed for long-term competitive success.

The Strategies of New Zealand Firms

We observed distinct patterns in the strategies followed by New Zealand firms. These patterns have been influenced by the goals and attitudes of managers and public policymakers. Although there are notable exceptions, New Zealand firms tend to have a mindset that is not well aligned to the requirements for competitive success in the global economy. This mindset is typically characterized by a short-term, static perspective of competition. Such a perspective is inadequate in a world where competition has become profoundly dynamic and where success depends on continuous improvement in all parts of the business.

This static view of competition is widely held in New Zealand business. It limits the range of strategic options for New Zealand firms. Many focus on improving performance within current constraints, rather than devising strategies that change the constraints and build new sources of advantage.

Cost-based Strategies. New Zealand firms tend to employ cost-based strategies with minimal efforts at differentiation of products and services. We tend to compete on price rather than on product or service quality. This is due in part to the industries and segments in which we compete. The majority of New Zealand's export industries are commodities. Fast-growing grass and trees, a favourable climate, spectacular scenery and other natural advantages give local producers viable cost positions in a number of industries.

In New Zealand, favourable natural-resource endowments have been coupled with continuing public and private investment in improving production efficiencies. Government research agencies such as the Department of Scientific and Industrial Research and the Ministry of Agriculture and Fisheries have figured prominently in these efforts, as have joint government industry agencies such as the Dairy Research Institute, the Wool Research Organization of New Zealand and the Forestry Research Institute.

The cost commodity mindset pervades a wide range of New Zealand industries. Indeed, many firms are not able to compete on any other basis than cost. New Zealand has produced world-class wines, yet much of our wine exports are in bulk containers. In construction, New Zealand firms tend to compete in relatively price-sensitive projects that require expertise that indigenous companies lack. Cost-based strategies are evident even in new industries, such as education services. Instead of focusing on gaining a sophisticated understanding of buyer needs and targeting segments where they might offer differentiated products at premium prices, New Zealand educators are focusing on offering basic courses at a lower cost than the Australians.

Only a few New Zealand industries compete by creating superior products based on sophisticated customer knowledge. In electric fencing, some software market segments and certain types of racing yachts, New Zealand companies are the world technology leaders. Return on sales in these industries are frequently ten to twenty times those of New Zealand's traditional industries. However, these industries make up less than 2% of our export earnings (see figure 63).

Production Focus. The economic challenge for New Zealand has traditionally been seen as increasing production. New Zealand, as Britain's farm, was the low-cost producer of wool, butter and lamb. Our cost advantages, Britain's ability to consume all we produced and a reliance on British companies to distribute the goods meant that New Zealand firms saw little need to develop new products, marketing skills or distribution systems. They have often seen their task as getting basic, simply processed products to the wharf.

Most New Zealand exporters use cost-based strategies

| | Competitive advantage through: | |
	Low cost	Differentiation
Broad **Competitive scope**	Sheepmeat Wool Butter Aluminium Pulp Education > 75% of NZ's exports	
Narrow		Software Ear tags Electric fences Roofing tiles Swimwear Yachts < 2% of NZ's exports

Figure 63

New Zealand management tends to be oriented to primary production. Inefficiencies in downstream processing within New Zealand, sometimes due to overmanning and low labour productivity, has reinforced the emphasis on primary production. This mindset is reflected in the large, and in some cases increasing, proportion of forest-product and meat exports that leave the country unprocessed. Indeed, a leading forest-products company recently undertook a public-relations campaign following the introduction of a debarking machine which was "adding value" to their logs prior to export.

Producer board structures have reinforced the production orientation in many of New Zealand's agricultural industries. Directors of the producer boards, predominately grower representatives, often focus on issues of selling what they produce rather than having a fundamental market orientation. Management is often understandably preoccupied with the requirements of the New Zealand producer rather than the international customer. Although increases in production have compensated for some declines in prices, price pressure continues to drive producers' incomes down in most of our agricultural industries. Innovations in product development, marketing and distribution often offer more potential as a means to improving returns, but in New Zealand these are seldom aggressively pursued. In contrast, foreign competitors like Nestlé and Dole are primarily marketing companies with directors with international business experience. The ability of these companies to introduce and market new and branded products is in sharp contrast to that of some of our producer boards.

In technology-intensive industries such as software, New Zealand firms are technically innovative but have difficulty in marketing. Most successful New Zealand software companies lack the finance, distribution and access to hardware necessary to market their own products overseas. Many have entered alliances with hardware vendors who promote their products overseas. This focus on production limits their potential to develop, distribute and market in a manner that meets consumers needs. As a result, New Zealand software companies often fail to develop a sophisticated understanding of their international customers. This, in turn, limits the potential for upgrading their products and improving their international position.

The typical New Zealand focus on production in traditional businesses has made it difficult for firms to compete in industries where heavy marketing or client cultivation is required. This mindset has begun to hurt some of our traditional industries, where value is increasingly created not in production, but in distribution and marketing. This is true in a number of industries, including the dairy industry, where developing and marketing new and differentiated products is becoming more and more important.

Managing for the Short-Term. A narrow and static conception of competition leads many companies in New Zealand to employ short-term strategies. As a result, low levels of investment to create new advantages, particularly in human-resource development, research and development, distribution channels and brands, is a common feature in many New Zealand industries.

While international competitive advantage is built over decades, a static view of competition causes New Zealand management to work within much shorter time frames. This short-term horizon compounds the constraints faced by New Zealand managers.

Reactive vs. Proactive Thinking. A static view of competition coupled with short-term strategies results in a tendency for New Zealand managers to be reactive rather than proactive. Many of the major initiatives undertaken by New Zealand business have been reactions to events rather than proactive development of opportunities. Our dairy industry began to significantly reduce its exposure to the vicissitudes of the commodity trade after Britain's entry into the European Community. The goat-fibre industry emerged because of the initiative of a major overseas buyer seeking an alternative source of supply, not through the efforts of New Zealand firms and entrepreneurs.

One of the more discouraging features of many of the industries we studied was the paucity of firms or individuals willing and able to make commitments and take risks to develop new markets. Examples of new industries developing from a careful analysis of international customers' requirements, or indeed of anticipating industry trends, were rare indeed.

The kiwifruit industry provides an example of a New Zealand industry that lacked strategic foresight. In the early eighties, large-scale planting of kiwifruit in Italy, Chile and elsewhere resulted in substantial additional supply. It was clear that a new and more sophisticated strategy was required if New Zealand was to maintain its profitable and pre-eminent position in the industry. Yet investments in creating new competitive advantages in production, packaging, distribution, marketing and quality assurance to improve our cost and market position came in response to the collapse in prices rather than in anticipation. The opportunity to shape the world kiwifruit industry in our favour passed. Sadly, this tends to be the pattern of strategic responses in New Zealand industry.

Eastern Europe's entry into the world economy could lead to similar supply shocks in a range of agricultural industries in which we compete. The commercial farming of deer was pioneered in New Zealand. This has resulted in our pre-eminent position in the world venison industry. A relatively small increase in production in the Soviet Union, let alone the rest of Eastern Europe, could have a major impact on the supply of venison to world markets and the long-term probability of a supply shock similar to that in the kiwifruit industry appears high (see figure 64).

Russia has potential to dramatically increase world venison export supply

If Russia exported 10 % of its venison production, world import demand
would need to increase by 43 % to absorb the additional volume

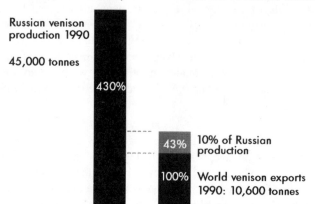

Source: Casewriter's estimates; UN trade statistics

Figure 64

The future prospects of New Zealand's venison industry depends on its ability to anticipate and prepare for these trends. To sustain its position, the industry will need to target specific market segments, differentiate New Zealand venison, and substantially improve New Zealand's cost position in production, processing and distribution. This will require heavy and sustained investment ahead of international competitors. There is still an opportunity for proactive long-term strategies to help industries such as venison build on their early lead and secure long-term competitive positions in the global industry.

Lack of an International Orientation. As the global economy becomes more integrated, company strategy needs to be developed with an intimate understanding of the world industry, particularly international customers and competitors. Although there are some notable exceptions, most New Zealand managers need to improve their understanding of the world industries in which they compete. This is not surprising given that New Zealand firms have only been allowed to have an international focus, at least from an investment point of view, since the mid 1980s.

In our interviews, senior executives were asked detailed questions about the identity and requirements of their final customer, product alternatives, the buying and selling process, competitor's distribution strategies, market shares and estimated profitabilities. Many managers were not able to answer these questions with any specificity or conviction. Relatively few had an intimate knowledge of competitors' strengths and weaknesses. One executive helpfully suggested that if these answers were really needed, the questions should be asked of one of the Japanese trading houses operating in New Zealand, who had more of this information than his or any other New Zealand firm.

This inward-looking focus is also reflected in the preoccupation of New Zealand management with New Zealand politicians rather than with international customers and competitors. This is partly attributable to the heavy politicization of the economy during the "Fortress New Zealand" era. The New Zealand business community tends to see government as both the source of and the solution to its problems. An extraordinary number of New Zealand's executive offices are within convenient walking distance of Parliament. The metaphor of bees clustered around the Beehive seeking honey is an apt one. Government subsidies, protection and incentives were critical to profitability and success within "Fortress New Zealand". Unfortunately, this inward focus is a considerable liability when the game is really about outperforming the world's best competitors in international markets.

The Contrast with Switzerland. The typical strategies of New Zealand firms contrasts with those adopted in another small country, Switzerland. Swiss firms tend to employ highly focused differentiation strategies in a range of industry segments that require sophisticated technical and marketing skills. These competitive positions are built and maintained through sustained investment. These kinds of strategies have provided for strong competitive positions and one of the highest standards of living in the world at the national level.

Swiss firms tend to succeed by seeking technical perfection through continuous improvement. The technical background and orientation of many top managers makes them more comfortable with and more desirous of technical change and innovation. Swiss companies are also extremely open to internationalization; it comes as second nature. Language skills, multiple cultures, a small home market and absence of government restrictions all contribute to this trait. Swiss firms have a strategic orientation and operating philosophy that grows out of their national circumstances and culture.

These differences are graphically illustrated in the differences in the mix of trade between New Zealand and Switzerland. Despite having precisely the same transportation difficulties, Swiss firms export to New Zealand more than four and a half times the value of New Zealand exports to Switzerland. Most importantly these products tend to be sophisticated and differentiated products in contrast to New Zealand's commodity exports to Switzerland. Several Swiss companies such as Nestlé and Ciba-Geigy have significant investments in New Zealand employing some hundreds of New Zealanders. The sales of Swiss companies in New Zealand is estimated to be at least equal in value to Swiss exports to New Zealand. New Zealand investment in Switzerland is negligible (see figure 65). This same pattern also applies for Sweden, Denmark, and several other small, distant nations.

New Zealand Trade with Switzerland

NZ Exports	(NZ $million)	NZ Imports	(NZ $million)
Meat	24.8	Pharmaceuticals	37.0
Wool	2.8	Aluminium foil	18.1
Fish	1.9	Machinery and machine tool	15.9
Kraft - paper	1.0	Electrical apparatus	13.4
Animal skins	1.0	Watches	3.8
Precious stones and jewellery	1.0	Sewing machines	3.4
Veterinary supplies	0.5	Chemicals	3.2
Wood pulp	0.3	Dyes and herbicides	3.2
Electric fences	0.3	Coated paper	1.2
Other	5.4	Other	74.9
Total exports	39.0	Total imports	174.1

Source: NZ Dept Stats. Provisional Data Jan.-Dec. 1990

Figure 65

Rivalry in New Zealand

Among the strongest empirical findings from Porter's international research is the association between vigorous domestic rivalry and the creation and persistence of competitive advantage. In Japan, for example, most internationally successful industries characteristically face fierce competition in the domestic and foreign markets (see figure 66). This contrasts with the popular misconception that the key to Japan's economic success has been widespread co-operation coordinated by government. Domestic rivalry is also important in small nations. In most industries where Switzerland is internationally successful, several competitors are engaged in active rivalry, often with directly competing strategies. Examples include banking (Union Bank, Crédit Suisse, Swiss Bank Corporation), chocolate (Nestlé, Jacobs-Suchard, Lindt and Sprungli) and pharmaceuticals (Sandoz, Ciba-Geigy, Hoffmann-LaRoche).

Estimated Number of Japanese Rivals in Selected Industries

Airconditioners	13	Motorcycles	4
Audio Equipment	25	Musical Instruments	4
Automobiles	9	Personal Computers	16
Cameras	15	Semiconductors	34
Car Audio	12	Sewing Machines	20
Carbon Fibers	7	Shipbuilding	33
Construction Equipment	15	Steel	5
Copiers	14	Synthetic Fibers	8
Facsimile Machines	10	Television Sets	15
Large-Scale Computers	6	Truck and Bus Tires	5
Lift Trucks	8	Trucks	11
Machine Tools	112	Typewriters	14
Microwave Equipment	5	Videocassette Recorders	10

Source: The Competitive Advantage of Nations, 1990

Figure 66

It is often argued in New Zealand and elsewhere that domestic competition is undesirable, particularly in a "small country". The belief that competition leads to duplication of effort and prevents firms from gaining economies of scale misses the fact that competition tends to force firms to improve and upgrade. Concentration is not the best way to achieve scale in small countries, export is. The notion that scale might be obtained through export to overseas markets is often foreign to many observers. Some also take the view that domestic rivalry is unimportant in global industries. The evidence from detailed analysis of over one hundred different industries in both large and small nations shows that domestic competition is vital to sustained international success.

Highly Concentrated Industries. The pursuit of economies of scale, efforts to counteract buyer power, and failure to facilitate new business formation have left New Zealand with highly concentrated industry structures. Figure 67 lists New Zealand's major export industries and the percent of exports controlled by the market leaders. New Zealand's export industries tend to be highly concentrated with either a producer board or a small number of firms dominating the business.

The buyers of resource-based commodities wield significant levels of bargaining power. New Zealand has established producer boards in an attempt to concentrate New Zealand sellers in order to counteract the power of overseas buyers. The New Zealand Dairy Board, the New Zealand Apple and Pear Marketing Board and the New Zealand Kiwifruit Marketing Board all have "single-desk" provisions which allow the boards to control all New Zealand

Most New Zealand export industries are highly concentrated

		# of major exporters	% of exports controlled by market leaders
Agriculture	Apples	1	100%
	Cut flowers	10	90%
	Dairy	1	100%
	Deer	3	90%
	Fish	4	65%
	Forestry	2	80%
	Goats	1	100%
	Kiwifruit	1	100%
	Meat	3	Sheep = 60% Beef = 75%
	Wine	2	90%
	Wool	10	65%
Manufacturing	Electr. fencing	4	100%
	Methanol	1	100%
	Yachts	10	90%
Services	Construction	3	100%
	Education	30	No dominant player
	Engineering con.	5	75%
	Software	4	75%
	Tourism	Many	No dominant player

Figure 67

exports in these industries. By contrast, the New Zealand Wool Board, until recently, only entered the market in attempts to smooth price fluctuations. Following the collapse of the Australian government's wool-price support scheme, however, the Board has discontinued this practice. The New Zealand Meat Board has the right to assume control of marketing; however, it typically restricts itself to a licensing role.

A high degree of concentration is tolerated in other major New Zealand industries not covered by producer boards. New Zealand's principal export sectors face little or no competition at home. The high, and sometimes legislated, barriers to entering New Zealand's key industries retard New Zealand's ability to respond to rapidly changing global markets. Rather than benefiting from multiple centres of initiative trying a multiplicity of new products and strategies, many New Zealand industries are dependent on a few large enterprises pursuing a very small number of strategies.

Concentrated Economic Power. Ownership of many of New Zealand's most successful private businesses is highly concentrated in a small number of groups which control a substantial and increasing share of New Zealand's economy. These firms tend to focus on different industries. Where they do participate in the same industry, they tend to operate in different segments. The net effect is that the incidence of sustained, direct, and active competition between the major New Zealand companies is limited.

The tendency toward economic concentration was reinforced in the mid 1980s with the government's privatization programme. Nearly all government's major assets were sold to either Fletcher Challenge (Petrocorp, Synfuels and the Rural Bank) or Brierley Investments (Air New Zealand), or to foreign companies. A programme of state-asset privatization that merely substitutes a private monopoly for a public monopoly is unlikely to produce companies with the dynamism to build international competitive advantage.

Weak Competition Policy. New Zealand lacks a tradition of strong competition policy. Official government policy in the 1980s, particularly as expressed by the Treasury, has been indulgent of monopoly practices. The alleged "economic efficiency" of market concentration has been used to justify a policy of "non-intervention" towards concentrations of market power. This reflects a fundamentally static view of the world that does not take into account the gains in dynamic efficiency that result from vigorous domestic rivalry.

The Commerce Commission is charged with ensuring that companies do not gain a "dominant position" in particular market segments, unless it can be shown that it is in the public's interest for them to do so. The Commission has taken a tolerant view of market dominance and has seldom prevented mergers or take-overs, even when market concentration has approached 100%.

Despite this, a paper prepared for the Treasury by the investment bank Jardens attacked the Commission for an alleged "bias towards intervention" against mergers and acquisitions. The Treasury contends that the sole purpose of competition policy should be "efficient resource utilization" and that the Commission tends to "overstate the economic costs of mergers and take-overs and non-standard contractual arrangements." The Treasury's paper charged that the Commission demands too high a standard of proof that particular instances of market concentration are in the public interest and that therefore the Commission's actions "are likely to result in too many efficient arrangements being deterred or precluded". This paper reflects a fundamentally static view of the world that does not take into account the dynamism and upgrading of firm capabilities that local rivalry engenders.

In different ways, the lack of emphasis on domestic competition, or its outright rejection, is also expressed by many of the major private-sector lobby groups. While these groups frequently disagree on a variety of matters, none has championed vigorous competition in the New Zealand market. This is perhaps not surprising since vigorous competition, while necessary, can be extremely uncomfortable and often does not favour the establishment.

Inadequate New Business Formation
New business formation is critical to maintaining and improving the vitality of a nation's economy. Upgrading the economy requires that some industries and segments be left behind for new industries and segments. An economy that does not develop new businesses is doomed to stagnation. New business formation also intensifies the level of domestic rivalry, stimulates the formation of related and supporting industries and facilitates the formation of clusters. New companies are often the source of new and innovative ideas. Vibrant new business formation is

vital to maintaining a competitive dynamic and ongoing upgrading in the economy.

However, stimulating new business formation in New Zealand has not been seen as a priority. New Zealand lacks specialist financing institutions to fund such businesses, and the banking system generally avoids new enterprises. Oligopolistic industry structures make new entry difficult, while legislated control of some significant industries makes new entry illegal. New Zealand lacks the small-business management-training courses that are common in the United States, for example. The amount and complexity of form filling for a multitude of government agencies makes it difficult for new businesses. Perhaps most importantly, negative attitudes towards risk taking and business failure in New Zealand inhibit entrepreneurship. These features contribute to a low level of net new business formation.

There are, however, a few examples of new entrants that are competing in traditional export industries. Fortex Meats is a relatively new and growing competitor in the meat industry. Fortex's innovations in human-resource management and marketing have allowed it simultaneously to improve productivity and open new markets to build a position in the industry. Unfortunately, this is still the exception in New Zealand rather than the rule.

Firm Strategy, Structure and Rivalry Summary

New Zealand's firms typically employ cost-based strategies that exploit its natural factor advantages. These were once sufficient to assure a high standard of living, but they are no longer adequate. New Zealand management has for too long been trapped in a mindset that the modern global economy has rendered inoperative. It has yet to make the quantum jump necessary to meet and beat the world's best competitors.

In part, this is due to the nature of our goals. The "Kiwi lifestyle" and the low status accorded business have blunted our willingness to make the sustained personal commitments necessary to achieve business success in a global economy. Our capital markets tend to shy away from making long-term investments in companies with ambitious strategies, particularly smaller enterprises. Part of rebuilding the competitive position of New Zealand will require fundamentally rethinking our goals as individuals, firms and as a nation.

While we revere competitive success in sport, we appear to have developed a notion that these benefits do not apply in business and the economy. We have consciously reduced the level of competition and rivalry in our economy in the misconception that this was in our interests. If New Zealand is to build a more prosperous and secure future, we need to take advantage of the invigorating force that domestic competition and rivalry can deliver to the process of upgrading our economy and developing broad-based competitive advantage.

Government Policy in New Zealand

The New Zealand government has historically played a prominent role in our economy. Its importance has been growing throughout the post-war era. In 1989, government expenditure accounted for 42% of GDP, the ninth highest in the OECD. Moves to limit the role of government in the mid-eighties, however, have led to some important reductions in the scope of government activities.

Government policy in New Zealand and elsewhere has had a wide range of social and economic impacts. During the post-war era, social goals have tended to dominate economic goals in New Zealand. Michael Joseph Savage, the first Labour Prime Minister, articulated this philosophy well when he said "Social justice must be the guiding principle and economic organization must adapt itself to social needs."[20] Historically, the focus of our government policy has been income redistribution and economic security rather than laying the foundations for a vibrant economy well suited to creating wealth for the nation.

The scope of government activities in New Zealand grew steadily until the election of the fourth Labour government in 1984. The foundations of the Welfare State, laid down by the first Labour government during the Great Depression, were steadily increased through the provision of health and education services as well as an increasing broad range of benefits. Government also attempted actively to manage the structure of the New Zealand economy through an increasingly complex array of protection, subsidy and tax-relief policies at industry level. Attempts were made to manage all the major macroeconomic variables, including wages, interest rates, exchange rates, money supply and inflation. Our politicians and bureaucrats appeared to believe that they could effectively manage almost every part of the New Zealand economy.

The advent of "Rogernomics", named after the Labour government's Minister of Finance, Roger Douglas, in 1984 signalled a fundamental change in philosophy as to government's role in the economy. Douglas's market-oriented approach was based on the idea that New Zealand's interests would be best served in the long term by allowing the economy to respond more freely to international market forces. It was a fundamental shift away from the previous attempts to insulate New Zealand from the rest of the world.

This philosophy led to the introduction of a range of dramatic policy changes designed to reduce the direct role of government in the economy and to integrate New Zealand into the world economy. The financial sector was deregulated and the New Zealand dollar floated. The Reserve Bank was granted more autonomy from the political wing of government and was given the maintenance of price stability as its key objective. Direct government participation in the economy was reduced through the privatization of state assets. Protectionism was reduced, widening consumer choice and opening New Zealand companies to direct international competition. Restrictions on foreign investment were relaxed to allow greater participation in our economy by overseas investors. Port reform and

---

[20] Keith Sinclair, *A History of New Zealand,* Pelican Books, 1980, p. 263.

deregulation of telecommunications, road, rail and air transportation were aimed at improving the performance of our national infrastructure.

Despite these reforms, the economy has not turned around and critical challenges lie ahead.

The New Zealand Government's Influence on the Determinants

Government can influence the four determinants of national competitive advantage in a positive or a negative fashion. In the next sections we will examine how government policies have influenced each of the determinants of national competitive advantage.

Government Influence on Factor Conditions

Education and Training. Overall, the government has not displayed a strong commitment to human-resource development. This has contributed to our present economic challenges. New Zealand has spent tens of billions of dollars in building an education system without a clear national consensus as to what we expect in return. Our educational goals and priorities continue to be developed independently from an understanding of our economy and its future development prospects. New Zealand's education system lacks specific focus on the kinds of knowledge and skills required to ensure that New Zealand remain a prosperous country. Striking the right balance between using education to help build a base for sustained wealth creation and using education to transmit societal values has been a source of intense debate in New Zealand, particularly in recent years.

Accurate and objective measures of the effectiveness of our education system are central to evaluating the effectiveness of this investment in addition to evaluating and motivating the performance of our young people. Standards need to be high and continually improving. They also need to be relevant. Legitimate concerns about the relevance of academically focused national examinations, such as School Certificate, that fail half the nation's teenagers each year, have led to a misguided move away from commitment to educational standards. The continuation of this trend could have an unfavourable impact on our industrial competitiveness in the long term.

Education and training in many advanced countries involves active participation and well-integrated co-operation of the public and private sectors. The limited role of private education and training facilities in New Zealand places a special focus on government education and training policies. Government involvement in sector-based training programmes tends to be quite limited. A system of training boards operates in several industries aimed at co-ordinating industry and government efforts, for example in boat building and textiles. The government recently had to incorporate the Tourism Human Resource Development Unit into the Tourism Department due to uncertain industry funding support. These efforts, while limited, offer considerable positive potential for government and industry to improve the skills base jointly.

Science and Technology. A relatively high proportion of New Zealand's research and development is funded by government and undertaken by government departments rather than universities or the private sector. Where government research and development has had a direct economic orientation it has tended to be focused on improving production efficiencies of our resource-based industries. DSIR Biological Industries Group has been prominent in plant breeding, plant productivity and related technologies. Similarly, MAFTech's research in animal production and health, soil and plant nutrition and irrigation is widely regarded by the resource-based industries as important to their competitive advantage. While these are all positive developments, research by these institutions into downstream processing, new product development and market research has been more limited.

Government support for advanced and specialized research institutes focused on the requirements of particular industries, such as the Dairy Research Institute, the Forest Research Institute and the Wool Research Organization of New Zealand, has provided a range of technological improvements. Government moves to increase the level of industry contribution to these institutes is likely to improve their integration into the further development of the respective industries.

The recent establishment of the Ministry of Research, Science and Technology and the introduction of contestability for government research funds is likely to contribute to better integration of public- and private-sector research efforts. Plans to establish a series of industry-focused research institutes could serve as the focal point for upgrading the technical base of the respective industries. It is also likely to focus more research on applications with direct commercial significance.

Infrastructure. The New Zealand government has played a major role in establishing the basic infrastructure of the country, including roads, rail, ports, telecommunications, airlines, shipping lines, hotels, hospitals, and electricity and gas supplies. Several of these were government monopolies with rigid labour practices that led to costs well in excess of those in most countries. Electricity was the only element in which New Zealand was cost competitive.

Since the early eighties, government has actively reduced its direct role in the development and provision of infrastructure through an ongoing programme of deregulation, corporatization (turning government agencies into state-owned companies) and privatization (selling state assets to private interests). In general, this has led to substantial improvements in the performance of our national infrastructure. Despite recent improvements, efficiencies in the ports and shipping, particularly on the trans-Tasman route, remain of concern. Overall, government policy has made significant improvements in infrastructural performance, though not to the extent that any aspect of New Zealand's infrastructure could be described as providing New Zealand firms with advantage over their competitors.

Capital Constraints. Government policy has influenced the household savings rate in a number of ways. The Welfare State has unintentionally dampened incentives for individuals to save. Generous housing allowances, unemployment payments, retirement benefits, educational funding and health care benefits limit the need for people to save. A combination of fiscal and monetary policies resulted in negative real interest rates for much of the seventies and early eighties, making it unwise to do so.

Government spending has grown far more rapidly than revenues, and as a percentage of GDP it has grown steadily. The accumulation of deficits and debts has become a structural feature of our economy. Funding these deficits has contributed to New Zealand's high interest rates and burgeoning overseas debt. Servicing of an ever higher level of debt itself contributes to the continuing government deficits. High levels of government debt have increased the risk premium attached to New Zealand investments and made it more difficult for firms to source capital from overseas.

In the mid 1980s, government moved aggressively to unravel a complex system of incentives and subsidies for exports and industries through a policy of investment neutrality. The central precept of these policies was to allow the capital flows in the economy to operate with the minimum of interference from the state. This led to a significant reduction in tax-driven investment and other measures that had previously been a central part of government economic policy. Unfortunately, it appears that much of the investment that did occur went into real-estate and share speculation rather than into productive investment.

Provision of Information. In New Zealand, the provision of information by government specifically for industry is limited. Those services that are provided have been helpful to industry. The field advisory service of the Ministry of Agriculture and Fisheries rapidly disseminated information in regard to agricultural and horticultural production. The Trade Development Board publishes a series of studies on trade-related issues. Little has been done to provide the public with information with which to make more discerning choices. While government supported the establishment and operation of the Consumers' Institute, this support was removed in 1989.

The reports and studies produced by the New Zealand government tend to be limited in number, scope and quality. This is in sharp contrast with the numerous reports, white papers, forecasts, technical studies and market reports provided by MITI and JETRO in Japan or the National Technical Information Service in the United States. There is considerable room for additional New Zealand government efforts in this area, especially given the fact that New Zealand companies tend to have limited knowledge of foreign markets and competitors.

Government Influence on Demand Conditions

Overall, New Zealand government policy towards demand has focused on management of aggregate demand. Upgrading the **quality** of domestic demand has not been a specific goal of New Zealand government policy. There are some isolated instances of government action leading to the improvement of local demand conditions and thereby to competitive advantage for New Zealand industry. However, these have not had a major impact on our competitive performance. Overall, government has had little positive impact on local-demand conditions.

Government Procurement. Government, with few exceptions, has done little to raise the quality of domestic demand. Government has been a major buyer of many goods and services. There are only a few instances where this has led to the development of competitive advantage for New Zealand firms. New Zealand engineering consulting firms' expertise in handling medium-sized infrastructural projects for the government within New Zealand has contributed to a strong position in this market segment in the Asia Pacific region. However, in this case and others, the advantage tends only to apply in less sophisticated markets. Generally, government is not known as a demanding purchaser.

Regulatory Standards. Government standards have not been aimed at encouraging the most demanding and sophisticated consumers in the world. Instances of where standards have had a favourable impact in New Zealand are relatively rare. Tough building standards relative to other nations have led to considerable upgrading in the construction industry, which has contributed in part to New Zealand's international position in that industry. The Ministry of Consumer Affairs, Standards Association and the Fair Trading Act all specify minimum standards that New Zealand firms have to meet in a range of areas. These standards are not considered particularly tough by international standards.

Government Influence on Related and Supporting Industries

Cluster Development. Despite the heavy involvement of the government in the economy, very little effort has gone into the enhancement of our few nascent industry clusters, such as in agricultural technology in Hamilton. Rather, the focus has been on the development of entirely new industries, often in areas where New Zealand has had little prospect of developing competitive advantage. A number of manufacturing industries developed behind the protectionist walls of "Fortress New Zealand". Many proved to be uncompetitive when protection was reduced. It is not surprising that firms insulated from the rigours of competition did not develop the skills necessary to engage foreign competitors.

Regional Development. Long-term investments by the state in regional development do not appear to have contributed to the development of self-sustaining clusters. Investments have often been made with a greater regard to political considerations than development of competitive advantage. It would appear that collectively these policies have contributed little to the upgrading of the New Zealand economy.

Media. Advanced media can provide important support for many marketing-intensive industries. Sophisticated domestic media can provide firms with the opportunity to develop sophisticated marketing techniques. In New Zealand, television remains highly concentrated, with the state-owned enterprise Television New Zealand holding an overwhelming market share. While the introduction of a third television channel has led to substantial improvements in performance, the strong grip of state television has been maintained. State run media often stunts the development of sophisticated marketing skills within a nation.

Government Influence on Firm Strategy and Structure

Government has traditionally been the single most important player in the New Zealand economy. As such, it has had a profound impact on the strategies of New

Zealand firms. Government policies have affected New Zealand industry in several ways. Government is a major purchaser of goods and services in New Zealand. For decades government protected some industries, promoted some industries and set up or protected monopolies in other industries. In some industries, it did all three. Government protected industries such as motor-car assembly, heavily subsidized agriculture and recently had to bail out the Bank of New Zealand. It also oversaw the central bargaining system in labour management negotiations.

The net effect of the extensive government involvement was to make a firm's political strategy as important, if not more important, than its business strategy. Government's traditional importance to firm strategy can easily be seen in the number of our leading companies, banks and producer boards that are headquartered within a short walk of Parliament.

Intervention in Factor Markets. The New Zealand government has a history of intervening in a variety of factor markets. Devaluations and a series of incentives for everything from kiwifruit to film making were undertaken to increase the size of the traded sector. These also reduced the need for New Zealand firms to be truly competitive. Government was an active participant in labour negotiations. It also exercised control over capital flows.

The fundamental change that took place in the mid-eighties exposed New Zealand firms to international competition and reduced government influence on investment decisions. The philosophy was that government should not "pick winners" but rather ensure a "level playing field" for competition. Government measures to integrate the New Zealand economy into the world economy in the mid 1980s led to the floating of the New Zealand dollar and removal of exchange controls. The principle of investment neutrality was also applied to the tax system to remove any incentives or disincentives for New Zealand firms to invest overseas.

The view was that New Zealand's long-term interests would be best served by exposing its firms to international competition without government having a particular view as to where investment should take place.

Floating the dollar and removal of exchange restrictions led to a significant increase in foreign investment by New Zealand firms. In fact, it allowed New Zealand companies to buy foreign assets, develop foreign distribution, attempt to exploit foreign markets and adopt multinational forms. Fletcher Challenge became a significant force in the international forest-products industry after acquiring assets in the US, the UK, Canada, Brazil and several other nations. The New Zealand Dairy Board invested in an international expansion programme designed to build its position in key markets.

The crash in 1987 led to a contraction of the momentum of international investment by New Zealand firms, particularly among the high-profile investment companies. However, the mindset of New Zealand business had been significantly changed by the combination of these measures to be more focused on competing on an international basis.

Influences on Labour. Labour laws have built rigidities into the economy. Compulsory unionism, organized by industry rather than by enterprise, led to inevitable demarcation disputes. The centralized bargaining system, now reduced, was heavily influenced by government. The centralized system often resulted in low differentials in wage rates for skills and labour inflexibility. Labour relations have been a source of friction between management and unions, especially in forestry, the meat industries and the port system. Recent reforms in the ports have improved their efficiency somewhat, though there is still a long way to go.

In a protected economy, wage increases were largely independent of international forces. There was little incentive for employers to restrict wage increases when any increases could be passed on in increased prices in the home market. The role of wages policy became a government rather than a private-sector prerogative.

Trade and Industrial Policy. Government trade and industrial policies have had particular impacts on firm strategy in New Zealand. Trade has been a central consideration in government economic policy given its critical role in New Zealand's economic welfare. With a managed exchange rate until the mid-eighties, the development and preservation of foreign exchange earnings was a central objective for government. The central role of government in the traded sector led to an inevitable focus by management on its dealings with the bureaucracy and politicians. This took the focus away from international customers and competition.

Historically, the goal of much of New Zealand trade policy was to encourage and subsidize New Zealand exports while protecting its firms at home and targeting particular industries for special favour. The Trade Commissioner Service was established to assist New Zealand exporters, particularly small to medium-sized businesses.

Government's major efforts in trade negotiations with other nations have centred on maintaining access for agricultural products into the EC and negotiating a free trade agreement with Australia. While these are appropriate, there has been little attempt to encourage firms to build competitive positions in sophisticated segments based on differentiated products and thereby to become less exposed to political developments in overseas markets.

Social Welfare and Incentives. A social-welfare system is a necessary part of any compassionate society. The most difficult challenge faced by any such system is in providing for those truly in need without reducing the incentives to work, save and upgrade one's skills for the rest of the population. New Zealand's social-welfare system tends to dampen the pressure for, and rewards from, skills upgrading. Non-contributory superannuation, comprehensive social security, subsidized housing, unemployment benefits, free health care and accident compensation have all unwittingly tended to dampen the urgency for individuals to improve their personal skills, productivity and living standards.

Full employment up until the 1980s reduced pressure for individuals to upgrade their skills while high marginal tax rates reduced the incentives to work longer hours. The low differential between unemployment benefits and paid work that has developed has the same effect. In some cases, the unemployment benefit has been more attractive than working, education or training.

New Zealand has one of the most comprehensive social-welfare systems in the world. Despite the persistence of government deficits and the increasing portion of the economy taken up by social-welfare spending, the nation's ability or otherwise to afford this system has received surprisingly little attention until recently.

Government Influence on Domestic Rivalry

The government has generally not stimulated domestic rivalry. New Zealand lacks a tradition of strong competition policy. The feeling has long been that New Zealand is too small to support multiple rivals in an industry. Competition is often regarded as unseemly or wasteful. Official government policy in the 1980s, particularly as expressed by the Treasury, has been indulgent of monopoly practices. The alleged "economic efficiency" of market concentration has been used to justify a policy of "non intervention" towards concentration of market power.

Government, in fact, has played a central role in the development of New Zealand's concentrated industry structures. Arguments for the need for small countries to achieve scale and countervailing bargaining power through concentration led to the legislative support for producer boards. These concepts also led to the toleration, and in some cases promotion, of industry consolidation, such as in the forest-products industry. Government's privatization programme has tended to reinforce the high levels of concentration in New Zealand industry. Several of the state's key assets, such as telecommunications, were sold as effective monopolies on the basis that if legislative protection of these companies was removed a competitive environment would be created. Privatization and deregulation were not followed up with ensuring that a truly competitive situation emerged, either through the sale process or through anti-trust type actions.

While government has moved aggressively to open up the economy to competitive forces within New Zealand in some industries such as finance, transportation and petroleum, there are many areas where it has been less active. Government's heavy involvement in health and education services has made the introduction of competition an emotionally charged issue, while strong professional bodies in law, medicine and stock broking have made the introduction of more competition in professional services difficult.

New Business Formation. New business formation is an integral part of upgrading competitive advantage in an economy. Several government policies influence new business formation. As part of its wide-ranging interventions in the economy, government historically has had a series of institutions and programmes targeted at new business formation, particularly concessional finance through the Development Finance Corporation. As part of the move towards a more neutral role in the economy, government has since reduced its activities in these areas. High interest rates make new business finance prohibitive. The academic focus of the education system does not develop a broad base of young people with business and/or technical qualifications that might provide an entrepreneurial basis for new business development. Government research tends to provide few new ideas and technologies on which new firms might be developed.

The tolerance of monopolies and oligopolies restricts, sometimes by law, the development of new businesses in those areas where New Zealand has the greatest potential to develop new competitive advantages. The multiplicity and complexity of form filling required by government agencies probably provides new businesses with an unneeded challenge. Bankruptcy laws have yet to be adjusted to reflect the greater flexibility accorded firms to reorganize their affairs that is a feature of the United States Chapter 11 provisions and has been incorporated into British and Australian law. In many ways, government policy has made the environment for new business formation perhaps more difficult than it need be.

Government Policy Summary
The effectiveness of government policy in improving the fundamental underpinning of the economy can be evaluated through the impact of government policy on the determinants of national competitive advantage. Often, key policies, such as in education, have been developed with wider considerations than the development of industrial advantage. However, we need to understand how these have influenced the ability of New Zealand industry continually to innovate and move to ever-higher forms of competitive advantage.

Historically, government policy has aimed to reduce our exposure to the rest of the world while encouraging exports to earn foreign exchange. Government has played the central role in the economy, attempting to influence almost all aspects of the economic equation to reduce pressure on firms and individual New Zealanders. Rather than building and extending upon our existing strengths, government has invested heavily in the development of industries where New Zealand has had little prospect of developing competitive advantage (see figure 68). We have found it difficult to accept that we are a very small part of a very

Government has reduced pressure and protected comparative advantage

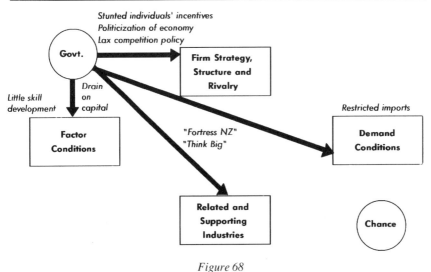

Figure 68

large global economy and that fewer and fewer decisions can be made in our economy within a purely New Zealand framework. In fact, we compete in a global economy.

Susceptibility to External Events

The development of the New Zealand economy has been heavily influenced by external events. Some of these have had a favourable impact on the economy but have not provided unique advantages. The introduction of wide-bodied jets, which significantly brought down the cost of air travel, is one such example. The introduction led to a major growth in tourist arrivals in New Zealand as well as elsewhere in the world.

Other chance events have been specific to New Zealand and have flourished as a result of the particular conditions present here. The discovery of a unique circuit-breaking system at Ruakura in the 1960s was quickly commercialized to offer New Zealand farmers improved fencing technology. The high level of education among our farmers and vigorous competition between local producers led to a continual stream of innovations and improvements. This environment has provided the fuel for the New Zealand industry to maintain its international leadership.

The Law of the Sea Conference gave New Zealand the seventh-largest exclusive economic zone. New Zealand's economic zone proved to be home to commercial quantities of a number of unique fish species. The present quota system allows the government and New Zealand firms to obtain rents from the fish resource. There have been limited attempts to upgrade the New Zealand industry beyond more effective management of the fish resource.

In other instances, the conditions have not been favourable in New Zealand for the continuing development of a firm or industry. In some cases, this has moved to more fertile environments elsewhere in the world. The software industry is one of the fastest-growing export industries in New Zealand. From negligible exports in 1980, software exports have reached over a hundred million dollars. However, the basis for this growth has been, in the main, the presence of a small number of outstanding entrepreneurs. These entrepreneurs have successfully commercialized their products despite the odds against them. However, several of the leading firms have left or been sold to foreign interests due to the lack of a favourable environment within New Zealand, including a lack of experienced personnel, leading-edge customers and venture capital.

New Zealand's economy has proven to be particularly vulnerable to external shocks. Recent declines in farm incomes show the precarious nature of a number of our export industries. Furthermore, we are often not well positioned to take advantage of opportunities that present themselves.

6

The Misaligned New Zealand System

There has been a growing misalignment between the structure of the New Zealand economy and the requirements for success in today's global economy. This is the fundamental cause of the continuing deterioration in our economic circumstances. The systemic nature of New Zealand's economic challenges underscores the magnitude of the task of turning the situation around.

The New Zealand economy was built to exploit our favourable growing conditions, originally for grass and animals and in more recent decades fruit and trees. The incentive to develop more sophisticated products, build international businesses or diversify into more technologically based industries was perhaps limited by our already high standards of living. It is readily apparent that high and rising living standards are unlikely to be maintained by an economy whose primary exports are price-sensitive commodities.

In order to understand the New Zealand economic system, and to identify its key leverage points, it is necessary to understand how the system came about. The system has a tight-knit internal logic that has developed over several decades and has become deeply ingrained into our economic and social fabric. This logic was developed for a time that has long since passed. It is poorly suited to the requirements of modern international competition and is simply failing to deliver the standards of living to which we aspire.

"Britain's Fertile Farm"

New Zealand's history as an agricultural producer serving principally the British market has imprinted the nation with a set of attitudes, institutions and strategies which are not suited to competition in advanced industries or segments.

New Zealand was originally "Britain's farm", exporting a narrow range of agricultural commodities, including wool, sheepmeat and butter, to Britain. In return we imported machinery and capital. The New Zealand economy complemented the British economy. We focused on low-cost production of basic commodities, while British interests controlled processing and distribution (early meat plants and shipping, for example).

Since Britain bought as much as we could produce, our principal economic challenge was to increase production in these commodities. There existed little pressure to upgrade the primary-sector industries by developing related and supporting industries. The result was a focus on production and cost reduction in New Zealand that lasts to today.

This trading relationship allowed New Zealand to achieve one of the highest per-capita incomes in the world, but left us with long-term structural weaknesses. New Zealand's prosperity, mild climate and beautiful natural environment all contributed to the "Kiwi lifestyle". These influences also had a major impact on shaping the strategic vision of New Zealand industry. Our attitudes, strategies, institutions and view of the world were influenced by this experience.

The relationship with Britain reduced opportunities for New Zealand companies to gain an intimate understanding of sophisticated consumers. Unsophisticated demand conditions in both New Zealand and the United Kingdom compounded matters. Even today, few New Zealand firms have world-class marketing skills, brands or distribution systems.

The fact that New Zealand was dependent on imported technology never seemed to be a concern. This was supplied from the "mother country". The result has been a New Zealand that develops little in the way of world-class technology outside of agriculture. The lack of related and supporting industries, such as agricultural machinery, has made it difficult to develop dynamic industry clusters that could provide economic growth.

Producer boards were gradually introduced in an attempt to improve the prices that fragmented New Zealand farmers received from concentrated international buyers through consolidation. These boards were responsible to primary producers for the sale of their products in international markets. Unwittingly, this further reinforced an emphasis on cost and production efficiencies within New Zealand. The pressures and abilities of New Zealand firms to develop new products, new distribution systems or new strategies, or to move offshore or diversify into related industries, were reduced. This approach, government involvement and industry concentration, became the model for a number of other New Zealand industries, even those with totally different economic drivers.

The position of primary producers, combined with exploitation of New Zealand farmers by British merchants earlier this century, contributed to a deep-seated suspicion of local and overseas participants in the value chain such as downstream processors and distributors. This was compounded by the fact that New Zealanders only participate in the primary-production end of the value chain. An attitude still widely held in New Zealand is that value is only really added in actually making the product (typically on the farm). This leads to the view that the interests of the producer, by which is meant the primary producer, should be paramount and enshrined in law if necessary. Indeed, it could be argued that in several important parts of our economy, a production focus has been legally mandated. This attitude has hampered efforts to compete in industries or segments that require a different focus, which in turn has limited opportunities to upgrade the New Zealand economy.

A Factor-driven Economy

The principal sources of competitive advantage in New Zealand's export industries are natural-factor advantages, such as favourable growing conditions, which allow New Zealand to produce temperate-climate commodities at low cost. This is characteristic of a factor-driven economy. In only a few small industries, such as custom racing yachts and electric fencing, do advantages in the determinants work together as a system to allow New Zealand firms to utilise multiple sources of advantage. (see figure 69).

New Zealand Custom-made Racing-yacht Industry Sources of Advantage

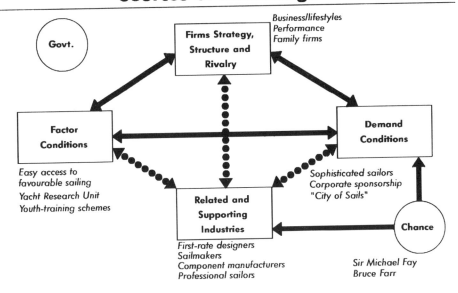

Figure 69

In many nations, factor advantages provided the initial impetus to the economy. In an upgrading economy, however, related and supporting industries develop, and demand widens and becomes more sophisticated. Domestic rivalry pushes the whole process along. New Zealand still largely produces commodity products. In its reliance on factor advantages, New Zealand's economy appears to be in a state of arrested development.

Our reliance on factor advantages has made many of our export industries vulnerable to entry by newcomers who can duplicate New Zealand's factor advantages but have lower wage levels. Chile and other nations have entered some of New Zealand's export industries, such as forest products and kiwifruit. Other advantages can be negated by improving technology. Dutch flower growers have overcome their unfavourable climate through innovations in greenhouse cultivation, new strains of flowers, energy conservation and in handling and transportation. Improvements in produce-storage technology, combined with extended growing seasons, have reduced the advantage of counter-seasonal production. Synthetics threaten our wool producers. Protection and subsidies have hurt our pastoral-farming industries. As a result of such pressures, over three-quarters of New Zealand's merchandise exports face fundamental and long-term pressures on profitability.

New Zealand's factor advantages have been a mixed blessing in the long term. While enabling New Zealand to be price competitive in bulk commodities, they have also reduced the pressure on industry to develop new and more sophisticated advantages. Paradoxically, New Zealand's comparative advantages in commodity production have contributed to attitudes, strategies and institutions that make up an overall system that is not well aligned with the requirements for an upgrading economy.

A Wealth-driven Ethos

New Zealand's natural endowments were so abundant relative to the size of the population that competing on the basis of factor advantages yielded a very high standard of living. A history of high standards of living resulted in attitudes on the part of government, industry, unions and the general public that reflects the wealth-driven stage of development. The focus of economic policy shifted from the creation of wealth to redistribution of wealth. Attitudes toward business, work and competition became those of a nation seeking to preserve rather than to build. The laudable and proper desire to provide for all of society's members has resulted in a social welfare-system that has unnecessarily limited incentives for individuals to save or to upgrade their skills and has outstripped the nation's ability to fund it. New Zealand's natural advantages provided for a high standard of living. As a result, the attitudes, institutions or skills necessary to drive forward the creation of broad-based competitive advantage have been poorly formed.

Government policy has implicitly assumed that New Zealand would always remain a wealthy society. In the complex policy trade-offs between maintaining living standards and egalitarian principles versus investing to build a more productive economy, social objectives have consistently been paramount. Politicians who have proposed a reordering of these priorities have been relegated to the annals of political history. New Zealand's commitment to social objectives is illustrated in its willingness to incur debt levels that would concern most Third World governments. These borrowings have been used to maintain government spending, which primarily goes to supporting the Welfare State. The tendency of government to "borrow and hope" has continued even since it has become apparent there is little sign of economic improvement and borrowing has become more and more problematic. Government has attempted to put patches on the system without realizing the need for fundamental change.

Vulnerability to Exogenous Shocks

Many of the shifts in New Zealand's economic direction over the years have been prompted by outside events. New Zealand's reliance on factor advantages in a small number of industries and limited investment in creating new, more sophisticated advantages has left us vulnerable to external shocks, especially in overseas markets. We tend to be in industries with poor profit potential. We often compete in the most precarious stage in the industries we are in. Our positions have become, in many instances, unsustainable or unprofitable.

Limited development of technology, brands and international distribution systems has left us exposed to the politics of the dairy industry, entry by Italy and Chile in the kiwifruit industry and undercutting by Third World construction firms. Our export revenues depend on whether the Chinese are buying wool, the Iranians mutton or the Russians dairy products.

New Zealand has been whipsawed by external events. Declining commodity prices, the oil shocks and the entry of Britain into the EC have all been particularly painful for New Zealand. Our vulnerability has not decreased. The 1987 stock market crash, for example, appears to have affected New Zealand to a greater extent than almost any other nation.

Repeated Intervention

The vulnerability of the New Zealand economy has led to a series of government interventions in the economy over the years. The Great Depression contributed to the introduction of the Social Security Act by the first Labour government in 1938. This Act dramatically expanded the state's role in assuring income levels and providing a wide range of social services. This was to be the foundation of an increasing state role in the economy.

A series of balance-of-payments problems led to the enactment of protectionist policies in the early 1950s. "Fortress New Zealand" policies ushered in widespread intervention. While these policies resulted in at least the appearance of industrial development, they also resulted in poor quality, high prices, a cost-plus mentality in industry, a focus on political strategy rather than business strategy, and continued failure to gain a close understanding of foreign markets. New Zealand did not fully participate in the subsequent growth of world trade.

The 1970s saw new shocks to the New Zealand economy. The entry of the United Kingdom into the EC in 1973 had dramatic repercussions. EC agricultural policy took away most of what had been our largest market for agricultural products, Britain. The oil shocks hit the nation particularly hard. Government responded with attempts to reduce New Zealand's dependence on foreign sources of energy. The "Think Big" projects signalled yet further expansion of government and resulted in multi-billion dollar write-offs.

External shocks have led to numerous government attempts to reduce our exposure to the outside world and to protect our factor-cost advantages. The desire to reduce foreign-buyer power, achieve economies of scale and enhance New Zealand's cost position have all contributed to government's willingness to reduce the level of competition in the New Zealand economy. However, over the long term this has reduced the number of new strategies being developed, impeding the momentum for upgrading in industry. Government tolerance and support for high levels of concentration in New Zealand industry have directly reinforced the focus on cost-based strategies.

As these strategies have become less successful in international markets, heavy political pressure has been exerted on government to pursue a range of policies to "assist" the export sector. Export incentives, agricultural subsidies, tax incentives, negative real interest rates, and devaluations have all been aimed at improving the position of exporters. As with government policies elsewhere in the world designed to attack the symptoms of poor competitive strategy in industry, they have tended to reduce the pressure on industry to upgrade its competitive position. Inevitably this has led to further requests for assistance, often couched in terms of becoming "competitive" or making up for "unfair" advantages elsewhere in the world.

In general, the responses of government and industry to external events have been aimed at relieving pressures in the short term rather than creating an environment in which a more vibrant economy could emerge. More often than not, such efforts have merely masked problems rather than solving them, and have impeded rather than fostered the development of long-term competitive advantage. In addition, they have fostered an attitude among both firms and individuals that it is the government, rather than themselves, that is responsible for maintaining their prosperity. A natural desire to insulate New Zealand from external shocks has left us more vulnerable than ever to new ones.

Loss of Promising Companies and Technologies

New Zealand's environment is not conducive to the formation of companies in technology-intensive industries. The fact that a number of the promising companies in these areas that were founded in New Zealand have left is therefore great cause for concern. Companies have left because they either cannot obtain required inputs or because they can achieve higher productivity and greater returns on innovation if they move their home base elsewhere. In software, for example, FACT and PAXUS, two promising New Zealand companies, have moved their headquarters overseas. Inadequate supplies of software professionals, limited finance and a lack of leading-edge demand all contributed to their departure.

Glaxo, now based in the United Kingdom, is one of the world's leading pharmaceutical companies. Glaxo was founded in New Zealand as a proprietary dairy company, specializing in dried-milk infant formulae foods in the 1920s. It began to manufacture pharmaceuticals for animal care, taking advantage of large and sophisticated home demand due to New Zealand's position in pastoral farming in the 1950s. The United Kingdom branch eventually became the head office. The UK offered a larger, more advanced market and a superior research environment. The New Zealand branch is now a subsidiary that serves the local market.

Two concerns arise from these examples. The first is that in order to upgrade the economy, we must provide an environment in which new firms can prosper in advanced industries. The second regards the structure of our traditional industries. Glaxo started as a dairy company before moving into a more advanced, related industry. This pattern of upgrading is very common in other nations. In New Zealand, however, the present structures of our traditional industries appears to hinder such development.

Consistent Patterns in the Economy

There have been several remarkably consistent patterns in the New Zealand economy over the last four decades which reflect our basic aspirations as New Zealanders. A commitment to egalitarian principles of social justice, and to maintaining a high standard of living, has underpinned much of the basic thrust of government policy. This has led to an emphasis on income distribution rather than long-term wealth creation. Even in the eighties when it began to dawn on the average Kiwi that all was not economically well, the debate has been focused on how to maintain our principles of a fair and prosperous society given our difficult economic circumstances.

Much government policy over recent decades has been aimed at reducing pressure on individuals (Welfare State) and industry (heavy protectionism and subsidy). Even when government policy opened up the New Zealand economy to foreign competition, little was done to open up the economy to domestic competition, or to upgrade the factor base through educational reform or to reduce government spending.

The New Zealand education system has placed a higher priority on the transmission of societal values and academic training than on providing economically useful skills. The resulting skill base makes it difficult for us to develop higher-order competitive advantages and reinforces a focus on price competition in industry. This focus is reflected in a reluctance to invest in research and human-resource development as these are seldom seen as central to competitive advantage. Limited skills also contribute to unfavourable demand conditions. This reduces the opportunity for New Zealand industry to use the local market as a proxy for demand elsewhere in the world.

Interventionist policies have diverted management attention away from building competitive advantage in a global economy to negotiating with New Zealand bureaucrats and politicians. The resulting investments have not served to upgrade the New Zealand economy or contribute to increased capital productivity. The continuing aftermath of the 1987 stock market crash illustrates the difficulties New Zealand managers have had coping in an open economy. The effects of a mindset that still tends not to focus on the development of higher-order advantages in global competition are readily apparent.

Rogernomics: Necessary, But Not Sufficient

By the early 1980s, the New Zealand system had clearly become unsustainable. Debt was spiralling out of control. Government hiring could no longer mask rising unemployment. In this atmosphere, the Labour government instituted a wide-ranging programme of reform. Rogernomics, which reduced the scope of government activity in the economy, eliminated a number of market distortions and integrated New Zealand into the world economy, represented a fundamental shift in policy.

Despite these measures, the New Zealand economy continued to languish. Many of the manufacturing companies that developed during the years of protection failed. The stock market crash of 1987 showed that the boom created by an immature, deregulated financial sector and easy credit was an illusion. The difficult economic circumstances that followed led to New Zealand seeking to bring forward by five years Closer Economic Relations with Australia. Continuing and accelerating problems with fiscal and current-account deficits increased the impetus for the sale of state assets.

Rogernomics was necessary, but not sufficient, to assure New Zealand of high and rising living standards. While Rogernomics swept away many of the distortions in our economy, it did not provide the basis for the development of broad-based competitive advantage. Government efforts to stimulate domestic rivalry and reshape the internal economic landscape remained less than enthusiastic. New business formation received little attention in government economic policy. The education system was not reformed to reflect better our economic needs. Government did not become a noticeably more discerning buyer, nor did it adopt particularly stringent or forward-looking product standards. Pressures and incentives for individuals to upgrade their skills were not provided.

New Zealand's economy was sheltered not only from the international economy but was sheltered internally. This, in many ways, was more important. New Zealand firms did not have to compete locally, and both managers and employees lacked pressures and incentives to work, to invest and to develop skills. Other important conditions for competitiveness were also missing.

By opening externally but leaving internal conditions largely unchanged, Rogernomics moved boldly in the right direction but in the wrong sequence. Rogernomics created forces that New Zealanders were ill prepared and unable to meet. The result has been near paralysis. A better means to the same end may have been instituting fundamental internal reforms first, and then phasing in external competition over a several-year period. This sequence of policy changes, while perhaps more politically difficult to sell, may have been more effective in upgrading the economy.[1] Internal then external opening was the approach that Japan, for example, in effect followed.

The Need for Systemic Change

Our economic system does not drive forward the creation of new technologies, products and strategies that could provide the basis for sustained competitive advantage. New Zealand generally lacks the dynamic interaction one finds in successful economies between a skilled workforce, rising levels of technology, sophisticated consumers, clusters of mutually reinforcing industries and vigorous domestic rivalry. Rather than propelling New Zealand industry forward, the low skills of our workforce hamper the development of new advantages and technological progress. Lack of sophisticated home demand means that New Zealand is a poor proxy for international markets. Concentration in industry stunts dynamism and reduces the number and rate of new developments of all kinds.

New Zealand has changed considerably in the last few years. The attitudes, strategies and institutions that worked so well when we were Britain's farm have become, in the main, liabilities. Our attitudes, strategies, institutions, and as a result our economy, have not changed sufficiently to assure New Zealand a high and rising standard of living. We need systematic changes to better align our economy with the requirements for success in the modern world.

---

[1] One can argue that, given New Zealand's attitudes and history, external pressures were needed to convince New Zealanders of the necessity to change internally at all. This argument has merit, but history has demonstrated the great cost of this course of action.

7

Implications for New Zealand

New Zealand's economy faces serious difficulties and our future prosperity is uncertain. New Zealand is heavily dependent on advantages based on natural resources which have become more fragile and unstable. In essence, instability has been built into the economy. Strategies designed to insulate New Zealand from the world economy, and heavy government intervention to try to create entirely new industries, have simply failed. Trying to do the same things better by increasing production efficiency, limiting competition and devaluing the currency has also failed to raise our relative standard of living. More recent steps to integrate the New Zealand economy into the world economy have not been sufficient to assure the country a secure and prosperous future. Clearly a new direction is needed.

New Zealand's economic position is the result of a complex system of attitudes, institutions and policies that developed when our economic challenges were different and much simpler, as the previous chapter has described. The world has changed, but New Zealand has not changed enough to keep pace. Restoring our prosperity demands that New Zealand industry upgrade and broaden its competitive advantages. This is a complex challenge that will require sustained and systemic change in our education system, attitudes towards competition, and prevailing management philosophies, to name but a few. Piecemeal solutions will simply not work.

There are no viable one-shot solutions. To pin our hopes on a short-term "kick start" of government incentives or devaluation is fundamentally to misunderstand the problem. We need to rebuild the base of our economy from the ground up so that we can compete successfully in today's global economy. Competitive advantage is built over decades. Effective solutions will, therefore, require a time frame of decades.

While there is much that can be learned from other nations' experiences, the specific circumstances facing New Zealand are unique. They have not been faced by previous generations of New Zealanders or by other nations. What is required is a new economic order that better matches our social aspirations with the mandates of modern economic competition. We need to develop distinctly New Zealand solutions to our current problems.

New Zealand has taken some promising steps to become better integrated into the world economy. Government now plays a less direct role in our economic affairs than previously. However, government spending remains higher than our capacity to finance it. Moreover, much of government spending contributes little to, and frequently impedes, the development of an upgrading economy. In many key areas, such as human-resource development, government efforts need to be refocused.

There is no inevitability about New Zealand's economic decline. We face fundamental choices about our economic future. Effective change will require a broad-based national consensus about the general thrust of the changes required. A turnaround will have to be driven by thousands of individuals behaving differently in their firms, schools, unions, industry associations and government agencies.

New Zealand's only constraint would be people's inability or unwillingness to adapt, change and thus compete more successfully in the global economy. We have a base of export industries from which positions in new segments and industries can be built. Several New Zealand corporations are emerging as significant international competitors. There is literally a world of opportunity. Rethinking our assumptions, values, attitudes, goals and policies can form the basis for re-engineering our company strategies, institutions and economy. The future is as bright as we wish it to be.

Implications for Company Strategy

Companies, not governments, are on the front line of international competition. They must increasingly compete globally. Yet globalization does not eliminate the importance of the nation. The home nation plays a central role in whether a firm can be internationally successful and the nature of the competitive advantage it can achieve.

The most important sources of national advantage are not passively available, but must be actively developed. The firms that succeed in international competition constantly seek out new competitive advantages. They invest in making their home nation an ever more favourable environment for competitive advantage by encouraging training, scientific activity and the development of local suppliers. They amplify their home-based advantages and offset home-based disadvantages through global strategies that selectively source capital, raw materials and ideas abroad. Competitive advantage ultimately results from an effective combination of national circumstances and company strategy. Conditions in a nation may create an environment in which firms can attain international competitive advantage, but it is up to firms to seize the opportunity.

The actions required to create and sustain international competitive advantage are challenging and often intensely uncomfortable. There are other ways to achieve profitability that have been chosen all too often in New Zealand, such as seeking monopolies, harvesting market position through under-investment, and avoiding global competition via protectionism. Such alternatives are damaging to the nation and, in a world of increasing global competition, even have their perils for the firms which are short-term beneficiaries. New Zealand firms must set their sights on gaining competitive advantage against the world's best rivals. The standards for performance are often set not in New Zealand, but elsewhere.

There is a lack of confidence evident in New Zealand business today. A mindset appears to be developing in some areas that a government "kick start" is needed to "get the economy going". However, the policies proposed, while appealing in the short term, will only make a further erosion of competitive advantage more likely. The tendency to turn to government to solve fundamental problems of company strategy is deeply rooted in New Zealand. It is likely to be as self-perpetuating and self-defeating in New Zealand as it has been elsewhere in the world.

New Zealand firms must take responsibility for assessing their sources of advantage and disadvantage and move aggressively themselves to deal with them. Some necessary steps would be taken most effectively through industry associations or in conjunction with government agencies, as we will describe. However, the primary responsibility for upgrading the competitive advantage of New Zealand must lie with New Zealand firms.

Each firm faces its own set challenges. Each industry has its own unique situation and its own sources of advantage and disadvantage. It is therefore difficult to provide specific recommendations that are applicable across the entire economy. From our research, however, a number of mandates apply to a broad range of New Zealand firms and industries.

We have worked with New Zealand managers to raise and explore the implications for their particular industries in a series of industry workshops that were part of our project. Many managers and some industries have made initial steps along the paths suggested by our research. We hope that other firms and industries will use these implications as a departure point for analysis and action in their own context.

Move Beyond Cost-based Strategies. Much of New Zealand industry employs, explicitly or implicitly, cost-based strategies involving commodity products that exploit basic-factor advantages. While such strategies are appropriate in some industries, they limit the prospects for success in many others. New Zealand firms need to seek out more sophisticated competitive advantages. They must move toward strategies that allow New Zealand to compete on quality, features or service rather than price. This is true in our traditional industries as well as in our newer industries.

In our traditional industries, New Zealand firms should explore the opportunities for branding, advances in marketing and distribution, and developing new products. In addition, New Zealand producers should determine what services might be profitably bundled with their products. Efforts to brand New Zealand venison (to take advantage of our "clean, green" image); improved packaging, shipping and presentation in the kiwifruit industry; the Dairy Board's increased focus on branding and overseas marketing — these are all steps in the right direction.

In newer industries, we should aim to serve segments where we can differentiate our products and price accordingly. New Zealand wines have won several international contests, which has formed the basis for successful differentiation strategies through specialist outlets in Britain and elsewhere. In higher education, demand in the AsiaPacific region far outstrips supply. Instead of developing the institutions and skills necessary to attract the price-insensitive customer through high quality, however, we seem to be focusing on the most price-sensitive markets, such as teaching English. In tourism, we need to improve the range and quality of amenities, attractions and quality of service in order to command high prices.

The challenge to New Zealand firms is to develop the skills, products, services and technologies that customers are willing to pay for. A greater focus on high-quality segments and differentiation strategies will require New Zealand firms to upgrade, and add to, their existing capabilities.

Seek Opportunities where New Zealand's Home Environment is Uniquely Favourable. New Zealand firms have not fully exploited unique advantages present in the nation. New Zealand does have some areas in which local customers and industries provide leading-edge demand for products, services, supplies and machinery. New Zealand firms can build on this world-class demand to succeed in new industries. Examples where this has already occurred include yachts, electric fencing and certain other agricultural inputs, and sporting equipment. New Zealand firms should seek out and serve pockets of world-class demand within New Zealand as a possible prelude to serving similar customers abroad.

There is also a surprising lack of competitive New Zealand firms in industries that are related to the nation's leading export industries. The only groups of related industries in which New Zealand succeeds are in pastoral farming and horticulture. Some of the related industries that have developed, such as goats and deer, were started with impetus from foreign rather than New Zealand sources. Dawsons PLC of the UK was instrumental in the formation of the New Zealand goat-farming industry. West German game importers were influential in the early days of the New Zealand deer-farming industry.

There are considerable opportunities in New Zealand to deepen and widen existing clusters in a number of our industries. The dairy industry has moved further downstream than most New Zealand industries, while the forestry, fishing, goat-fibre and wool industries, for the most part, have not. New Zealand has achieved significant positions in racing yachts, with has opened the door for increased exports of marine components. New Zealand marine-equipment exporters are active in jet-propulsion units, anchor winches, marine-plumbing components, buoyancy aids, wet-weather gear, sails, spars, oars, marine electronics, rudders, ropes, winches and galley pumps.

Diversification is one way in which a nation's firms can create successful related industries. Related diversification often improves a company's competitive position in the core business as well as offering opportunities for growth. In several industries, including the home-appliance, food and consumer packaged-good industries, related diversifiers can obtain significant economies of scope. This has not proven to be a significant factor in New Zealand. Much of the diversification of some of our larger firms has been unrelated, while the mandates of the producer boards dampen the drive to diversify into related and supporting industries.

Become More Knowledgeable Competitors. Many New Zealand firms simply need to raise the level of their game in order to compete effectively in international markets. They need to develop a clearer understanding of the structure of their industry, the needs of their customers, and the strategies and strengths of their competitors. This knowledge and perspective is essential to the formation of effective strategies.

New Zealand firms should define their goal as international competitive advantage and act accordingly. This will require a higher level of professional skills and commitment. New Zealand's food industries lack the requisite skills to compete head on in key markets with the world's finest food multinationals such as Nestlé or Dole. The relaxed "Kiwi lifestyle" often means New Zealanders are unwilling to make the commitments necessary to compete successfully overseas. The "cottage industry" wine maker will find it difficult to sell against foreign competitors with more aggressive attitudes. New Zealand sailing enthusiasts compete effectively in the racing segments of the yacht markets, where their very love of the sport is a key advantage, but compete less effectively in mass production segments where business skills are more important.

Effective competitors put the onus for developing the skills and making the investments necessary to compete on themselves rather than on government. They move aggressively to try to influence events rather than waiting to be whipsawed by them. The New Zealand kiwifruit industry may have lost the opportunity to determine its forward path. The New Zealand deer industry may lose its chance soon. The New Zealand forest-products industry will be forever at the mercy of commodity cycles unless it begins a massive, sustained programme to upgrade its competitive position. New Zealand firms must develop the skills, attitudes and commitment necessary to shape their own destiny.

A Greater Focus on Innovation. The scope of innovation within New Zealand industry has been limited. While New Zealand has been innovative in some areas (especially agricultural production), few New Zealand firms employ proprietary technology and even fewer have been innovative marketers. Innovation, in its widest sense, is at the heart of competitive advantage. We must broaden our notion of innovation to encompass not only innovation in primary production, but also in new products, processes, marketing and logistics. Continuous investment is necessary to gain and maintain innovation-based advantages.

New Zealand firms should seek out pressures for innovation, not avoid them. They should sell to the most sophisticated and demanding buyers and channels, develop products to meet the most stringent customer needs, establish norms that exceed the toughest product standards, source from the most advanced suppliers and invest in upgrading employee skills. This requires the development of corporate cultures where innovation and change is encouraged and can flourish.

The advancement of employees with technical or business backgrounds will aid innovation. Too many New Zealand firms have managements populated by accountants who are good cost controllers but lack the forward-looking orientation necessary to the innovative process. This is in stark contrast with the technical backgrounds of the managements of most German and Japanese firms. Greater commitment to research and development, close liaison with local universities and polytechnics, and participation in local-management programmes will also benefit the innovation process.

New Zealand firms and institutes can be innovators. LYNX and Linc in software, cashgora in goat fibres, ear tags and electric fencing in agricultural technology, and the mass marketing of kiwifruit are all examples of successful New Zealand innovations. New Zealanders are an innovative people. We need to unleash this potential throughout the economy.

Invest in Human-resource Development. New Zealand firms have not invested aggressively in human-resource development. This is due in part to a static view of competition. Employee skills are less critical when firms keep producing the same products with the same processes. Too many New Zealand firms seem all too willing to leave the development of human resources to others, such as government or foreign multinationals. In addition, New Zealand business has tended to look to immigration to fill key skill shortages rather than training New Zealanders.

In today's economy, human-resource development is simply too important for firms to ignore or leave to someone else. The quality and productivity of a firm's human resources is fundamental to its competitive advantage and its ability to move beyond competing solely on the basis of natural resources. Continual skill upgrading at all levels in the enterprise, from the shop floor to the boardroom, is needed. Training in all facets of the enterprise must become a central part of strategy. This will require a fundamental change in thinking in many of our firms to making human-resource development a central priority.

After one of our project presentations, one Chief Executive told us he had decided to reinstitute a company training programme that was to be eliminated as a cost-cutting measure. This is the type of longer-range thinking that New Zealand firms need and the type of rethinking we hope to stimulate with this book.

Forge Closer Links with Educational Institutions. There is a glaring mismatch between the skills needed to upgrade the New Zealand economy and those provided by our education system. Many in the New Zealand business community understand that this mismatch exists, but few have taken an active role in assisting to adapt the system to support New Zealand's economic goals. This will require significant business participation and investment. Rather than standing on the sidelines, New Zealand's business men and women must make an active contribution.

Closer linkages between the education system and industry need to be formed. Direct input to course development that reflects the needs of industry will improve the relevance of the education process at all levels. New Zealand and foreign software companies should provide greater input to courses in computer science. IBM's commitment to Auckland University's Centre for Information Science is a prototype that needs to be replicated more broadly. Engineering firms should provide greater input to the development of engineering programs, and so on. Our courses should provide a better balance between practical and theoretical training.

Firms and industry associations should explore the opportunities for apprenticeship and co-operative education. The German or Swiss type of apprenticeship programme, which provides a high-quality education and work experience to the participants, could serve as a better model for New Zealand industry. Co-operative education programmes, in which students work part time or alternate work and schooling, can forge close links between education and industry, as well as provide a well-trained workforce.

Increased joint industry/university research will benefit both industry and academia. Joint research will provide some companies with a more rigorous basis for their in-house research. It will also help focus university research on commercially valuable areas. The genetic engineering skills of the Animal Husbandry Department at Massey University have contributed to the improvement of the genetic base of New Zealand's sheep and cattle industries, as well as the development of new breeds such as the Perendale. These kinds of programmes can be an important source of competitive advantage.

Increasing government budgetary difficulties within New Zealand may require business to contribute financially to develop specialized education and research programmes, or even to ensure the maintenance and improvement of the general education system. New Zealand firms have a large stake in the quality of the New Zealand education system, and must play their part in making the system work.

Adopt a More Global Approach to Strategy. New Zealand firms need to become more international in focus. Few New Zealand firms possess an intimate knowledge of their foreign customers and competitors. Fewer still use such knowledge actively to develop global strategies.

New Zealand firms need to have a meaningful sales business in those parts of the world where demand conditions in the industry are the toughest. They must have direct contact with leading-edge buyers in foreign markets in order to keep up with the latest in customer needs. Tapping into pockets of sophisticated demand elsewhere in the world can partially compensate for poor domestic-demand conditions. The Dairy Board, for example, has located research-and-development centres close to leading-edge demand in the United States, Europe and Japan.

New Zealand enjoys a position in the rapidly growing Pacific Basin, and is an efficient producer of products that will be in demand as industrialization progresses in the region. Despite this fact, too many New Zealand industries still focus on the UK and European markets. Japan is already our principal trading partner, and its importance, and that of our other Asian neighbours, is growing.

Every New Zealand exporter or potential exporter should have an Asian strategy to take advantage of the potential of the Asian market.

Some of our industries have adopted a more Asian outlook, while some have had a more Asian outlook forced upon them. Asian markets represent significant growth potential for the tourism industry. Our construction firms mainly serve the regional market. Much of our pulp and newsprint goes to Japan. A large portion of our wool is purchased by China. Iran has been an important customer for lamb. The Dairy Board has made a number of strategic investments in Asian markets. These exceptions must become the rule.

New Zealand has only a handful of multinational firms. This is due in part to our history of isolation and in part to an inward focus on the part of companies and management. Global strategies can be used to tap into favourable conditions elsewhere in the world to complement strengths in the New Zealand environment. While the initial phase in internationalizing a firm will be to export from a New Zealand home base, complementary businesses offshore should be developed into an effective global organization. It will be interesting to see how our large companies, such as Fletcher Challenge, meet this challenge.

Seek International Success rather than Local Dominance. There is a tendency in New Zealand business to seek to dominate the local market rather than compete internationally. Yet success in much larger international markets usually offers far greater profit potential than dominance at home. Such dominance is unlikely to lead to the development of the skills necessary to succeed abroad.

Corporate Leadership rather than Administration. As a result of New Zealand's long period of protectionism, there is a tendency for New Zealand businesses to be administered rather than led. Managing within existing constraints has produced a management culture that is neither used to building, nor equipped to build, new advantages on a continual basis. Overcoming the tendency simply to administer and preserve the present business will require the creation of a new management philosophy in New Zealand business.

It is a task of leadership at all levels to create an approach that is adaptable and aggressive in the search for new advantage. The CEO has a special responsibility in setting the tone throughout the organization. Today's competitive realities demand leadership.

Implications for Industry Associations

Historically, most New Zealand industry associations have seen their prime role as lobbying government. It is time to change this conception. Industry associations should be charged with identifying opportunities to improve the New Zealand context, especially in factor creation, in ways that firms themselves would find difficult or less efficient. Their memberships should be expanded to include participants from related and supporting industries, as they have a central role to play in the creation and maintenance of competitive advantage.

Adopt Human-resource Development as a Central Goal. Human-resource development should be a central priority for industry associations. New Zealand's industry associations need to be more proactive in establishing their own training programmes and working with educators at the local and national level. Industry has an interest in the creation of pools of specialized skills closely related to its needs. This can be enhanced through closer interaction between local schools and local industry associations through career days, internships and a more active involvement in curriculum development.

Apprenticeship schemes, vocational programmes and short courses for management should be developed in conjunction with local polytechnics and universities. This will benefit both industry and educators. Industry associations in Germany, for example, have been active in providing training which has resulted in the development of skilled workers that provide the nation's firms with advantages in a broad range of industries.

Set High Product and Process Standards. Industry associations can play a key role in setting and enforcing the high product and service standards for all participants in the New Zealand market. Industry associations can influence standards in two ways. First, associations can set standards for their member companies. Second, associations can influence standards set by government.

In either case, New Zealand industry associations should seek to guarantee the local customer that a local product is the best value for money in the world. This will require strictly enforced quality-assurance programmes. The goal should be to develop a reputation for quality and reliability. "Made in New Zealand" should become a mark of quality, both at home and abroad, just as "Made in Japan" has become.

Provide a Clearinghouse for Information. Industry associations can also serve as clearinghouses for information. Consumer information and education on product features and usage should be aimed at improving local-demand conditions. In addition, regular industry-association briefings for bankers on an industry's prospects and difficulties may facilitate improved understanding among financiers and better risk assessment.

Co-ordinate Business Support for Member Firms. Industry associations are often active in co-ordinating investments that are useful for the entire industry but beyond the means of a single firm. Industry initiatives are usually far more effective in these matters than government efforts, since the industry initiatives tend to be focused far more on investments that create true value for members. In some nations, industry associations co-ordinate investments in basic research and infrastructure that provide advantages to the entire industry.

Generic marketing of New Zealand industries' products in foreign markets is another function that industry associations can perform. Italian industry associations, for example, co-ordinate participation in trade shows, undertake market research in foreign countries, buy advertising space, and maintain contact and prospective customer lists.

Improving the availability of finance can be another useful role for industry associations. Specialist financing techniques and instruments can be adapted from overseas through joint task forces of industry and finance markets representatives.

Other functions that may be performed by industry associations include bulk purchasing and even clerical functions, such as payroll and systems development, for member firms.

Focus on Upgrading Competition, not Eliminating It. An important challenge for industry associations will be ensuring that the right balance is struck between co-operation in the provision of certain supporting or infrastructure functions and maintaining vigorous local competition. Industry associations can perform activities valuable to member firms without reducing competition in the product market. It is important that they do not degenerate into umbrellas for reducing competition. The focus should be on developing the competitive advantage of an industry rather than lobbying government.

Implications for Government Policy

Government can play a significant, though partial, role in creating and sustaining national advantage. Without the presence of underlying national circumstances that support competitive advantage in a particular industry, the best policy intentions will fail. Government does not control national competitive advantage; government can only influence it.

New Zealand's government has played a prominent role in the economy, but frequently it has been the wrong one. Our economic policy has operated under a faulty paradigm and, as a result, has often been counterproductive. The central role of government economic policy should be to set the stage so that New Zealand firms can achieve high and rising levels of productivity. To stimulate such dynamism, government should try to create an environment in which firms can upgrade competitive advantages in established industries and enter new industries where higher productivity can be achieved. The objective should be the creation of long-term competitive advantage for New Zealand rather than to shore up profits or reduce short-term market pressure.

The upgrading process requires that some industries will inevitably fail. In New Zealand, there has been a tendency to try to preserve and protect established industries, particularly those with political power. Such efforts have locked us into a limited set of industries that are increasingly threatened. This in turn has limited our capacity to upgrade the economy and has constrained New Zealand's standard of living. A system that tries too hard to preserve the old makes it difficult to create the new.

Much of the economic policy debate in New Zealand focuses on devaluation and wage rates. Attempts to boost "competitiveness" through devaluation or artificially forcing down wages are not the answer. Currency and wage rates should reflect market conditions. We should be concerned with the capacity of our nation's firms to innovate and upgrade. This is something that goes far beyond wage rates, interest rates and the exchange rate. If policies are measured in terms of their effects on dynamism and sustained productivity growth, the chances of working at cross purposes to true economic growth are much reduced.

A consistent programme is needed in a wide range of areas, because seemingly discrete policies are interdependent. The systemic nature of national competitive advantage means that the effect of choices in one policy area depends on those made in others. Choices concerning our education system affect the level of skills in our workforce. Social programmes may affect the incentives for individuals to save or invest in upgrading their own skills. Measures to protect and preserve particular industries may limit our ability to create new industries.

In New Zealand, social-policy considerations have tended to be pre-eminent over economic-policy considerations. We have tended to separate social and economic policy. Yet social and economic policy are inextricably tied. New Zealand's social policies have often needlessly undermined our economy. We must set our social policies in a way that creates the skills and incentives we need, without losing commitment to our ideals. Government policy at all levels needs to integrate macroeconomic and microeconomic policy, social and economic policy within the overall context of New Zealand's social aspirations and economic circumstances.

Below we provide a list of recommendations for the policies most in need of change. We offer these as a starting point for debate. Each broad area must be translated into specific policy programmes. Many of these recommendations are not new, though they have not been put into a coherent framework that can form a basis for action. We have lacked an overall view of our competitive position in the global economy.

The bottom line is that in assessing any government policy that affects the economy, we must ask: Does this policy provide the incentives, pressures and/or opportunities for our firms to innovate and upgrade? If the answer is no, the policy is unlikely to contribute to long-run prosperity.

Move Beyond Macroeconomic Policy. The economic debate in New Zealand has traditionally focused on macroeconomic variables. This debate has, for the most part, missed the point. Sound macroeconomic policy is necessary but not sufficient to bring success to the New Zealand economy. Debate over macroeconomic policy has deflected attention from the steps necessary to build competitive advantage in industry. Assertions such as "A devaluation of 12.83% will ensure prosperity" would be amusing if they were not taken so seriously.

New Zealand's macroeconomic-policy framework should remain market oriented. A floating dollar and market-determined interest rates should be maintained. Concerns with the levels of interest rates and exchange rates must be addressed through tackling the root causes of the problem — limited capital resources, low productivity, high-country risk premium, the accumulated debt burden and government deficits. The focus of the Reserve Bank on price stability should be maintained. However, the overall role of monetary policy in the fight against inflation should be reduced, with greater emphasis on productivity improvements and reductions in government spending.

Wages should be allowed to rise or fall with productivity. New Zealand workers should not be pressured into real wage sacrifices where productivity improvements are being achieved. Nor should they be paid artificially high wages or wage increases that do not reflect underlying levels of productivity or productivity growth.

New Zealand should settle quickly on a stable macroeconomic framework so we can get on with the real work of transforming the microeconomic structure of the economy. New Zealand faces greater challenges in building a world-class education system, world-class companies and world-class industries than it does in reducing inflation. Macroeconomic policy should support long-term upgrading in New Zealand industry rather than work against this process through uncertainty over the stability of the macroeconomic-policy framework.

Avoid the Devaluation Trap. There are those who would argue that devaluation offers a simple solution to New Zealand's complex and difficult economic problems. They argue that a devaluation, by making New Zealand firms more price competitive in world markets, would boost exports. Devaluation is extremely seductive for government. With a single move, its proponents would have us believe, our firms would immediately become more competitive.

These arguments overlook the fact that continuing and substantial depreciation of the New Zealand dollar in recent decades has not led to any significant improvement in New Zealand's competitive position. In 1975 one New Zealand dollar was worth one American dollar and thirty cents. Today, one New Zealand dollar is worth around sixty American cents. In fact, devaluation sets up the conditions for further devaluations, and reduces the probability of the development of sustainable competitive advantage.

Devaluation is not the road to prosperity because it does not attack the underlying causes of New Zealand's economic difficulties. Devaluation would not provide us with better skills, improve our product mix, or give us more inspired company strategies. Instead, devaluation would be likely to make us even more dependent on industries and segments with limited potential for profits or growth.

Devaluation, more than simply not working, would have negative consequences for the economy. It would lower our standard of living, which is already under pressure, by making our imports more expensive. Profits generated through devaluation will soon be appropriated by our customers and lost as international markets adjust. Inelastic demand for many of our export commodities significantly limits the potential for major market share gains. As New Zealand incomes drop, emigration becomes a more attractive option for the talented, qualified and motivated. New Zealand will need to continue to import critical technologies, machinery and other inputs in order to upgrade the economy. Devaluation would make these more expensive, reducing the probability of firms making these investments. It would also increase the burden of national-debt repayments.

Most importantly, devaluation would reduce the pressures on New Zealand firms to upgrade their competitive position and differentiate their products. Moreover, it would actually reinforce our tendency to compete on cost in commodity industries. It would provide short-term relief by temporarily masking long-term problems.

The goal should be to create an economy that supports a strong currency. This means making New Zealand's products and services attractive enough to command high prices, rather than selling goods only because they are cheap. Many of the nations that have significantly upgraded their competitive capacity, such as Japan, Germany and Switzerland, have had strong and rising currencies.

Exchange-rate difficulties should be addressed by attacking their fundamental causes. Sustained improvements in national productivity and reductions in government spending will do far more for us than artificial devaluation.

Upgrade New Zealand's Human Resources. The skill base of the New Zealand workforce is low relative to that of other advanced economies, and the trends are not encouraging.

Set High Standards. Appropriate standards need to be developed that evaluate and motivate performance at the individual level as well as that of our educational institutions and the education system as a whole. Legitimate concerns of the relevance of academically focused national examinations, such as School Certificate, that fail half the nation's fifteen-year-olds each year, have led to a misguided move away from commitment to educational standards. The continuation of this trend could have an unfavourable impact on our industrial competitiveness in the long term.

Skill Formation. A central priority of our education system should be providing young New Zealanders with the skills necessary to become productive members of society in an increasingly competitive world. This means an increased focus on mathematics, technological subjects and languages. We must expand our notion of education to include economic goals as well as social and academic goals.

Interactions with industry through curriculum development, internships and joint research should be promoted to assist in the realignment of the education system to the needs of industry. Closer liaison between local education facilities and local industry can lead to well-targeted training and research programmes. For example, schools and polytechnics in the Nelson area could focus on the development of skills for the fishing industry, those in Rotorua on skills for forestry, and so on.

Improve Vocational Training. Vocational training should be upgraded to provide relevant and excellent training for the bulk of young New Zealanders who do not require academic qualifications for their working careers. The status and resources of the polytechnics should be improved so that they provide a true alternative to universities for students and educators. Curricula should be developed with input from appropriate industry associations to ensure relevant skills are being developed. Vocational training should also provide ongoing opportunities for individuals to upgrade their skills.

Improve Management Education. The state of management education in New Zealand must be improved. We must provide managers with the skills needed to lead firms in modern competition. At present, the university and polytechnic schools of business administration, particularly graduate schools, are frequently insufficiently funded to meet teaching demands yet alone undertake research. This situation needs to be remedied. Business-studies options need to be better integrated into other programmes such as computer science, agriculture and engineering. Development of centres of excellence in areas central to the competitive advantage of New Zealand, such as international food marketing, could become central to the upgrading process across a broad base of industries. In addition, a series of high-quality short courses and part-time courses should be developed to provide additional training opportunities to as many managers as possible.

Upgrade Workforce Skills. A central focus of labour-market policy must be on upgrading workforce skills. Firms need to be encouraged to invest in continual training programmes for employees at all levels. Programmes should be developed for all levels of the workforce with a life-long learning perspective. These efforts can be integrated with those of industry associations on a joint-funded basis. Government studies of skills levels in New Zealand industry compared to those of international competitors, in association with industry associations, can act as a motivator to improve local skill levels. Polytechnics and universities should focus on the requirements for skills upgrading in their local areas. Each Business Development Centre throughout the country should be required to develop and implement a strategy for the upgrading of key skills in their local areas.

Determine the Causes of Emigration. New Zealand loses tens of thousands of people each year who emigrate on a permanent basis. These emigrants tend to be the better qualified and most productive in our society. A government task force should be formed to identify the reasons for this large-scale emigration of talented New Zealanders and determine a plan of action to reverse the flow.

Targeted Immigration. Some in New Zealand believe that mass immigration can help restore the nation's prosperity. Immigration can have a role, but it is a different one from that typically supposed. Carefully targeted immigration of highly skilled people, particularly those with entrepreneurial experience, can help the upgrading process. Immigration of those with particular skills might help to reinforce nascent clusters. Similarly, people with skills that may improve the competitiveness of our present industries, such as those with specialized skills in marketing, engineering or software, should be given priority. Immigrants are frequently more willing to approach business using new strategies and approaches. Dalmatian immigrants have been critical to the wine industry, as have Dutch immigrants to the development of New Zealand's cut-flower exports.

Stimulate Domestic Competition. Domestic competition is one of the most powerful means of stimulating innovation and upgrading in an economy. While government policy has opened up New Zealand to international competition, there has been uneven attention given to domestic competition. Domestic competition not only stimulates innovation, it also opens up opportunities and provides a means for new ideas to develop within the economy.

Establish an Effective Competition Agency. Large areas of the New Zealand economy remain under the control of private monopolies and oligopolies. This has slowed the move away from factor-cost competition and contributed to a tendency among New Zealand firms not to develop more sophisticated sources of competitive advantage.

Deregulation and privatization on their own will not be successful without vigorous domestic rivalry. There needs to be greater recognition of the benefits that competition brings to the process of upgrading the economy. This requires a strong and consistent competition policy as well as a well-resourced competition agency. While it is fashionable today to call for mergers and alliances in the name of globalization and the small size of the New Zealand market, these often undermine the creation of competitive advantage. Real national competitiveness requires that governments disallow mergers, acquisitions and alliances that involve industry leaders.

Approach to Privatization. In New Zealand, privatization has often replaced public monopolies with private monopolies. Privatizing state-owned enterprises must be accomplished in a way that assures effective competition. The goals of privatization should be to ensure the maximum amount of dynamism in the New Zealand economy, not just the removal of assets from government control or obtaining the highest possible price.

Many in New Zealand believe that the absence of government restrictions on entry also means the absence of monopoly, even if a single firm has a 100% market share. Monopoly means control of the market, not the absence of government restrictions. Privatized entities must not be able effectively to prevent or reduce significant competition. This means that state enterprises should, whenever possible, be privatized into equally sized, equally powerful competitors so that a competitive industry structure is created. It also means that state enterprises should be sold to independent owners, not existing players. While "contestability" may provide efficiency gains at the margin, direct competition among equals forces firms to seek efficiency gains at the core. Effective competition policy is essential to this process.

State Monopolies. There continues to be a number of state-owned enterprises with monopolies or significant market power in certain industries. Government can quickly improve the competitive dynamism in the economy through privatization, allowing, or in some cases encouraging, new entrants into these respective industries, such as electricity generation and postal services. Instances where state-owned enterprises enjoy significant market power, such as Television New Zealand, should be curtailed unless the case against this is overwhelming. The private sector could also play a greater role in the provision of health and education services as well as infrastructural support, areas which are currently dominated by protected, state-funded entities.

Re-engineer the Producer Board Concept. The producer-board structure emerged earlier this century to meet the challenges of a particular set of circumstances. Today's vastly different circumstances, and the poor performance of New Zealand's agricultural industries, call for a deep rethinking of the role of the producer boards.

Producer boards, in their present forms, have been unable to stem the decline in prices of most of New Zealand's agricultural exports. The producer-board structure has, on occasion, also constrained the development of more sophisticated and/or specialized products, and impeded development of other industries related to New Zealand's agricultural strengths.

Each producer board is different and operates in a different industry context. Until recently, the Wool Board entered the market to support wool prices, but did not intervene otherwise. Since the collapse of the Australian government's wool-price support scheme, however, the Board has ceased to do this. The Apple and Pear Marketing Board, on the other hand, has monopoly selling rights for apples in both domestic and foreign markets.

Each producer board should be examined separately. We recommend the government convene a task force that should include disinterested representatives from New Zealand, international industry experts, as well as representatives from upstream, downstream and related industries. This effort should be supported by sufficient research capability to offset the monopoly on industry information held by some producer boards.

The following questions should be addressed:

- What is the competitive position of each industry and how can it be upgraded?
- What industry structure would be most conducive to the rapid upgrading of New Zealand's agricultural industries in the long term given fundamental changes in the world economy?
- Are there activities now carried out by producer boards that can be effectively carried out by industry associations and therefore allow the entry of new competitors while protecting the interests of farmers?
- How can domestic competition accelerate the upgrading process? Are producer boards the optimal structure to promote the development of new products and markets? Are they the optimal structures to launch new brands or to promote related and supporting industries in New Zealand?
- Why should some boards have exclusive selling rights in New Zealand? Do these rights risk these industries putting all their eggs in one basket?
- Do single desks make sense in the present economic environment? Would establishing separate boards or co-operative market divisions by product or geographic area provide some of the benefits of competition while still protecting farmers interests?
- Should firms be freed to compete with producer boards and each other in selling differentiated products and non-commodities?

The onus should be on the boards that operate as single desks, or which control new initiatives in their industry, to justify their monopoly position. Our research indicates that the concept of the producer board needs to be re-engineered to fit better with today's competitive realities.

Maintaining an Open Economy. Protectionist policies have had a major adverse effect on the competitiveness of New Zealand firms at home and abroad. They have also reinforced poor demand conditions in New Zealand, as New Zealanders and New Zealand industries have been cut off from products that would force local suppliers to improve.

The opening up of the New Zealand economy to imports has provided consumers with wider choice and New Zealand firms with the motivation to improve performance. The principles of an open economy should be maintained.

Improve Business Access to Capital. The limited availability and high cost of capital represent important constraints to the development of the New Zealand economy. Small and medium-sized companies are particularly disadvantaged by this situation.

Eliminate the Government Deficit. Government demands on the nation's capital resources have helped make New Zealand's real interest rates among the highest in the world. There are few investment opportunities that can compete with government bonds to obtain funds. Government crowding-out of private-sector investment needs to be reduced through a substantial reduction in the levels of government spending. Raising the proportion of investment decisions made by firms rather than government will assist in improving New Zealand's capital productivity.

An essential first step is that the government spending be reduced to levels at which meaningful reductions in the accumulated government debts can be achieved. This means the elimination of government deficits. Otherwise, the present debt crisis will continue to hinder needed investment. This will require achieving real government surpluses without tax increases.

Rethink the Structure of Government Expenditures. Reducing the deficit will require us to rethink the entire way in which government spends. We must understand that New Zealand's economic difficulties are not a temporary aberration but the accumulation of decades of deep-seated structural problems. All aspects of government expenditure need to be reviewed with a view to achieving our objectives more efficiently and effectively.

We must determine what types and levels of government spending are sustainable, realistic and fair for the wider community. In particular, we need to reassess the magnitude and extensiveness of the Welfare State. We simply cannot afford the present system. In 1990 over $17 billion was spent by Government on health, education and welfare. This was 62% of all government spending. Our goal of high and rising standards of living for all New Zealanders cannot be achieved if government continues to divert billions of dollars from the productive sector to support a welfare system that reduces savings and distorts incentives. Sustainable prosperity will only be achieved if we create incentives and focus resources on building the productive capacity of our economy.

Unfortunately, a social-welfare system that we cannot finance will hurt our welfare in the long run. The choice is between maintaining levels of consumption that are bankrupting the nation or shifting to an investment-led economy. This is a choice for government.

Restructure Superannuation. New Zealand's superannuation is one of the most generous in the world. It makes up the largest part of the welfare expenditures, which are the largest part of New Zealand government expenditures. It represents the largest single transfer of cash in the economy. The level of expenditures on superannuation places tremendous pressure on national capital resources. Perhaps even more importantly, non-contributory superannuation reduces the incentives to save and invest for retirement. Efforts to develop a sustainable and fair superannuation system to provide for those in genuine need without draining the economy need to be redoubled.

One solution might be a partially contributory system in which each employee contributes a small percentage of his or her wage towards retirement. The funds collected under such a plan should not be used to finance current government expenditure, as has become practice in the US, but should be invested in the New Zealand economy. Clearly such a system would have to be phased in so as not to burden unduly those who are close to retirement age.

Tackle Financial Market Weaknesses. The deregulation of the financial sector through floating the dollar and opening the banking sector to greater competition have been positive moves. However, our research identified areas where New Zealand's capital markets could make an improved contribution to economic development. These issues are inevitably complex and would best be tackled through a government/industry task force.

The limited availability of equity capital to enterprises of all sizes needs special attention. It has been several years since any significant public equity has been raised in New Zealand. The causes of this reluctance to invest need to be analysed and a plan of action developed.

The adequacy of finance for new small to medium-sized enterprises is also a priority. Given the importance of these types of firms to New Zealand's future, the government may need to provide special incentives for the establishment of venture capital funds and for bank lending to small and medium-sized firms.

Provide the Proper Incentives. New Zealand government policies have shaped incentives for individuals and firms in ways that work against the economy. In particular, government policies have inadvertently resulted in disincentives for individuals to save and, for some, disincentives to obtain training or to work. Policies have also limited the incentives for firms to invest in long-term development.

All policies that affect incentives in the New Zealand economy should be examined for their impact on the ability of individual companies to upgrade their capabilities. Sustainable reductions in state dependency will require that an appropriate mix of pressures, incentives and opportunities are developed to facilitate self-sufficiency.

A major problem in New Zealand has been labour laws which have impeded innovation, lowered incentives for skill building and blocked upgrading. Although recent government legislation aimed at significantly reducing labour-market rigidities was a step in the right direction. However, there remains much to be done. Labour-market policy should also ensure that the opportunities and incentives are in place to facilitate skills upgrading. Audits of the skills levels in particular industries should be undertaken in conjunction with relevant unions and companies. These should form the basis for co-ordinated action by government, unions and companies to upgrade the skill base.

Incentives for Savings. A history of negative real interest rates, non-contributory superannuation and housing allowances have reduced incentives to save which we should try to reverse. A more proactive approach is required to stimulate the development of private savings to reduce foreign debt and bring down interest rates. Incentives for saving need to be built into our economic policies. Positive encouragement should be provided for people to save for their retirement and health requirements. Government policies that provide disincentives for saving, such as many provisions of the Welfare State, should be re-examined along the lines suggested above for superannuation. One might envisage a plan that modestly raised individual tax rates, but also provided tax deductions or credits for savings. The idea is to increase the incentive to save and invest rather than spend the marginal dollar of income.

Replace Unemployment Benefits with Training Benefits. The number of unemployed in New Zealand is unprecedented. One clear long-term reason for the high and rising levels of unemployment is the low level of skills in our population. Government has an obligation to provide the unemployed with the incentives and opportunities to upgrade their personal skills so they are better able to join or rejoin the workforce.

Unemployment benefits need to be tied to participation in training or retraining to rejoin the workforce. Those not wishing to participate in training should receive less than those in training. In addition, there should be a meaningful difference between working wages and unemployment benefits to provide an incentive for all who are able to participate in the workforce.

Promote Long-term Corporate Investment. The government should create incentives that favour long-term investments in corporate equities. Sustained investment in our economy will be required to provide the foundation for innovation and upgrading. The introduction of a short-term capital-gains tax could assist in the development of long-term investment attitudes in New Zealand.

Upgrade the Technological Base. New Zealand's technological base is, for the most part, weak by international standards. An upgrading economy demands a steadily rising standard of technology and technological expertise.

New Zealand should ensure that government research institutes and programmes are focused on the important technologies affecting specific industry clusters. Such institutes and programmes should be used to solve industry problems and prompt more individual company research. The goal should not be to fund blue-sky "high technology" or "key technology" research for its own sake, but to focus on research that can improve the competitive position of New Zealand industry.

Each institute must be jointly funded by industry to build ownership, not solely paid for by government. Participation by government, universities and the private sector should be encouraged. The move to contestability between public and private research institutions for government research funds has the potential to improve the integration of government efforts with those of industry and should be continued. Explicit dissemination mechanisms will be required to ensure that scientific knowledge is available throughout industry.

Improve New Zealand's Transportation and Communication Infrastructure. New Zealand is located far from many of its major trading partners. Our transportation and communications infrastructure is therefore vital to our ability to compete. A series of government policies have improved the performance of the national infrastructure over the last decade. There have been significant improvements in the efficiency in the ports, in the provision of telecommunications services, in the Railways Corporation and in the Post Office.

With privatization, government's direct role in infrastructure has been reduced. However, given the critical importance of the performance of our national infrastructure to competitiveness in a wide range of industries, the need for government attention in this area remains. Each component of our national infrastructure should be regularly assessed to identify opportunities for improvement. Government should ensure that each element of the national infrastructure has active competition to improve efficiency and service quality. These assessments should be undertaken in conjunction with industry. The objective should be to achieve a level of performance in our national infrastructure that surpasses that of other nations and thus provides a source of competitive advantage to New Zealand firms. Despite recent improvements, the performance of New Zealand's ports and shipping services will need to remain an area of focus for some time.

Upgrade Local-demand Conditions. Advanced and sophisticated home demand is essential to competitive advantage in industry, as the New Zealand racing-yacht industry indicates. Government's traditional focus has been on influencing aggregate demand through government spending or manipulating the availability and cost of credit. What is more important, however, is raising the quality of home demand to challenge industry.

Government Procurement. The most direct effect of government on demand conditions is via its role as a buyer of many goods and services. The government should purchase the best-value products, even if they come from abroad. High standards and competition will provide positive stimulus for upgrading in New Zealand industry. While some preference might be given to a fraction of purchases from local firms, procurement must ensure competition among New Zealand firms and provide for some foreign competition.

High Regulatory Standards. Government influences local-demand conditions through regulations that affect product standards and the processes by which products are made, such as those governing product performance, product safety, environmental impact and the operating conditions for employees (such as working conditions). Stringent standards for product performance, product safety and environmental impact, that anticipate standards elsewhere, contribute to creating and upgrading competitive advantage. They pressure firms to improve quality, upgrade technology and provide features in areas of important customer (and social) concern. Standards must be set in ways that encourage innovation.

Equally important is to put in place a standard setting-and-enforcement process that is timely and predictable. Under these conditions, high standards, rather than harming New Zealand industry, can be a source of competitive advantage.

Strict Environmental Standards. New Zealanders tend to be environmentally conscious. New Zealand should aim to be a world leader in its environmental standards. Such an approach would contribute directly to our quality of life. In addition, it would force our companies to perform to high standards that could lead to the creation of internationally competitive products and services. New Zealand's "clean, green" image is already an attraction for tourists and is being used to market New Zealand venison in Europe.

A National Commitment to Quality. Government can also influence both consumer and firm standards for product quality through awarding prizes for quality excellence. The Deming Prize in Japan led to sustained improvements in quality among Japanese firms, and helped make the Japanese consumer more quality conscious. While it took years to develop, sophisticated home demand is now a source of considerable advantage to Japanese industry. Similar programmes to raise the quality of New Zealand products and services could have a major positive impact.

Stimulate Development via Clusters. National advantage resides as much in clusters as in individual industries. Outside of the agricultural sector, New Zealand has not been able to create competitive clusters of industries. Even in the agricultural sector, New Zealand's clusters tend to be relatively shallow; they lack strength in machinery, services and specialty inputs.

Government policy, both at the national and local level, has an important role to play in cluster development. The stimulation of clusters should form the basis for regional development strategies. Central and local governments should encourage investments that develop, or attract, specialist suppliers and industries related to our current areas of success.

Government investments in factor creation, such as research institutions, training centres, data banks and specialized infrastructure, must be responsive to the needs of clusters. Government can work with industry associations in a number of ways to aid cluster development. It can help collect and disseminate information and research on technology and market opportunities. It can co-ordinate research carried out by universities, polytechnics and government research institutions. In addition, policies that promote new business formation and ensure vigorous domestic rivalry in our successful export industries would also assist in the development of dynamic clusters.

Stimulate New-business Formation. The climate for new-business formation in New Zealand is inadequate. This is a very serious matter for New Zealand, since new-business formation is integral to the process of upgrading the economy. Legislated monopolies, state-owned enterprises and private oligopolies dominate many of the areas of the New Zealand economy that could be fertile ground for new companies. New entry is prohibited or blocked in large sectors of the economy. Government can contribute to the climate for new business in a number of ways. New-business formation can not flourish without a strong commitment to competition.

Investments in management training will improve the probabilities of success in new enterprise. Specialist financing mechanisms such as venture capital are required to facilitate the development of new businesses. Reduction in the amount of paperwork required by government agencies will assist in reducing the hurdles of establishing a new business. A review of company, securities and insolvency laws is necessary to reduce the risks of establishing a new enterprise.

The "tall poppy" syndrome and "Kiwi knocking machine" are significant inhibitors to a willingness to try new things that is central to entrepreneurship. A programme to raise the profile of some of New Zealand's success stories would assist in the development of new and more favourable attitudes to entrepreneurship.

Form a New Business Government Relationship. The traditional relationship between business and government in New Zealand has been one of dependence. Government has attempted to control virtually all aspects of the economy. While some groups and companies have done well under this arrangement, the economy as a whole has suffered. The future prosperity of even the groups that have benefited is in question.

Fundamental changes in the world economy call for equally fundamental changes in the relationship between business and government in New Zealand. Moves towards a more market-oriented economy show that the New Zealand government has realized that it lacks the ability to micromanage the economy.

In moving to a more market-oriented economy, however, government has overlooked some of its legitimate and important responsibilities, such as in factor creation, shaping incentives, setting high standards and ensuring domestic competition.

The New Zealand government should move forcefully to embrace a new role, one that focuses on creating an environment in which New Zealand firms can prosper. Government must put in place the institutions and policies that provide the pressures, incentives and opportunities for New Zealand firms to improve and upgrade. This is a very different role from, and a far more subtle one than, either heavy intervention or a strictly hands-off policy. This new role will also require a change in mindset in both government and a business community that too often sees government as both the source of and the solution to its problems.

Summary

The New Zealand economy is not well suited to the imperatives of the modern global economy. Despite recent reforms, our economy has continued to languish. The weak competitive position of many of our industries remains essentially unchanged. Government spending has become an even larger drain on the national economy.

If New Zealand is to be a prosperous nation in the next century, broad-based systemic change is required — in attitudes, institutions, policies and strategies. These changes will take decades fully to bear fruit, but must begin immediately. Their very character demands that New Zealanders develop a broad-based understanding of their situation and a consensus on what needs to be done.

As we have said before, there is nothing inevitable about New Zealand's economic decline. There are few constraints on New Zealand's future prosperity other than our limited ability to compete successfully in the global economy. Indeed, the levels of prosperity that are possible today are unprecedented. What is needed is a fundamental upgrading of the competitive position of our industry. Some significant upgrading has taken, and is taking, place. However, the pace and urgency will not be sufficient unless we act now. Unlike many nations, we still have the luxury of a choice. We can choose to make the tough decisions necessary for our future, or we can opt for a system that may seem secure, but is really not secure at all.

Statistics

Many sets of statistics were used to examine the state of the New Zealand economy and its position in world trade. Trade statistics were acquired principally from the *United Nations International Trade Statistic Yearbook*, which uses the Standard International Trade Classifications (SITC) codes.

Trade statistics and cluster charts for eight of the ten countries in the original Harvard study appear in Appendix 2 of Michael Porter's *The Competitive Advantage of Nations*. The same methodology was employed to calculate New Zealand's world export shares, top fifty export and import industries by value, trade balances and so on.

Similar statistics were also compiled for Australia and Chile, two countries with whom New Zealand competes in world markets. The top fifty industries by export value or export share give a picture of where a nation competes in international trade. The stark conclusion from this analysis is that there is virtually no overlap between the competitive industries of Australia, Chile and New Zealand, and the competitive industries of Sweden, Switzerland, the US, Germany, Italy, the UK, Japan and Korea. Some iron-related exports industries are common to Australia and Germany, and some forest-products industries are common to New Zealand, Sweden and Chile, but that is about where the similarities cease.

From this relatively raw data, cluster charts were prepared which classified industries into groups. This information was then analysed over time (1979 to 1985), by vertical stage, and for the relative importance of each industry within the cluster. This information can be found on the cluster charts.

The 1985 information provides the opportunity for direct comparison with the data appearing in *The Competitive Advantage of Nations*. As more recent data were available for New Zealand, the information was updated to 1987, showing a relative reduction in the number of competitive New Zealand industries since 1985. This information is also included.

Also identified were the imports into New Zealand and, for comparison, into Australia and Chile. These lists again provide valuable insight into the nature of New Zealand trade patterns.

Appendices

TOP 50 NEW ZEALAND INDUSTRIES IN TERMS OF
EXPORT VALUE
1985

	COMMODITY	DESCRIPTION	WORLD EXPORT SHARE (%)	R	NZ EXPORTS ($US'000)	NZ IMPORTS ($US'000)	TRADE BALANCE ($US'000)	NZ EXPORT SHARE (%)
1	011.20	SHEEP MEAT, FRESH, CHILLED OR FROZEN	55.2%		$577,506	$21	$577,485	10.1%
2	011.12	BEEF, FRESH, CHILLED OR FROZEN, BONELESS	13.0%		$439,514	$297	$439,217	7.7%
3	268.20	SHEEP/LAMBS WOOL SCOURED NOT CARDED	38.4%		$417,139	$1,386	$415,753	7.3%
4	023.00	BUTTER	15.7%		$331,354	$15	$331,339	5.8%
5	268.10	SHEEP/LAMBS WOOL, GREASY	12.1%		$279,378	$48	$279,330	4.9%
6	684.10	ALUMINIUM AND ALUMINIUM ALLOYS, UNWROUGHT	3.7%		$243,607	$1,622	$241,985	4.2%
7	211.70	LAMB AND SHEEP PELTS (WITHOUT WOOL)	12.6%	♦	$165,360	$4,990	$160,370	2.9%
8	022.43	BUTTERMILK, WHOLE MILK IN GRANULES OR POWDER	13.0%		$156,091	$4	$156,087	2.7%
9	592.22	ALBUMINOIDAL SUBSTANCES (CASEIN)	9.8%	♦	$143,339	$3,115	$140,224	2.5%
10	024.00	CHEESE	3.4%		$131,737	$1,757	$129,980	2.3%
11	057.98	KIWIFRUIT, FRESH	60.0%		$119,855	$0	$119,855	2.1%
12	022.42	SKIMMED MILK IN GRANULES OR POWDER	9.6%		$115,998	$4	$115,994	2.0%
13	036.00	SHELLFISH, NOT PRESERVED OR PREPARED	2.0%		$99,903	$1,761	$98,142	1.7%
14	034.40	FISH FILLETS, FROZEN	5.7%		$78,834	$99	$78,735	1.4%
15	411.32	TALLOW	6.0%		$55,562	$930	$54,632	1.0%
16	251.20	MECHANICAL WOOD PULP, WASTE PAPER	3.7%	♦	$54,161	$933	$53,228	0.9%
17	057.40	FRESH APPLES	4.8%		$53,992	$1,537	$52,455	0.9%
18	034.20	FISH, FROZEN	3.2%		$52,844	$150	$52,694	0.9%
19	659.42	WOOL CARPETS AND LINOLEUMS	3.6%	♦	$52,037	$4,982	$47,055	0.9%
20	651.26	TEXTILE YARN, OTHER THAN SILK OR COTTON (WOOLLEN)	3.2%	♦	$45,973	$4,337	$41,636	0.8%
21	291.93	SAUSAGE CASINGS	11.0%		$44,611	$2,116	$42,495	0.8%
22	011.60	EDIBLE OFFALS	6.4%		$44,339	$46	$44,293	0.8%
23	611.40	BOVINE AND EQUINE LEATHER	1.6%		$41,354	$1,518	$39,836	0.7%
24	054.51	OTHER VEGETABLES, FRESH OR PRESERVED (ONIONS, PEAS, CORN)	0.9%	♦	$40,381	$5,565	$34,816	0.7%
25	001.50	LIVE HORSES (RACING)	2.2%		$37,894	$37,071	$823	0.7%
26	081.99	ANIMAL FOOD PREPARATIONS	1.2%	♦	$36,217	$1,585	$34,632	0.6%
27	634.92	LAMINATED OR SIMPLY SHAPED WOOD PRODUCTS	5.2%	♦	$35,351	$287	$35,064	0.6%
28	248.22	WOOD OF CONIFERS, PLANED, TONGUED, GROOVED ETC	1.0%		$30,471	$68	$30,403	0.5%
29	897.31	ARTICLES OF JEWELLERY AND PARTS OF PRECIOUS METALS	0.6%		$29,499	$2,937	$26,562	0.5%
30	251.71	CHEMICAL WOOD PULP, SODA OR SULPHATE, UNBLEACHED	10.1%		$28,966	$188	$28,778	0.5%
31	248.21	WOOD OF CONIFERS, SAWN LENGTHWISE, SLICED OR PEELED	0.9%		$28,609	$6,209	$22,400	0.5%
32	211.10	BOVINE AND EQUINE HIDES	1.2%		$26,073	$122	$25,951	0.5%
33	674.61	ROLLED SHEETS/PLATES OF IRON/STEEL LESS THAN 3MM	0.5%		$25,837	$75,930	($50,093)	0.5%
34	512.11	ACYCLIC HYDROCARBONS (METHANOL)	0.8%	♦	$25,443	$7,166	$18,277	0.4%
35	699.79	BASE METAL MANUFACTURES N.E.S. (ROOF-TILES)	0.3%	♦	$24,903	$26,948	($2,045)	0.4%
36	697.32	DOMESTIC HEATING, COOKING APPLIANCES (WOOD BURNERS)	2.2%	♦	$22,257	$3,497	$18,760	0.4%
37	892.89	POSTCARDS, PRINTED MATTER N.E.S.	0.8%	♦	$22,171	$11,547	$10,624	0.4%
38	322.20	COAL, LIGNITE, PEAT, NOT AGGLOMERATED (BITUMINOUS COAL)	0.3%	♦	$21,706	$71	$21,635	0.4%
39	011.11	BEEF, FRESH, CHILLED OR FROZEN, WITH BONE IN	0.7%		$21,379	$100	$21,279	0.4%
40	247.11	SAWLOGS AND VENEER LOGS OF CONIFERS, ROUGH	1.4%		$21,102	$13	$21,089	0.4%
41	251.72	CHEMICAL WOOD PULP, SODA OR SULPHATE, BLEACHED	0.4%		$20,082	$6,711	$13,371	0.4%
42	081.41	ANIMAL MEALS OF MEAT OR OFFAL	10.4%		$19,993	$0	$19,993	0.3%
43	641.32	SACK KRAFT PAPER, KRAFT PAPER AND PAPERBOARD	1.5%	♦	$19,709	$256	$19,453	0.3%
44	281.50	IRON ORE AND CONCENTRATES, NOT AGGLOMERATED	0.4%		$19,415	$9	$19,406	0.3%
45	611.50	CALF, SHEEP AND OTHER LEATHER (LAMB SKIN)	1.0%	♦	$19,398	$3,878	$15,520	0.3%
46	641.61	HARDBOARD, PAPER AND PAPERBOARD N.E.S.	0.5%	♦	$19,198	$8,402	$10,796	0.3%
47	553.00	PERFUMERY, COSMETICS, TOILET PREPARATIONS	0.6%		$19,196	$7,233	$11,963	0.3%
48	043.00	BARLEY, UNMILLED	0.7%		$18,476	$0	$18,476	0.3%
49	058.99	FRUIT AND NUTS, PREPARED OR PRESERVED N.E.S.	0.8%	♦	$18,399	$13,462	$4,937	0.3%
50	054.20	DRIED BEANS, PEAS, LENTILS, OTHER LEGUMES	1.5%		$18,090	$2,070	$16,020	0.3%

♦ SOURCE : NEW ZEALAND KIWIFRUIT MARKETING BOARD
R = RESIDUAL

NEW ZEALAND'S TOP 50 COMPETITIVE INDUSTRIES
IN TERMS OF WORLD EXPORT SHARE
1985

	COMMODITY	DESCRIPTION	WORLD EXPORT SHARE (%)	R	NZ EXPORTS ($US'000)	NZ IMPORTS ($US'000)	TRADE BALANCE ($US'000)	NZ EXPORT SHARE (%)
1	057.98	KIWIFRUIT, FRESH	# 60.0%		$119,855	$0	$119,855	2.1%
2	011.20	SHEEP MEAT, FRESH, CHILLED OR FROZEN	55.2%		$577,506	$21	$577,485	10.1%
3	268.20	SHEEP/LAMBS WOOL SCOURED NOT CARDED	38.4%		$417,139	$1,386	$415,753	7.3%
4	023.00	BUTTER	15.7%		$331,354	$15	$331,339	5.8%
5	022.43	BUTTERMILK, WHOLE MILK IN GRANULES OR POWDER	13.0%		$156,091	$4	$156,087	2.7%
6	011.12	BEEF, FRESH, CHILLED OR FROZEN, BONELESS	13.0%		$439,514	$297	$439,217	7.7%
7	211.70	LAMB AND SHEEP PELTS (WITHOUT WOOL)	12.6%	•	$165,360	$4,990	$160,370	2.9%
8	268.10	SHEEP/LAMBS WOOL, GREASY	12.1%		$279,378	$48	$279,330	4.9%
9	291.93	SAUSAGE CASINGS	11.0%		$44,611	$2,116	$42,495	0.8%
10	081.41	ANIMAL MEALS OF MEAT OR OFFAL	10.4%		$19,993	$0	$19,993	0.3%
11	251.71	CHEMICAL WOOD PULP, SODA OR SULPHATE, UNBLEACHED	10.1%		$28,965	$188	$28,778	0.5%
12	592.22	ALBUMINOIDAL SUBSTANCES (CASEIN)	9.8%	•	$143,339	$3,115	$140,224	2.5%
13	022.42	SKIMMED MILK IN GRANULES OR POWDER	9.6%		$115,998	$4	$115,994	2.0%
14	011.60	EDIBLE OFFALS	6.4%		$44,339	$46	$44,293	0.8%
15	411.32	TALLOW	6.0%		$55,562	$930	$54,632	1.0%
16	034.40	FISH FILLETS, FROZEN	5.7%		$78,834	$99	$78,735	1.4%
17	047.02	CEREAL, GROATS, MEAL AND PELLETS OTHER THAN WHEAT	5.4%	•	$13,310	$78	$13,232	0.2%
18	634.92	LAMINATED OR SIMPLY SHAPED WOOD PRODUCTS	5.2%	•	$35,351	$287	$35,064	0.6%
19	057.40	FRESH APPLES	4.8%		$53,992	$1,537	$52,455	0.9%
20	684.10	ALUMINIUM AND ALUMINIUM ALLOYS, UNWROUGHT	3.7%		$243,607	$1,622	$241,985	4.2%
21	251.20	MECHANICAL WOOD PULP, WASTE PAPER	3.7%	•	$54,161	$933	$53,228	0.9%
22	659.42	WOOL CARPETS AND LINOLEUMS	3.6%	•	$52,037	$4,982	$47,055	0.9%
23	024.00	CHEESE	3.4%		$131,737	$1,757	$129,980	2.3%
24	651.26	TEXTILE YARN, OTHER THAN SILK OR COTTON (WOOLLEN)	3.2%	•	$45,973	$4,337	$41,636	0.8%
25	034.20	FISH, FROZEN	3.2%		$52,844	$150	$52,694	0.9%
26	091.49	MARGARINE, IMITATION LARD AND OTHER EDIBLE FATS	2.5%	•	$15,524	$318	$15,206	0.3%
27	001.11	BREEDING CATTLE (DAIRY)	2.3%		$6,917	$0	$6,917	0.1%
28	697.32	DOMESTIC HEATING, COOKING APPLIANCES (WOOD BURNERS)	2.2%	•	$22,257	$3,497	$18,760	0.4%
29	001.50	LIVE HORSES (RACING)	2.2%	•	$37,894	$37,071	$823	0.7%
30	036.00	SHELLFISH, NOT PRESERVED OR PREPARED	2.0%		$99,903	$1,761	$98,142	1.7%
31	775.22	DEEP FREEZERS OF HOUSEHOLD TYPE	1.7%		$5,100	$72	$5,028	0.1%
32	611.40	BOVINE AND EQUINE LEATHER	1.6%		$41,354	$1,518	$39,836	0.7%
33	011.89	MEAT AND EDIBLE OFFALS (VENISON)	1.5%	•	$10,184	$29	$10,155	0.2%
34	054.20	DRIED BEANS, PEAS, LENTILS, OTHER LEGUMES	1.5%		$18,090	$2,070	$16,020	0.3%
35	641.32	SACK KRAFT PAPER, KRAFT PAPER AND PAPERBOARD	1.5%	•	$19,709	$256	$19,453	0.3%
36	247.11	SAWLOGS AND VENEER LOGS OF CONIFERS, ROUGH	1.4%		$21,102	$13	$21,089	0.4%
37	541.62	GLYCOSIDES, GLANDS AND EXTRACTS	1.2%	•	$13,865	$6,233	$7,652	0.2%
38	081.99	ANIMAL FOOD PREPARATIONS	1.2%	•	$36,217	$1,585	$34,632	0.6%
39	211.10	BOVINE AND EQUINE HIDES	1.2%		$26,073	$122	$25,951	0.5%
40	291.16	CRUDE ANIMAL MATERIALS, NOT SAUSAGE CASINGS (HORNS, ANTLERS)	1.2%	•	$9,605	$4,131	$5,474	0.2%
41	848.31	ARTICLES OF FURSKIN (SHEEPSKIN RUGS, JACKETS)	1.1%		$12,101	$3	$12,098	0.2%
42	292.50	SEED, FRUIT AND SPORES N.E.S. USED FOR SOWING	1.1%		$8,271	$3,589	$4,682	0.1%
43	793.21	YACHTS AND OTHER PLEASURE CRAFT (SAIL YACHTS)	1.0%		$13,259	$1,179	$12,080	0.2%
44	611.50	CALF, SHEEP AND OTHER LEATHER (LAMB SKIN)	1.0%	•	$19,398	$3,878	$15,520	0.3%
45	034.10	FISH, LIVE OR DEAD, FRESH OR CHILLED	1.0%		$14,711	$57	$14,654	0.3%
46	248.22	WOOD OF CONIFERS, PLANED, TONGUED, GROOVED ETC	1.0%		$30,471	$68	$30,403	0.5%
47	721.39	DAIRY AND OTHER AGRICULTURAL MACHINERY	0.9%	•	$8,086	$4,645	$3,441	0.1%
48	037.20	SHELLFISH, PREPARED OR PRESERVED	0.9%		$8,035	$4,845	$3,190	0.1%
49	212.09	FURSKINS, RAW, NOT MINK (OPOSSUM)	0.9%		$5,858	$184	$5,674	0.1%
50	022.30	FRESH MILK, CREAM, YOGHURT, SKIMMED MILK, ETC	0.9%		$7,793	$0	$7,793	0.1%

# SOURCE : NEW ZEALAND KIWIFRUIT MARKETING BOARD
R = RESIDUAL

CLUSTERS OF INTERNATIONALLY COMPETITIVE NZ INDUSTRIES 1985

	MATERIALS/ METALS	FOREST PRODUCTS	PETROLEUM/ CHEMICALS	SEMICONDUCTORS/ COMPUTERS	MULTIPLE BUSINESS
Primary Goods:	*Iron & Steel:* Iron, Steel Blooms Iron, Steel Wire, Rod Iron, Steel Plates, Thin Iron Steel Wire	*Wood Products:* SAWLOGS, CONIFER, ROUGH SAWN CONIFER TIMBER# SHAPED CONIFER TIMBER# PLYWOOD# RECONSTITUTED WOOD# WOODEN BEADINGS, MOULDINGS*	*Organic:* METHANOL		
	Fabricated Iron & Steel:		*Polymers:* Plastic Bags, Sachets		
	Non-Ferrous Metals: UNWROUGHT ALUMINIUM ALLOYS Aluminium Bars, Rods ALUMINIUM FOIL	*Pulp:* MECHANICAL WOOD PULP, WASTEPAPER* CHEMICAL WOOD PULP, UNBLEACHED CHEMICAL WOOD PULP, BLEACHED#			
	Metal Manufacturers: STRUCTURES, PARTS OF ALUMINIUM Base Metal Mnfrs NES (Rooftiles)*	*Paper:* KRAFTLINER, BULK# SACK KRAFT PAPER, PAPERBOARD*# HARDBOARD, PAPER & PAPERBOARD*# NEWS PRINT#			
Machinery					Metalworking Machine Tools
Specialty Inputs	Iron Ores, Concentrates, Not Aggl. Coal White Portland Cement				
Services				INSURANCE SOFTWARE † PROGRAMMER PRODUCTIVITY TOOLS† PRODUCTION CONTROL SYSTEMS	CONSTRUCTION TOURISM† ENGINEERING CONSULTING† INVESTMENT MANAGEMENT† Education Services†

	TRANSPORTATION	POWER GENERATION & DISTRIBUTION	OFFICE PRODUCTS	TELECOMMUNICATION	DEFENCE
Primary Goods:	*Vehicle Equipment:* MOBILE CRANES		POSTCARDS,*		
Machinery:					
Specialty Inputs:					
Services					

KEY:	BOLD CAPS:	1.2% world export share or above	†	Added due to in-country research
	CAPS	0.6% world export share or higher, but less than 1.2%		
	Mixed Case	0.3% world export share or higher, but less than 0.6% share	#	Upgraded due to Foreign Direct Investment
	*	Calculated Residuals		

	FOOD/BEVERAGES		TEXTILES/APPAREL	HOUSING/HOUSEHOLD	HEALTH CARE
Primary Goods:	*Basic Food:* BEEF WITH BONE IN BEEF, BONELESS SHEEP MEAT EDIBLE OFFAL VENISON* FRESH MILK & CREAM FISH, FRESH, FISH, FROZEN, Fish Fillet, fresh, FISH FILLET, FROZEN SHELLFISH, FROZEN BARLEY DRIED PEAS ONIONS, PEAS, CORN & SQUASH* APPLES KIWIFRUIT Fresh Stone & Berry Fruits	*Processed Food:* Canned Meat SKIMMED MILK POWDER WHOLEMILK BUTTER CHEESE SHELLFISH, PREPARED Fish Fingers, PASTRY, CAKES, ETC Asparagus, Corn (Preserved)* PRESERVED FRUIT, JAM* CHOCOLATE Milk Biscuits, Ice Cream etc* *Beverages:* FRUIT JUICE* Beer *Edible Oils:* MARGARINE TALLOW	SHEEP LEATHER* Furskins, tanned or dressed TEXTILE ARTICLES NES* SHEEPSKIN RUGS, JACKETS, COATS	*Furniture:* CARPETS, LINOLEUMS* Wood Furniture NES *Appliances:* DOMESTIC HEATING, COOKING APP* REFRIGERATORS, DOMESTIC DEEP FREEZERS *Other Household Products:* SOAPS, POLISHES & CREAMS LAWN MOWERS* *Builders Woodwork:* BUILDERS' WOODWORK, PREFABRICATED	*Pharmaceuticals:* GLYCOSIDES, GLANDS & EXTRACTS*
Machinery:	DAIRY MACHINERY PARTS*				
Specialty Inputs:	ANIMAL CONTROL SYSTEMS† BREEDING CATTLE UNMILLED BARLEY MEAT MEAL FODDER ANIMAL FOOD PREPARATIONS ANIMAL MATERIALS (HORNS, ANTLERS, VELVET, ETC)* SAUSAGE-CASINGS SEEDS FOR PLANTING UREA CASEIN, ALBUMINS, ETC GLASS BOTTLES Paper Containers, Bags		HIDES, RAW SHEEP PELTS OPPOSUM SKINS WOOL GREASY WOOL, SCOURED LEATHER WOOLLEN YARN*	POTTERY CLAY	
Services	AGRICULTURAL CONSULTING GENETIC MANAGEMENT SYSTEMS†				

	PERSONAL	ENTERTAINMENT/LEISURE
Primary Goods:	PERFUMERY, COSMETICS PRECIOUS METAL/ JEWELLERY	Cut Flowers YACHTS INDOOR GAME EQUIPMENT RACEHORSES*
Machinery:		
Specialty Inputs:		

KEY:	BOLD CAPS:	1.2% world export share or above	†	Added due to in-country
	CAPS	0.6% world export share or higher, but less than 1.2%		research
	Mixed Caps	0.3% world export share or higher, but less than 0.6% share	#	Upgraded due to Foreign
	*	Calculated Residuals		Direct Investment

NEW ZEALAND INDUSTRIES WITH DISPRORTIONATE WORLD MARKET SHARE WITH GAINS OR LOSSES OF WORLD EXPORT SHARE OF 15 PERCENT OR MORE BETWEEN 1979 AND 1985

UPSTREAM INDUSTRIES

	Materials/Metals			Forest Products			Petroleum/Chemicals			Semiconductors/Computers			UPSTREAM INDUSTRIES		
	Industries	Gains	Losses	Industries	Gains	Losses	Industries	Gains	Losses	Industries	Gains	Losses	Indus.	Gains	Los.
	9	7	1	13	6	6	2	2	0	0	0	0	24	15	
	0	0	0	0	0	0	0	0	0	0	0	0	0	0	
	3	2	1	0	0	0	0	0	0	0	0	0	3	2	
total	12	9	2	13	6	6	2	2	0	0	0	0	27	17	

INDUSTRIAL AND SUPPORTING FUNCTIONS

	Multiple Business			Transportation			Power Generation & Distribution			Office			Telecommunications			Defence			INDUSTRIAL AND SUPPORTING FUNCTIONS		
	Indus.	Gains	Losses	Indus.	Gains	Losses	Indus.	Gains	Losses	Indus.	Gains	Losses	Indus.	Gains	Losses	Indus.	Gains	Losses	Indus.	Gains	Los.
	0	0	0	1	1	0	0	0	0	1	1	0	0	0	0	0	0	0	2	2	
	1	1	0	0	0	0	0	0	0	0	0	0	0	0	0	0	0	0	1	1	
	0	0	0	0	0	0	0	0	0	0	0	0	0	0	0	0	0	0	0	0	
total	1	1	0	1	1	0	0	0	0	1	1	0	0	0	0	0	0	0	3	3	

FINAL CONSUMPTION GOODS AND SERVICES

	Food/Beverages			Housing/Household			Textiles/Apparel			Health Care			Personal			Entertainment/Leisure			FINAL CONSUMPTION GOODS AND SERVICES		
	Indus.	Gains	Losses	Indus.	Gains	Losses	Indus.	Gains	Losses	Indus.	Gains	Losses	Indus.	Gains	Losses	Indus.	Gains	Losses	Indus.	Gains	Los.
	34	29	1	8	6	1	4	2	1	1	1	0	2	2	0	4	3	0	53	43	
	1	0	1	0	0	0	0	0	0	0	0	0	0	0	0	0	0	0	1	0	
	10	7	2	1	1	0	7	2	4	0	0	0	0	0	0	0	0	0	18	10	
	45	36	4	9	7	1	11	4	5	1	1	0	2	2	0	4	3	0	72	53	

* Included were industries exceeding the cutoff in 1987, or that had first achieved sufficient share to exceed the cutoff in 1987.

PERCENTAGE OF NEW ZEALAND EXPORTS OF COMPETITIVE INDUSTRIES BY BROAD CLUSTER

UPSTREAM INDUSTRIES

	Materials/Metals	Forest Products	Petroleum/Chemicals	Semiconductors/Computers	UPSTREAM INDUSTRIES
Share of Country Exports:	6.6 (1.6)	4.7 (-1.3)	0.6 (0.5)	-	12.0 (0.9)
Share of World Cluster Exports:	0.2 (0.0)	0.5 (-0.2)	0.0 (0.0)	-	0.1 (0.0)

INDUSTRIAL & SUPPORTING FUNCTIONS

	Multiple Business	Transportation	Power Generation & Distribution	Office	Telecommunications	Defence	INDUSTRIAL & SUPPORTING FUNCTIONS
Share of Country Exports:	0.1 (0.1)	0.1 (0.1)	-	0.4 (0.2)	-	-	0.6 (0.4)
Share of World Cluster Exports:	0.0 (0.0)	0.0 (0.0)	-	0.1 (0.1)	-	-	0.0 (0.0)

FINAL CONSUMPTION GOODS & SERVICES

	Food/Beverages	Textiles/Apparel	Housing/Household	Health Care	Personal	Entertainment/Leisure	FINAL CONSUMPTION GOODS & SERVICES
Share of Country Exports:	49.4 (1.0)	18.0 (-6.2)	2.2 (0.7)	0.2 (0.2)	0.8 (0.7)	1.4 (-0.8)	71.9 (-4.5)
Share of World Cluster Exports:	1.4 (0.0)	0.8 (-0.4)	0.3 (0.1)	0.1 (0.0)	0.1 (0.1)	0.1 (-0.1)	0.8 (0.1)

NOTE: Numbers in parentheses are changes between 1979 and 1985.
Exports are those of competitive industries, not all industries.

PERCENTAGE OF EXPORTS BY CLUSTER AND VERTICAL STAGE
NEW ZEALAND

Upstream Industries

	Materials/Metals SCE	Δ SCE	SWCE	Δ SWCE	Forest Products SCE	Δ SCE	SWCE	Δ SWCE	Petroleum/Chemicals SCE	Δ SCE	SWCE	Δ SWCE	Semiconductors/Computers SCE	Δ SCE	SWCE	Δ SWCE	Upstream SCE	Upstream SWCE
Pri. Gds.	5.8	1.4	0.3	0.1	4.7	-1.3	0.6	-0.2	0.6	0.5	0.0	0.0	-	-	-	--	11.1	0.1
Mach.	-	-	-	-	-	-	-	-	-	-	-	-	-	-	-	-	-	-
Spec. Inp.	0.9	0.2	0.1	0.0	-	-	-	-	-	-	-	-	-	-	-	-	0.9	0.1
Total	6.6	1.6	0.2	0.0	4.7	-1.3	0.5	-0.2	0.6	0.5	0.0	0.0	-	-	-	-	12.0	0.1

Industrial & Supporting Functions

	Multiple Business SCE	Δ SCE	SWCE	Δ SWCE	Transportation SCE	Δ SCE	SWCE	Δ SWCE	Power Generation & Distribution SCE	Δ SCE	SWCE	Δ SWCE	Office SCE	Δ SCE	SWCE	Δ SWCE	Telecommunications SCE	Δ SCE	SWCE	Δ SWCE	Defence SCE	Δ SCE	SWCE	Δ SWCE	Ind. SCE	Ind. SWCE
Pri. Gds.	-	-	-	-	0.1	0.1	0.0	0.0	-	-	-	-	0.4	0.2	0.1	0.1	-	-	-	-	-	-	-	-	0.5	0.1
Mach.	0.1	0.1	0.0	0.0	-	-	-	-	-	-	-	-	--	-	-	-	-	-	-	-	-	-	-	-	0.1	0.0
Spec. Inp.	-	-	-	-	-	-	-	-	-	-	-	-	-	-	-	-	-	-	-	-	-	-	-	-	-	-
Total	0.1	0.1	0.0	0.0	0.1	0.1	0.0	0.0	-	-	-	-	0.4	0.2	0.1	0.1	-	-	-	-	-	-	-	-	0.6	0.0

Final Consumption Goods & Services

	Food/Beverages SCE	Δ SCE	SWCE	Δ SWCE	Textiles/Apparel SCE	Δ SCE	SWCE	Δ SWCE	Housing/Household SCE	Δ SCE	SWCE	Δ SWCE	Health Care SCE	Δ SCE	SWCE	Δ SWCE	Personal SCE	Δ SCE	SWCE	Δ SWCE	Entertainment/Leisure SCE	Δ SCE	SWCE	Δ SWCE	Final SCE	Final SWCE
Pri. Gds.	44.0	0.6	2.0	0.1	0.9	-0.1	0.1	0.0	2.1	0.7	0.3	0.1	0.2	0.2	0.1	0.0	0.8	0.7	0.1	0.1	1.0	0.4	0.1	0.0	49.0	0.8
Mach.	0.1	-0.1	0.1	0.0	-	-	-	-	-	-	-	-	-	-	-	-	-	-	-	-	-	-	-	-	0.1	0.0
Spec. Inp.	5.2	0.5	0.5	0.0	17.1	-6.2	2.4	-1.0	0.1	0.1	0.0	0.0	-	-	-	-	-	-	-	-	0.3	-1.1	0.2	-0.9	22.7	0.9
Total	49.4	1.0	1.4	0.0	18.0	-6.2	0.8	-0.4	2.2	0.7	0.3	0.1	0.2	0.2	0.1	0.0	0.8	0.7	0.1	0.1	1.4	-0.8	0.1	-0.1	71.9	0.3
																									84.5	0.3

Note: Totals may not add due to rounding.

Key

Pri. Gds.	Primary Goods	SCE	Share of country's total exports 1985
Mach.	Machinery	Δ SCE	Change in share of country's exports 1979-1985
Spec. Inp.	Specialty Inputs	SWCE	Share of world cluster exports 1985
		Δ SWCE	Change in share of world cluster exports 1979-1985

TOP 50 NEW ZEALAND INDUSTRIES IN TERMS OF
IMPORT VALUE
1985

	COMMODITY	DESCRIPTION	WORLD IMPORT SHARE (%)	R	NZ IMPORTS ($US'000)	NZ EXPORTS ($US'000)	TRADE BALANCE ($US'000)	NZ IMPORT SHARE (%)
1	781.00	MOTOR CARS (ASSEMBLED & UNASSEMBLED)	0.4%		$344,494	$498	$343,996	5.7%
2	334.11	GASOLINE	2.1%		$203,779	$13	$203,766	3.4%
3	333.00	CRUDE PETROLEUM	0.1%		$193,239	$65,615	$127,624	3.2%
4	334.30	GAS OILS	0.7%		$164,291	$26	$164,265	2.7%
5	782.10	TRUCKS AND VANS	0.6%		$129,783	$40	$129,743	2.1%
6	752.40	AUTOMATIC DATA PROCESSING MACHINES	0.6%	•	$119,131	$5,905	$113,226	2.0%
7	287.32	ALUMINIUM OXIDE	4.7%		$100,041	$0	$100,041	1.6%
8	764.10	TELEPHONE EQUIPMENT	2.0%		$96,100	$1,547	$94,553	1.6%
9	334.21	KEROSENE	2.2%		$91,759	$3	$91,756	1.5%
10	752.50	EDP PERIPHERAL UNITS	0.8%		$84,520	$2,840	$81,680	1.4%
11	784.20	MOTOR VEHICLE BODIES, PARTS AND ACCESSORIES	0.2%	•	$79,713	$13,578	$66,135	1.3%
12	674.61	IRON & STEEL SHEETS & PLATES (LESS THAN 3 MM)	2.0%		$75,931	$25,837	$50,094	1.2%
13	951.07	WAR FIREARMS, AMMUNITION	2.8%	•	$75,204	$1,006	$74,198	1.2%
14	541.79	MEDICAMENTS, NOT INCLUDING ANTIBIOTICS	0.9%	•	$72,908	$9,930	$62,978	1.2%
15	874.83	MEASURING AND CONTROLLING INSTRUMENTS	0.5%	•	$66,298	$9,015	$57,283	1.1%
16	892.11	BOOKS	1.6%		$63,095	$8,654	$54,441	1.0%
17	652.24	WOVEN FABRICS (MAINLY COTTON)	1.4%	•	$61,027	$119	$60,908	1.0%
18	641.22	WRITING PAPER (MAINLY CLAY-COATED)	1.7%		$56,920	$1,191	$55,729	0.9%
19	792.40	AIRCRAFT EXCEEDING 15000 KGS	0.7%		$52,632	$0	$52,632	0.9%
20	772.10	ELECTRICAL CIRCUIT APPARATUS	0.4%		$50,987	$11,427	$39,560	0.8%
21	737.21	ROLLING MILLS	0.7%		$50,351	$177	$50,174	0.8%
22	583.11	POLYETHYLENE	1.4%		$49,479	$453	$49,026	0.8%
23	722.40	TRACTORS	1.3%		$48,495	$573	$47,922	0.8%
24	653.41	FABRICS, WOVEN, SYNTH. FIBRES (DISCONTINUOUS)	1.1%	•	$47,846	$2,474	$45,372	0.8%
25	764.93	TELECOMMUNICATION EQUIPMENT N.E.S.	0.3%	•	$47,198	$7,375	$39,823	0.8%
26	752.20	DIGITAL DATA PROCESSING MACHINES	1.3%		$41,766	$1,038	$40,728	0.7%
27	759.90	OFFICE, ADP MACHINERY PARTS AND ACCESSORIES	0.2%	•	$40,159	$5,869	$34,290	0.7%
28	749.20	TAPS, COCKS, VALVES & SIMILAR APPLIANCES	0.6%		$40,011	$8,561	$31,450	0.7%
29	274.10	SULPHUR AND UNROASTED IRON PYRITES	2.1%	•	$37,640	$0	$37,640	0.6%
30	001.50	LIVE ANIMALS, NOT BOVINE (RACE HORSES)	1.8%	•	$37,285	$37,894	($609)	0.6%
31	657.33	SPECIAL TEXTILE FABRICS AND RELATED PRODUCTS	1.0%	•	$37,060	$3,455	$33,605	0.6%
32	061.10	SUGAR, RAW	2.5%		$36,326	$0	$36,326	0.6%
33	775.86	DOMESTIC APPLIANCES (MAINLY MICROWAVE OVENS)	0.5%	•	$35,989	$20,175	$15,814	0.6%
34	598.99	WOOD, RESIN-BASED & ORGANIC CHEMICAL PRODUCTS	0.4%	•	$34,968	$3,481	$31,487	0.6%
35	728.49	MACHINERY FOR SPECIALISED INDUSTRIES N.E.S.	0.4%	•	$34,696	$8,109	$26,587	0.6%
36	583.91	OTHER POLYMERIZATION & COPOLYMERIZATION PRODUCTS	0.7%	•	$32,265	$1,065	$31,200	0.5%
37	893.99	MISC. SANITARY, ORNAMENTAL & LIGHTING ARTICLES	0.4%	•	$32,223	$26,040	$6,183	0.5%
38	334.40	FUEL OILS	0.1%		$31,902	$5,993	$25,909	0.5%
39	582.91	CONDENSATION AND POLYADDITION PRODUCTS	0.6%	•	$30,454	$1,912	$28,542	0.5%
40	334.51	LUBRICATING PETROLEUM OILS	0.5%		$29,815	$329	$29,486	0.5%
41	271.32	CALCIUM PHOSPHATES	6.8%		$29,052	$0	$29,052	0.5%
42	726.71	PRINTING MACHINERY (NOT PRINTING PRESSES)	1.1%	•	$28,004	$1,765	$26,239	0.5%
43	723.90	PARTS AND MACHINERY FOR CIVIL ENGINEERING	1.8%	•	$27,813	$75	$27,738	0.5%
44	699.79	IRON AND STEEL PRODUCTS (NOT CHAINS & LOCKS)	0.4%	•	$26,948	$24,903	$2,045	0.4%
45	892.20	NEWSPAPERS, JOURNALS AND PERIODICALS,	1.5%		$26,598	$2,258	$24,340	0.4%
46	674.70	TINNED SHEETS & PLATES OF STEEL	1.5%		$26,491	$0	$26,491	0.4%
47	515.69	OTHER HETEROCYCLIC COMPOUNDS	0.5%	•	$25,308	$240	$25,068	0.4%
48	682.21	WIRE RODS OF COPPER	1.2%		$24,457	$3,768	$20,689	0.4%
49	653.15	FABRICS, WOVEN (CONTINUOUS)	0.6%	•	$24,451	$508	$23,943	0.4%
50	763.81	TELEVISION SETS	0.3%		$24,416	$1,822	$22,594	0.4%

R = RESIDUAL

NEW ZEALAND'S TOP 50 COMPETITIVE INDUSTRIES
IN TERMS OF WORLD IMPORT SHARE
1985

	COMMODITY	DESCRIPTION	WORLD IMPORT SHARE (%)	R	NZ IMPORTS ($US'000)	NZ EXPORTS ($US'000)	TRADE BALANCE ($US'000)	NZ IMPORT SHARE (%)
1	271.32	CALCIUM PHOSPHATES	6.8%		$29,052	$0	$29,052	0.5%
2	287.32	ALUMINIUM OXIDE	4.7%		$100,041	$0	$100,041	1.6%
3	951.07	WAR FIREARMS, AMMUNITION	2.8%	*	$75,204	$1,006	$74,198	1.2%
4	057.52	GRAPES, DRIED	2.5%		$10,149	$60	$10,089	0.2%
5	061.10	SUGAR, RAW	2.5%		$36,326	$0	$36,326	0.6%
6	744.19	PARTS, NES OF THE TRUCKS AND TRACTORS	2.4%		$17,027	$260	$16,767	0.3%
7	334.21	KEROSENE	2.2%		$91,759	$3	$91,756	1.5%
8	274.10	SULPHUR AND UNROASTED IRON PYRITES	2.1%	*	$37,640	$0	$37,640	0.6%
9	334.11	GASOLINE	2.1%		$203,779	$13	$203,766	3.4%
10	764.10	TELEPHONE EQUIPMENT	2.0%		$96,100	$1,547	$94,553	1.6%
11	674.61	IRON & STEEL SHEETS & PLATES (LESS THAN 3 MM)	2.0%		$75,931	$25,837	$50,094	1.2%
12	655.22	KNITTED OR CROCHETED FABRICS	2.0%	*	$14,225	$721	$13,504	0.2%
13	723.90	PARTS AND MACHINERY FOR CIVIL ENGINEERING	1.8%		$27,813	$75	$27,738	0.5%
14	001.50	LIVE ANIMALS, NOT BOVINE (RACE HORSES)	1.8%	*	$37,285	$37,894	($609)	0.6%
15	641.22	WRITING PAPER (MAINLY CLAY-COATED)	1.7%		$56,920	$1,191	$55,729	0.9%
16	583.41	POLYVINYL CHLORIDE	1.6%		$23,501	$135	$23,366	0.4%
17	892.11	BOOKS	1.6%		$63,095	$8,654	$54,441	1.0%
18	664.40	GLASS (MAINLY PLATE AND BODY TINTED)	1.6%		$13,021	$178	$12,843	0.2%
19	651.66	YARN OF DISCONT. SYNTH. FIBRES, 85% BY WEIGHT OR LESS	1.5%	*	$14,663	$4	$14,659	0.2%
20	892.20	NEWSPAPERS, JOURNALS AND PERIODICALS,	1.5%		$26,598	$2,258	$24,340	0.4%
21	674.70	TINNED SHEETS & PLATES OF STEEL	1.5%		$26,491	$0	$26,491	0.4%
22	792.30	AIRCRAFT, MECHANICALLY PROPELLED, UNLADEN	1.4%		$13,760	$584	$13,176	0.2%
23	652.24	WOVEN FABRICS (MAINLY COTTON)	1.4%	*	$61,027	$119	$60,908	1.0%
24	583.11	POLYETHYLENE	1.4%		$49,479	$453	$49,026	0.8%
25	657.32	TEXTILE FABRICS IMPREGNATED, COATED,	1.4%		$13,118	$691	$12,427	0.2%
26	752.80	OFF LINE DATA PROCESSING EQUIPMENT NES.	1.3%		$15,473	$1,910	$13,563	0.3%
27	722.40	TRACTORS	1.3%		$48,495	$573	$47,922	0.8%
28	752.20	DIGITAL DATA PROCESSING MACHINES	1.3%		$41,766	$1,038	$40,728	0.7%
29	686.10	ZINC , UNWROUGHT	1.2%		$20,198	$0	$20,198	0.3%
30	725.20	PAPER, PAPERBOARD CUTTING MACHINES	1.2%		$9,791	$18	$9,773	0.2%
31	682.21	WIRE RODS OF COPPER	1.2%		$24,457	$3,768	$20,689	0.4%
32	751.11	ELECTRIC TYPEWRITERS	1.2%		$8,048	$118	$7,930	0.1%
33	541.71	ANTIBIOTICS	1.1%		$14,091	$1,096	$12,995	0.2%
34	726.71	PRINTING MACHINERY (NOT PRINTING PRESSES)	1.1%	*	$28,004	$1,765	$26,239	0.5%
35	657.73	WADDING, WICKS & TEXTILE FABRICS FOR MACHINERY	1.1%	*	$10,189	$222	$9,967	0.2%
36	271.11	NATURAL CALCIUM PHOSPHATES, ALUMINIUM	1.1%		$14,371	$0	$14,371	0.2%
37	728.42	MACHINES FOR THE RUBBER & PLASTIC INDUSTRIES	1.1%		$20,747	$476	$20,271	0.3%
38	653.41	FABRICS, WOVEN, SYNTH. FIBRES (DISCONTINUOUS)	1.1%	*	$47,846	$2,474	$45,372	0.8%
39	335.42	PETROLEUM COKE	1.0%		$14,036	$0	$14,036	0.2%
40	657.33	SPECIAL TEXTILE FABRICS AND RELATED PRODUCTS	1.0%	*	$37,060	$3,455	$33,605	0.6%
41	655.10	KNITTED OR CROCHETED FABRICS,NOT ELASTIC	1.0%		$10,474	$793	$9,681	0.2%
42	121.21	TOBACCO, WHOLLY OR PARTLY STRIPPED	1.0%		$13,252	$0	$13,252	0.2%
43	896.05	COLLECTIONS,COLLECTORS PIECES	1.0%		$7,690	$1,226	$6,464	0.1%
44	562.31	POTASSIUM CHLORIDE	0.9%		$13,627	$1	$13,626	0.2%
45	724.31	SEWING MACHINES	0.9%		$10,710	$589	$10,121	0.2%
46	583.43	POLYVINYL CHLORIDE IN PLATES, SHEETS, STRIPS, ETC	0.9%		$12,054	$2,222	$9,832	0.2%
47	541.79	MEDICAMENTS, NOT INCLUDING ANTIBIOTICS	0.9%	*	$72,908	$9,930	$62,978	1.2%
48	716.21	ELECTRIC MOTORS (INCLUDING UNIVERSAL	0.9%		$15,453	$75	$15,378	0.3%
49	874.30	INSTRUMENTS & APPARATUS FOR MEASURING	0.8%		$12,226	$2,356	$9,870	0.2%
50	112.49	SPIRITS & DISTILLED ALCOHOLIC BEVERAGES,	0.8%		$9,286	$5,540	$3,746	0.2%

R = RESIDUAL

TOP 50 AUSTRALIAN INDUSTRIES IN TERMS OF
EXPORT VALUE
1985

	COMMODITY	DESCRIPTION	WORLD EXPORT SHARE (%)	R	AUSTRALIAN EXPORT VALUE ($US'000)	AUSTRALIAN IMPORT VALUE ($US'000)	TRADE BALANCE VALUE ($US'000)	AUSTRALIAN EXPORT SHARE (%)]
1	322.00	COAL, BRIQUETTES AND SIMILAR SOLID FUELS FROM COAL	25.6%	*	$3,562,719	$759	$3,561,960	16.0%
2	041.20	WHEAT, OTHER THAN DURUM (INCL. SPELT)	21.7%		$1,876,859	$0	$1,876,859	8.5%
3	268.10	SHEEPS' OR LAMBS' WOOL, GREASY OR FLEECE-WASHED	69.7%		$1,631,070	$388	$1,630,682	7.3%
4	281.50	IRON ORE AND CONCENTRATES, NOT AGGLOMERATED	44.6%		$1,312,526	$517	$1,312,009	5.9%
5	333.00	PETROLEUM OILS, CRUDE AND CRUDE OILS FROM BITUMINOUS MINERALS	0.7%		$1,147,106	$535,727	$611,379	5.2%
6	287.32	ALUMINA	51.1%		$998,969	$1,948	$997,021	4.5%
7	011.12	BEEF, BONELESS	24.3%		$833,085	$6,428	$826,657	3.8%
8	684.10	ALUMINIUM AND ALUMINIUM ALLOYS, UNWROUGHT	8.5%		$600,185	$0	$600,185	2.7%
9	971.01	GOLD, NON-MONETARY (EXCL. ORES AND CONCENTRATES)	7.8%	*	$464,975	$63,732	$401,243	2.1%
10	043.00	BARLEY, UNMILLED	17.9%		$453,445	$0	$453,445	2.0%
11	061.11	SUGAR, CANE	5.5%		$370,125	$0	$370,125	1.7%
12	341.31	LIQUIFIED PROPANE, BUTANE	3.9%		$343,321	$0	$343,321	1.5%
13	268.20	SHEEPS' OR LAMBS' WOOL, DEGREASED, NOT CARDED OR COMBED	29.7%		$320,015	$32,713	$287,302	1.4%
14	036.00	CRUSTACEANS AND MOLLUSCS, FRESH, CHILLED, FROZEN, SALTED, BRINE OR DRIED	6.0%		$291,605	$49,044	$242,561	1.3%
15	287.22	NICKEL, MATTES, SINTERS, ETC	28.9%		$231,745	$603	$231,142	1.0%
16	286.00	URANIUM, THORIUM ORES AND CONCENTRATES	56.3%		$225,575	$1	$225,574	1.0%
17	263.10	COTTON, NOT CARDED OR COMBED	4.5%		$223,142	$0	$223,142	1.0%
18	334.21	KEROSENE	3.9%		$197,937	$28,146	$169,791	0.9%
19	685.11	LEAD, UNREFINED	26.8%	*	$187,681	$0	$187,681	0.8%
20	686.10	ZINC AND ZINC ALLOYS, UNWROUGHT	9.6%		$170,210	$0	$170,210	0.8%
21	001.50	SHEEPS, GOATS, POULTRY, HORSES, MULES, ASSES, HINNIES AND OTHERS, LIVE	10.8%	*	$168,883	$36,767	$132,116	0.8%
22	287.50	ZINC ORES AND CONCENTRATES	16.9%		$165,024	$1,073	$163,951	0.7%
23	334.30	GAS OILS (AUTOMOTIVE, INDUSTRIAL AND MARINE DIESEL)	0.9%		$160,808	$153,729	$7,079	0.7%
24	287.60	LEAD, TIN ORES AND CONCENTRATES, AND OTHER BASE METALS	23.4%	*	$151,367	$3,892	$147,475	0.7%
25	246.02	PULPWOOD IN CHIPS OR PARTICLES	33.8%		$150,569	$0	$150,569	0.7%
26	287.93	MOLYBDENUM, NIOBIUM, TANTALUM, VANADIUM & ZIRCONIUM ORES AND CONCENTRATES	12.5%		$139,470	$921	$138,549	0.6%
27	211.60	HIDES AND SKINS, RAW (NOT BOVINE OR HORSE)	10.4%	*	$128,068	$204	$127,864	0.6%
28	024.00	CHEESE AND CURD	3.2%		$123,888	$47,572	$76,316	0.6%
29	011.20	MEAT OF SHEEP, LAMBS' AND GOATS'	11.1%		$123,401	$0	$123,401	0.6%
30	045.92	SORGHUM	9.7%		$122,906	$0	$122,906	0.6%
31	211.10	BOVINE AND EQUINE HIDES (OTHER THAN CALF SKINS)	5.1%		$114,919	$204	$114,715	0.5%
32	713.20	ENGINES, INTERNAL COMBUSTION PISTON TYPE FOR PROPELLING ROAD VEHICLES	2.4%		$113,913	$83,823	$30,090	0.5%
33	684.20	ALUMINIUM ALLOYS, WORKED	1.7%		$111,286	$0	$111,286	0.5%
34	683.10	NICKEL, ALLOYS, UNWROUGHT	9.2%		$106,155	$2,729	$103,426	0.5%
35	334.11	PETROL (AUTOMOTIVE GASOLINE) AVIATION SPIRIT	1.1%		$104,986	$87,896	$17,090	0.5%
36	334.51	LUBRICATING PETROLEUM OILS, FROM BITUMINOUS MINERALS, NES	1.9%	*	$97,627	$29,150	$68,477	0.4%
37	682.12	COPPER, REFINED, UNWROUGHT (INCL. COPPER ALLOYS OTHER THAN MASTER ALLOYS)	3.8%		$95,317	$0	$95,317	0.4%
38	672.51	IRON/STEEL BLOOMS, BILLETS, SLABS & SHEET BARS (NOT HIGH CARBON ALLOY STEEL)	3.5%		$95,186	$4,321	$90,865	0.4%
39	674.91	UNIVERSAL PLATES OF IRON AND STEEL AND OTHER SHEETS & PLATES	2.0%	*	$89,884	$72,319	$17,565	0.4%
40	081.12	HAY AND FODDER, BRAN, SHARPS AND FOOD WASTES	7.7%	*	$89,556	$19,131	$70,425	0.4%
41	287.11	COPPER ORES AND CONCENTRATES	4.8%		$89,142	$1	$89,141	0.4%
42	651.20	YARN OF WOOL OR ANIMAL HAIR	3.5%		$79,594	$51,910	$27,684	0.4%
43	278.30	OTHER CRUDE MINERALS (NOT CLAY)	3.2%	*	$78,212	$12,740	$65,472	0.4%
44	411.32	TALLOW	7.3%		$67,583	$0	$67,583	0.3%
45	022.43	MILK AND CREAM, IN POWDER OR GRANULES, MORE THAN 1.5% BY WEIGHT OF FAT	5.2%		$62,002	$0	$62,002	0.3%
46	667.50	PEARLS, PRECIOUS AND SEMI-PRECIOUS STONES, WORKED AND UNWORKED	0.5%	*	$59,482	$43,949	$15,533	0.3%
47	023.00	BUTTER	2.8%		$58,404	$0	$58,404	0.3%
48	022.42	MILK, IN POWDER OR GRANULES, 1.5% BY WEIGHT OF FAT OR LESS (NOT WHEY)	4.8%		$58,138	$0	$58,138	0.3%
49	281.60	IRON ORE AGGLOMERATES	5.6%		$54,110	$3	$54,107	0.2%
50	057.52	GRAPES, DRIED (RAISINS)	11.1%		$51,741	$2,464	$49,277	0.2%

R = RESIDUAL

AUSTRALIA'S TOP 50 COMPETITIVE INDUSTRIES
IN TERMS OF WORLD EXPORT SHARE
1985

	COMMODITY	DESCRIPTION	WORLD EXPORT SHARE (%) R	AUSTRALIAN EXPORT VALUE ($US'000)	AUSTRALIAN IMPORT VALUE ($US'000)	TRADE BALANCE VALUE ($US'000)	AUSTRALIAN EXPORT SHARE (%)]
1	268.10	SHEEPS' OR LAMBS' WOOL, GREASY OR FLEECE-WASHED	69.7%	$1,631,070	$388	$1,630,682	7.3%
2	286.00	URANIUM, THORIUM ORES AND CONCENTRATES	56.3%	$225,575	$1	$225,574	1.0%
3	287.32	ALUMINA	51.1%	$998,969	$1,948	$997,021	4.5%
4	281.50	IRON ORE AND CONCENTRATES, NOT AGGLOMERATED	44.6%	$1,312,526	$517	$1,312,009	5.9%
5	246.02	PULPWOOD IN CHIPS OR PARTICLES	33.8%	$150,569	$0	$150,569	0.7%
6	268.20	SHEEPS' OR LAMBS' WOOL, DEGREASED, NOT CARDED OR COMBED	29.7%	$320,015	$32,713	$287,302	1.4%
7	287.22	NICKEL, MATTES, SINTERS, ETC	28.9%	$231,745	$603	$231,142	1.0%
8	685.11	LEAD, UNREFINED	26.8% *	$187,681	$0	$187,681	0.8%
9	322.00	COAL, BRIQUETTES AND SIMILAR SOLID FUELS FROM COAL	25.6% *	$3,562,719	$759	$3,561,960	16.0%
10	011.12	BEEF, BONELESS	24.3%	$833,085	$6,428	$826,657	3.8%
11	287.60	LEAD, TIN ORES AND CONCENTRATES, AND OTHER BASE METALS	23.4% *	$151,367	$3,892	$147,475	0.7%
12	041.20	WHEAT, OTHER THAN DURUM (INCL. SPELT)	21.7%	$1,876,859	$0	$1,876,859	8.5%
13	043.00	BARLEY, UNMILLED	17.9%	$453,445	$0	$453,445	2.0%
14	287.50	ZINC ORES AND CONCENTRATES	16.9%	$165,024	$1,073	$163,951	0.7%
15	287.93	MOLYBDENUM, NIOBIUM, TANTALUM, VANADIUM & ZIRCONIUM ORES AND CONCENTRATES	12.5%	$139,470	$921	$138,549	0.6%
16	011.20	MEAT OF SHEEP, LAMBS' AND GOATS'	11.1%	$123,401	$0	$123,401	0.6%
17	057.52	GRAPES, DRIED (RAISINS)	11.1%	$51,741	$2,464	$49,277	0.2%
18	001.50	SHEEPS, GOATS, POULTRY, HORSES, MULES, ASSES, HINNIES AND OTHERS, LIVE	10.8% *	$168,883	$36,767	$132,116	0.8%
19	211.60	HIDES AND SKINS, RAW (NOT BOVINE OR HORSE)	10.4% *	$128,068	$204	$127,864	0.6%
20	045.20	OATS, UNMILLED (NOT SORGHUM)	10.2% *	$29,742	$0	$29,742	0.1%
21	045.92	SORGHUM	9.7%	$122,906	$0	$122,906	0.6%
22	686.10	ZINC AND ZINC ALLOYS, UNWROUGHT	9.6%	$170,210	$0	$170,210	0.8%
23	683.10	NICKEL, ALLOYS, UNWROUGHT	9.2%	$106,155	$2,729	$103,426	0.5%
24	684.10	ALUMINIUM AND ALUMINIUM ALLOYS, UNWROUGHT	8.5%	$600,185	$0	$600,185	2.7%
25	081.12	HAY AND FODDER, BRAN, SHARPS AND FOOD WASTES	7.7% *	$89,556	$19,131	$70,425	0.4%
26	048.20	MALT	8.0%	$45,016	$0	$45,016	0.2%
27	971.01	GOLD, NON-MONETARY (EXCL. ORES AND CONCENTRATES)	7.8% *	$464,975	$63,732	$401,243	2.1%
28	592.12	STARCHES, INULIN AND WHEAT GLUTEN	7.6% *	$22,820	$1,491	$21,329	0.1%
29	411.32	TALLOW	7.3%	$67,583	$0	$67,583	0.3%
30	011.60	OFFALS, EDIBLE OF CATTLE, SHEEP, GOATS, PIGS, HORSES, ETC (EXCL. GUTS, BLADDERS)	7.0%	$48,468	$0	$48,468	0.2%
31	036.00	CRUSTACEANS AND MOLLUSCS, FRESH, CHILLED, FROZEN, SALTED, BRINE OR DRIED	6.0%	$291,605	$49,044	$242,561	1.3%
32	061.50	MOLASSES, NATURAL HONEY, AND OTHER SUGARS	5.8% *	$20,520	$0	$20,520	0.1%
33	281.60	IRON ORE AGGLOMERATES	5.6%	$54,110	$3	$54,107	0.2%
34	061.11	SUGAR, CANE	5.5%	$370,125	$0	$370,125	1.7%
35	022.43	MILK AND CREAM, IN POWDER OR GRANULES, MORE THAN 1.5% BY WEIGHT OF FAT	5.2%	$62,002	$0	$62,002	0.3%
36	211.10	BOVINE AND EQUINE HIDES (OTHER THAN CALF SKINS)	5.1%	$114,919	$204	$114,715	0.5%
37	022.42	MILK, IN POWDER OR GRANULES, 1.5% BY WEIGHT OF FAT OR LESS (NOT WHEY)	4.8%	$58,138	$0	$58,138	0.3%
38	287.11	COPPER ORES AND CONCENTRATES	4.8%	$89,142	$1	$89,141	0.4%
39	263.10	COTTON, NOT CARDED OR COMBED	4.5%	$223,142	$0	$223,142	1.0%
40	291.93	GUTS, BLADDERS AND STOMACHS	4.1%	$15,864	$5,377	$10,487	0.1%
41	058.99	FRUIT, PRESERVED AND PREPARED (NOT INCL. JUICES)	4.0% *	$46,895	$25,979	$20,916	0.2%
42	334.21	KEROSENE	3.9%	$197,937	$28,146	$169,791	0.9%
43	681.14	SILVER (INCL. ROLLED SILVER), UNWROUGHT	3.9% *	$38,543	$348	$38,195	0.2%
44	341.31	LIQUIFIED PROPANE, BUTANE	3.9%	$343,321	$0	$343,321	1.5%
45	682.12	COPPER, REFINED, UNWROUGHT (INCL. COPPER ALLOYS OTHER THAN MASTER ALLOYS)	3.8%	$95,317	$0	$95,317	0.4%
46	651.20	YARN OF WOOL OR ANIMAL HAIR	3.5%	$79,594	$51,910	$27,684	0.4%
47	672.51	IRON/STEEL BLOOMS, BILLETS, SLABS & SHEET BARS (NOT HIGH CARBON ALLOY STEEL)	3.5%	$95,186	$4,321	$90,865	0.4%
48	037.20	CRUSTACEANS AND MOLLUSCS, PREPARED OR PRESERVED, N.E.S.	3.4%	$29,039	$33,163	($4,124)	0.1%
49	278.30	OTHER CRUDE MINERALS (NOT CLAY)	3.2% *	$78,212	$12,740	$65,472	0.4%
50	024.00	CHEESE AND CURD	3.2%	$123,888	$47,572	$76,316	0.6%

R = RESIDUAL

TOP 50 AUSTRALIAN INDUSTRIES IN TERMS OF
IMPORT VALUE
1985

	COMMODITY	DESCRIPTION	WORLD IMPORT SHARE (%)	R	AUSTRALIAN IMPORT VALUE ($US'000)	AUSTRALIAN EXPORT VALUE ($US'000)	TRADE BALANCE ($US'000)	AUSTRALIAN IMPORT SHARE (%)
1	781.00	MOTOR CARS (ASSEMBLED AND UNASSEMBLED)	1.1%		$959,730	$68,647	$891,083	4.1%
2	782.10	TRUCKS AND VANS	4.7%		$929,886	$13,799	$916,087	4.0%
3	931.00	SPECIAL TRANSACTIONS AND COMMODITIES	3.0%		$774,365	$541,514	$232,851	3.3%
4	334.40	FUEL OILS	2.2%		$674,872	$252,365	$422,507	2.9%
5	333.00	CRUDE PETROLEUM	0.3%		$533,797	$1,125,486	($591,689)	2.3%
6	752.50	EDP PERIPHERAL UNITS	4.3%		$472,317	$0	$472,317	2.0%
7	784.90	BODIES, PARTS AND ACCESSORIES, N.E.S. FOR MOTOR VEHICLES	1.1%	*	$453,564	$87,523	$366,041	2.0%
8	874.83	MEASURING & CONTROLLING INSTRUMENTS, PARTS, ACCESSORIES N.E.S.	2.3%	*	$344,603	$38,820	$305,783	1.5%
9	759.90	DATA PROCESSING MACHINE PARTS	1.6%	*	$321,364	$27,767	$293,597	1.4%
10	764.91	TELECOMMUNICATIONS EQUIPMENT N.E.S.	1.8%		$252,694	$11,172	$241,522	1.1%
11	892.11	BOOKS	6.3%		$239,215	$18,895	$220,320	1.0%
12	775.86	DOMESTIC APPLIANCES (MAINLY MICROWAVE OVENS)	3.1%	*	$219,037	$158,782	$60,255	0.9%
13	772.10	ELECTRICAL CIRCUIT APPARATUS	1.8%		$214,508	$20,010	$194,498	0.9%
14	752.20	DIGITAL DATA PROCESSING MACHINES	6.3%		$214,078	$0	$214,078	0.9%
15	652.24	WOVEN FABRIC (MAINLY COTTON)	4.5%	*	$200,895	$2,216	$198,679	0.9%
16	722.40	TRACTORS, WHEELED	5.0%		$193,970	$435	$193,535	0.8%
17	752.30	DIGITAL CENTRAL PROCESSING UNITS	3.6%		$193,339	$0	$193,339	0.8%
18	728.48	SPECIALISED MACHINERY AND MECHANICAL APPLIANCES	2.0%	*	$187,742	$12,775	$174,967	0.8%
19	723.43	PARTS AND MACHINERY FOR CIVIL ENGINEERING (NOT BULLDOZERS)	1.8%	*	$164,743	$23,607	$141,136	0.7%
20	723.42	MECHANICAL SHOVELS AND EXCAVATORS	6.7%		$159,190	$1,882	$157,308	0.7%
21	763.81	TV IMAGE AND SOUND RECORDERS OR REPRODUCERS	1.9%		$155,290	$235	$155,055	0.7%
22	334.30	DIESEL OIL, AUTOMOTIVE	0.7%		$153,729	$160,808	($7,079)	0.7%
23	893.99	MISC. PLASTICS, SANITARY & TOILET, & ELECTRICAL LIGHTING ARTICLES	2.0%	*	$153,163	$8,768	$144,395	0.7%
24	541.79	MEDICAMENTS (NOT INCLUDING HORMONES, ANTIBIOTICS)	1.6%	*	$133,025	$22,129	$110,896	0.6%
25	515.68	HETEROCYCLIC COMPOUNDS, N.E.S; NUCLEIC ACIDS	2.6%	*	$131,817	$209	$131,608	0.6%
26	641.22	PRINTING AND WRITING PAPER, COATED, IMPREGNATED, COLOURED ETC.	3.9%		$130,814	$3,326	$127,488	0.6%
27	641.80	PAPER AND PAPERBOARD, COATED, IMPREGNATED, COLOURED ETC	3.4%		$129,144	$7,051	$122,093	0.6%
28	764.10	TELEPHONE EQUIPMENT	2.5%		$128,708	$7,823	$120,885	0.6%
29	894.23	TOYS (WORKING MODELS)	2.2%	*	$127,087	$1,080	$126,007	0.5%
30	749.20	TAPS, COCKS, VALVES AND SIMILAR APPLIANCES	2.1%		$125,202	$9,988	$115,214	0.5%
31	598.99	CHEMICAL PRODUCTS AND PREPARATIONS, N.E.S.	1.4%	*	$123,824	$16,616	$107,208	0.5%
32	248.21	WOOD, CONIFEROUS, SAWN LENGTHWISE, SLICED OR PEELED	2.7%		$121,135	$896	$120,239	0.5%
33	582.90	CONDENSATION AND POLYADDITION PRODUCTS(NOT ALKYDS, POLYMIDES)	2.5%	*	$120,165	$6,283	$113,882	0.5%
34	792.90	AIRCRAFT PARTS, N.E.S. (NOT TYRES, ENGINES OR ELECTRICAL PARTS)	1.4%		$118,076	$33,134	$84,942	0.5%
35	641.59	PAPER, PAPERBOARD, FIBRE BOARD OF WOOD & OTHER VEGE. MATERIALS	2.7%	*	$114,183	$12,351	$101,832	0.5%
36	641.10	NEWSPRINT	1.8%		$110,668	$1,663	$109,005	0.5%
37	851.02	FOOTWEAR WITH OUTER SOLES OF LEATHER, RUBBER OR PLASTIC	1.0%		$110,408	$2,443	$107,965	0.5%
38	713.90	PARTS, N.E.S. OF INTERNAL COMBUSTION PISTON ENGINES	1.7%		$110,285	$6,424	$103,861	0.5%
39	598.20	ANTI-KNOCK PREPARATIONS & PREPARED ADDITIVES OF MINERAL OILS	5.4%		$107,226	$0	$107,226	0.5%
40	743.10	AIR PUMPS, VACUUM PUMPS AND AIR OR GAS COMPRESSORS	3.5%		$104,761	$2,895	$101,866	0.5%
41	749.30	TRANSMISSION SHAFTS, CRANKS, GEARS, PULLEYS, CLUTCHES ETC.	2.8%		$104,348	$4,168	$100,180	0.5%
42	699.79	IRON/STEEL ARTICLES, N.E.S. (EXCL. LOCKS, SAFES, AND CHAINS)	1.3%	*	$102,679	$34,252	$68,427	0.4%
43	653.41	WOVEN FABRICS, SYNTHETIC FIBRES (DISCONTINUOUS)	2.1%	*	$102,648	$58	$102,590	0.4%
44	831.09	CASES AND PURSES (NOT HANDBAGS)	4.5%	*	$98,404	$248	$98,156	0.4%
45	894.72	NON-MILITARY ARMS/AMMUNITION, SPORTS GOODS, OTHERS, N.E.S.	2.6%	*	$98,080	$9,310	$88,770	0.4%
46	334.11	GASOLINE (MOTOR AND AVIATION)	0.9%		$91,535	$101,261	($9,726)	0.4%
47	898.31	PREPARED MEDIA FOR SOUND OR SIMILAR RECORDING	2.4%		$85,213	$2,241	$82,972	0.4%
48	778.86	ELECTRIC MACHINERY/APPARATUS, NES (NOT HAND TOOLS WITH MOTORS)	1.5%	*	$85,056	$16,999	$68,057	0.4%
49	785.10	MOTOR CYCLES, AUTO-CYCLES AND CYCLES WITH AUXILIARY MOTORS	4.2%		$84,886	$82	$84,804	0.4%
50	713.20	INTERNAL COMBUSTION PISTON ENGINES FOR TRANSPORT VEHICLES	1.2%		$83,554	$113,534	($29,980)	0.4%

R = RESIDUAL

AUSTRALIA'S TOP 50 COMPETITIVE INDUSTRIES
IN TERMS OF WORLD IMPORT SHARE
1985

	COMMODITY	DESCRIPTION	WORLD IMPORT SHARE (%)	R	AUSTRALIAN IMPORT VALUE ($US'000)	AUSTRALIAN EXPORT VALUE ($US'000)	TRADE BALANCE VALUE ($US'000)	AUSTRALIAN IMPORT SHARE (%)
1	723.41	BULLDOZERS, ANGLEDOZERS AND LEVELLERS	13.8%		$83,036	$1,882	$81,154	0.4%
2	248.52	WOOD, NON-CONIFEROUS, PLANED, GROOVED, V-JOINTED AND THE LIKE	8.8%		$24,839	$36	$24,803	0.1%
3	651.66	TEXTILE YARN, MIXED WITH WOOL OR ANIMAL HAIR (OTHER THAN COTTON)	8.6%	▾	$80,755	$11	$80,744	0.3%
4	723.42	MECHANICAL SHOVELS AND EXCAVATORS	6.7%		$159,190	$1,882	$157,308	0.7%
5	752.20	DIGITAL DATA PROCESSING MACHINES	6.3%		$214,078	$0	$214,078	0.9%
6	892.11	BOOKS	6.3%		$239,215	$18,895	$220,320	1.0%
7	653.97	WOVEN FABRICS OF MAN-MADE SYNTH. AND REGENERATED FIBRES	6.1%	▾	$28,334	$122	$28,212	0.1%
8	716.22	ALTERNATING CURRENT GENERATORS	5.9%		$26,341	$591	$25,750	0.1%
9	721.22	COMBINED HARVESTER-THRESHERS	5.6%		$45,300	$151	$45,149	0.2%
10	678.10	CAST IRON TUBES AND PIPES	5.5%		$61,574	$928	$60,646	0.3%
11	598.20	ANTI-KNOCK PREPARATIONS & PREPARED ADDITIVES OF MINERAL OILS	5.4%		$107,226	$0	$107,226	0.5%
12	562.92	FERTILISERS, CONTAINING NITROGEN AND PHOSPHORUS	5.3%		$63,197	$0	$63,197	0.3%
13	271.31	CRUDE FERTILISERS, UNDERGROUND N.E.S.	5.2%		$65,580	$1	$65,579	0.3%
14	722.40	TRACTORS, WHEELED	5.0%		$193,970	$435	$193,535	0.8%
15	782.10	TRUCKS AND VANS	4.7%		$929,886	$13,799	$916,087	4.0%
16	751.11	ELECTRIC TYPEWRITERS	4.6%		$32,483	$300	$32,183	0.1%
17	583.43	POLYVINYL CHLORIDE, IN PLATES, SHEETS, STRIPS, FILM OR FOIL	4.5%		$38,898	$2,374	$36,524	0.2%
18	652.24	WOVEN FABRIC (MAINLY COTTON)	4.5%	▾	$200,895	$2,216	$198,679	0.9%
19	745.11	HAND-TOOLS, PNEUMATIC OR WITH SELF-CONTAINED NON-ELECTRIC MOTOR	4.5%		$42,127	$932	$41,195	0.2%
20	831.09	CASES AND PURSES (NOT HANDBAGS)	4.5%	▾	$98,404	$248	$98,156	0.4%
21	659.41	FLOOR COVERINGS, ETC (MAINLY CARPETS OR RUGS)	4.5%	▾	$64,405	$4,750	$59,655	0.3%
22	752.50	EDP PERIPHERAL UNITS	4.3%		$472,317	$0	$472,317	2.0%
23	785.10	MOTOR CYCLES, AUTO-CYCLES AND CYCLES WITH AUXILIARY MOTORS	4.2%		$84,886	$82	$84,804	0.4%
24	666.50	TABLEWARE ETC FOR DOMESTIC AND TOILET USE (EXCL. PORCELAIN CHINA)	4.2%		$28,228	$469	$27,759	0.1%
25	724.31	SEWING MACHINES	4.2%		$50,002	$100	$49,902	0.2%
26	778.40	HAND-TOOLS, WITH SELF-CONTAINED ELECTRIC MOTORS, PARTS, N.E.S.	4.1%		$52,959	$298	$52,661	0.2%
27	726.41	ROTARY PRINTING PRESSES	4.1%		$59,591	$327	$59,264	0.3%
28	582.41	POLYAMIDES IN PRIMARY FORMS	4.1%		$38,856	$314	$38,542	0.2%
29	892.20	NEWSPAPERS, JOURNALS AND PERIODICALS	4.1%		$72,324	$10,804	$61,520	0.3%
30	641.22	PRINTING AND WRITING PAPER, COATED, IMPREGNATED, COLOURED ETC.	3.9%		$130,814	$3,326	$127,488	0.6%
31	658.10	SACKS, TARPAULINS, RUGS, OTHER MADE-UP ARTICLES OF TEXTILE FABRICS	3.7%	◂	$73,635	$2,142	$71,493	0.3%
32	071.20	EXTRACTS, ESSENCES AND CONCENTRATES OF COFFEE	3.7%		$32,606	$16,994	$15,612	0.1%
33	894.24	GAMES (PARLOUR, TABLE, FUNFAIR) EQUIPMENT FOR ADULTS AND CHILDREN	3.7%		$27,344	$8,974	$18,370	0.1%
34	034.40	FISH FILLETS, FROZEN	3.6%		$51,795	$1,183	$50,612	0.2%
35	752.30	DIGITAL CENTRAL PROCESSING UNITS	3.6%		$193,339	$0	$193,339	0.8%
36	665.20	GLASSWARE FOR KITCHEN, TABLE, TOILET, DECORATION AND OFFICE USE	3.6%		$57,801	$2,438	$55,363	0.2%
37	628.20	ARTICLES OF RUBBER, N.E.S.	3.6%	◂	$28,168	$940	$27,228	0.1%
38	037.20	CRUSTACEANS AND MOLLUSCS, PREPARED OR PRESERVED, N.E.S.	3.6%		$33,044	$28,752	$4,292	0.1%
39	778.12	ELECTRIC ACCUMULATORS	3.5%		$33,968	$156	$33,812	0.1%
40	037.10	CAVIAR AND CAVIAR SUBSTITUTES (FISH)	3.5%		$70,058	$539	$69,519	0.3%
41	662.45	GLAZED CERAMIC SETTS, FLAGS AND PAVING, HEARTH AND WALL TILES	3.5%		$58,366	$221	$58,145	0.3%
42	743.10	AIR PUMPS, VACUUM PUMPS AND AIR OR GAS COMPRESSORS	3.5%		$104,761	$2,895	$101,866	0.5%
43	783.20	ROAD TRACTORS FOR SEMI-TRAILERS	3.4%		$47,265	$15	$47,250	0.2%
44	744.11	WORK TRUCKS AND TRACTORS USED IN WAREHOUSES, DOCK AREAS, ETC	3.4%		$57,763	$516	$57,247	0.2%
45	641.80	PAPER AND PAPERBOARD, COATED, IMPREGNATED, COLOURED ETC	3.4%		$129,144	$7,051	$122,093	0.6%
46	881.39	PHOTOGRAPHIC AND CINEMATOGRAPHIC APPARATUS AND EQUIPMENT, N.E.S.	3.4%	◂	$47,408	$1,702	$45,706	0.2%
47	764.30	TV, RADIO-BROADCASTING, RADIO-TELEGRAPHIC TRANSMITTERS	3.3%		$76,002	$440	$75,562	0.3%
48	898.32	RECORDED TAPES, RECORDS, ETC	3.3%		$60,342	$2,758	$57,584	0.3%
49	792.30	AIRCRAFT, BETWEEN 2,000 KG AND 15,000 KG (EXCL. HELICOPTERS)	3.3%		$31,890	$0	$31,890	0.1%
50	666.40	PORCELAIN OR CHINA TABLEWARE ETC, FOR DOMESTIC OR TOILET PURPOSES	3.2%		$26,650	$187	$26,463	0.1%

R = RESIDUAL

TOP 50 CHILEAN INDUSTRIES IN TERMS OF
EXPORT VALUE
1985

	COMMODITY	DESCRIPTION	WORLD EXPORT SHARE (%)	CHILE IMPORT VALUE ($US'000)	CHILE EXPORT SHARE (%)
1	682.11	COPPER, UNREFINED	64.1%	$1,223,980	32.0%
2	287.11	COPPER ORES AND CONCENTRATES	20.5%	$316,383	8.3%
3	081.42	FISH MEAL (FOR ANIMALS)	32.4%	$273,311	7.1%
4	288.21	COPPER WASTE AND SRAP	16.4%	$237,380	6.2%
5	057.51	FRESH GRAPES	27.1%	$224,847	5.9%
6	251.60	CHEMICAL WOOD PULP, DISSOLVING GRADES	17.6%	$149,349	3.9%
7	287.93	MOLYBDENUM, NIOBIUM, TANTALUM, ETC	13.1%	$144,875	3.8%
8	681.11	SILVER, UNWROUGHT, UNWORKED OR SEMI-MANUFACTURED	5.7%	$97,860	2.6%
9	281.00	IRON ORE AND CONCENTRATES	1.5%	$91,658	2.4%
10	971.00	GOLD	1.0%	$85,256	2.2%
11	057.40	FRESH APPLES	7.1%	$74,427	1.9%
12	289.00	ORES AND CONCENTRATES OF PRECIOUS METALS	6.4%	$56,694	1.5%
13	641.10	NEWSPRINT	0.8%	$48,622	1.3%
14	057.93	FRESH STONE FRUIT	8.7%	$46,949	1.2%
15	248.21	WOOD OF CONIFERS, SAWN LENGTHWISE, SLICED OR PEELED	1.3%	$42,398	1.1%
16	247.11	SAWLOGS AND VENEER LOGS OF CONIFERS, ROUGH	2.6%	$39,433	1.0%
17	054.20	DRIED BEANS, PEAS, LENTILS, OTHER LEGUMES	3.0%	$36,904	1.0%
18	411.00	FATS AND OILS OF FISH AND MARINE MAMMALS	12.3%	$35,432	0.9%
19	522.10	CHEMICAL ELEMENTS	1.7%	$35,173	0.9%
20	271.00	FERTILISERS, CRUDE	1.9%	$32,893	0.9%
21	292.00	CRUDE VEGETABLE MATERIALS (INC. SEEDS FOR SOWING)	0.6%	$32,772	0.9%
22	034.20	FROZEN FISH, EXCLUDING FILLETS	1.8%	$32,319	0.8%
23	037.20	SHELLFISH, PREPARED OR PRESERVED	3.6%	$30,287	0.8%
24	036.00	SHELLFISH, NOT PREPARED OR PRESERVED	0.6%	$27,644	0.7%
25	523.00	OTHER CHEMICALS, COMPOUNDS OF PRECIOUS METALS	0.4%	$19,806	0.5%
26	562.90	FERTILISERS, MANUFACTURED N.E.S.	0.7%	$17,571	0.5%
27	081.93	BEET-PULP, BAGASSE AND OTHER SUGAR WASTE	2.0%	$15,992	0.4%
28	682.21	COPPER BARS, RODS, WIRE ETC	0.8%	$15,004	0.4%
29	287.50	ZINC ORES AND CONCENTRATES	1.2%	$12,012	0.3%
30	268.10	SHEEP/ LAMBS WOOL, GREASY	0.5%	$11,534	0.3%
31	672.51	IRON/STEEL, BLOOMS, BILLETS, SLABS AND BARS	0.5%	$11,359	0.3%
32	112.12	WINE	0.3%	$10,986	0.3%
33	784.00	MOTOR VEHICLE PARTS AND ACCESSORIES	0.0%	$10,826	0.3%
34	037.10	FISH, PREPARED, PRESERVED, N.E.S.	0.6%	$10,743	0.3%
35	583.00	POLYMERISATION AND COPOLYMERISATION PRODUCTS ETC	0.1%	$10,293	0.3%
36	248.30	WOOD OF NON-CONIFERS, SAWN, PLANED ETC	0.5%	$10,227	0.3%
37	057.70	EDIBLE NUTS, FRESH OR DRIED	0.5%	$8,656	0.2%
38	671.60	FERRO-ALLOYS	0.2%	$7,450	0.2%
39	635.00	WOOD MANUFACTURES N.E.S.	0.3%	$7,441	0.2%
40	048.20	MALT	1.2%	$6,823	0.2%
41	056.00	VEGETABLES, PREPARED OR PRESERVED, N.E.S.	0.3%	$6,596	0.2%
42	278.00	OTHER CRUDE MINERALS	0.2%	$5,808	0.2%
43	057.20	LEMONS, LIMES AND GRAPEFRUIT	0.8%	$5,742	0.2%
44	512.10	ACYCLIC ALCOHOLS AND THEIR DERIVATIVES	0.2%	$5,516	0.1%
45	674.70	TINNED SHEETS AND PLATES OF STEEL	0.3%	$5,373	0.1%
46	058.50	FRUIT JUICE	0.2%	$5,187	0.1%
47	054.40	TOMATOES	0.6%	$4,822	0.1%
48	892.20	NEWSPAPERS, PERIODICALS	0.3%	$4,374	0.1%
49	034.40	FISH FILLETS, FROZEN	0.3%	$3,924	0.1%
50	672.71	IRON AND STEEL COILS FOR RE-ROLLING	0.1%	$3,884	0.1%

R = RESIDUAL

CHILE'S TOP 50 COMPETITIVE INDUSTRIES
IN TERMS OF WORLD EXPORT SHARE
1985

	COMMODITY	DESCRIPTION	WORLD EXPORT SHARE (%)	CHILE EXPORT VALUE ($US'000)	CHILE EXPORT SHARE (%)
1	682.11	COPPER, UNREFINED	64.1%	$1,223,980	32.0%
2	081.42	FISH MEAL (FOR ANIMALS)	32.4%	$273,311	7.1%
3	057.51	FRESH GRAPES	27.1%	$224,847	5.9%
4	287.11	COPPER ORES AND CONCENTRATES	20.5%	$316,383	8.3%
5	251.60	CHEMICAL WOOD PULP, DISSOLVING GRADES	17.6%	$149,349	3.9%
6	288.21	COPPER WASTE AND SCRAP	16.4%	$237,380	6.2%
7	287.93	MOLYBDENUM, NIOBIUM, TANTALUM, ETC	13.1%	$144,875	3.8%
8	411.00	FATS AND OILS OF FISH AND MARINE MAMMALS	12.3%	$35,432	0.9%
9	057.93	FRESH STONE FRUIT	8.7%	$46,949	1.2%
10	057.40	FRESH APPLES	7.1%	$74,427	1.9%
11	289.00	ORES AND CONCENTRATES OF PRECIOUS METALS	6.4%	$56,694	1.5%
12	681.11	SILVER, UNWROUGHT, UNWORKED OR SEMI-MANUFACTURED	5.7%	$97,860	2.6%
13	037.20	SHELLFISH, PREPARED OR PRESERVED	3.6%	$30,287	0.8%
14	054.20	DRIED BEANS, PEAS, LENTILS, OTHER LEGUMES	3.0%	$36,904	1.0%
15	247.11	SAWLOGS AND VENEER LOGS OF CONIFERS, ROUGH	2.6%	$39,433	1.0%
16	081.93	BEET-PULP, BAGASSE AND OTHER SUGAR WASTE	2.0%	$15,992	0.4%
17	271.00	FERTILISERS, CRUDE	1.9%	$32,893	0.9%
18	034.20	FROZEN FISH, EXCLUDING FILLETS	1.8%	$32,319	0.8%
19	522.10	CHEMICAL ELEMENTS	1.7%	$35,173	0.9%
20	281.00	IRON ORE AND CONCENTRATES	1.5%	$91,658	2.4%
21	248.21	WOOD OF CONIFERS, SAWN LENGTHWISE, SLICED OR PEELED	1.3%	$42,398	1.1%
22	287.50	ZINC ORES AND CONCENTRATES	1.2%	$12,012	0.3%
23	048.20	MALT	1.2%	$6,823	0.2%
24	971.00	GOLD	1.0%	$85,256	2.2%
25	641.10	NEWSPRINT	0.8%	$48,622	1.3%
26	057.20	LEMONS, LIMES AND GRAPEFRUIT	0.8%	$5,742	0.2%
27	682.21	COPPER BARS, RODS, WIRE ETC	0.8%	$15,004	0.4%
28	562.90	FERTILISERS, MANUFACTURED N.E.S.	0.7%	$17,571	0.5%
29	292.00	CRUDE VEGETABLE MATERIALS (INC. SEEDS FOR SOWING)	0.6%	$32,772	0.9%
30	037.10	FISH, PREPARED, PRESERVED, N.E.S.	0.6%	$10,743	0.3%
31	054.40	TOMATOES	0.6%	$4,822	0.1%
32	036.00	SHELLFISH, NOT PREPARED OR PRESERVED	0.6%	$27,644	0.7%
33	672.51	IRON/STEEL, BLOOMS, BILLETS, SLABS AND BARS	0.5%	$11,359	0.3%
34	057.70	EDIBLE NUTS, FRESH OR DRIED	0.5%	$8,656	0.2%
35	268.10	SHEEP/ LAMBS WOOL, GREASY	0.5%	$11,534	0.3%
36	248.30	WOOD OF NON-CONIFEROUS, SAWN, PLANED ETC	0.5%	$10,227	0.3%
37	523.00	OTHER CHEMICALS, COMPOUNDS OF PRECIOUS METALS	0.4%	$19,806	0.5%
38	682.25	COPPER TUBES, PIPES, ETC	0.4%	$3,039	0.1%
39	674.70	TINNED SHEETS AND PLATES OF STEEL	0.3%	$5,573	0.1%
40	112.12	WINE	0.3%	$10,986	0.3%
41	635.00	WOOD MANUFACTURES N.E.S.	0.3%	$7,441	0.2%
42	034.40	FISH FILLETS, FROZEN	0.3%	$3,924	0.1%
43	011.20	SHEEP MEAT	0.3%	$2,912	0.1%
44	034.10	FISH, LIVE OR DEAD, FRESH OR CHILLED	0.3%	$3,821	0.1%
45	056.00	VEGETABLES, PREPARED OR PRESERVED, N.E.S.	0.3%	$6,596	0.2%
46	892.20	NEWSPAPERS, PERIODICALS	0.3%	$4,574	0.1%
47	671.60	FERRO-ALLOYS	0.2%	$7,450	0.2%
48	058.50	FRUIT JUICE	0.2%	$5,187	0.1%
49	682.22	COPPER PLATES, SHEETS AND STRIPS	0.2%	$2,071	0.1%
50	291.00	CRUDE ANIMAL MATERIALS	0.2%	$2,345	0.1%

TOP 50 CHILEAN INDUSTRIES IN TERMS OF
IMPORT VALUE
1985

	COMMODITY	DESCRIPTION	WORLD IMPORT SHARE (%)	CHILE IMPORT VALUE ($US'000)	CHILE IMPORT SHARE (%)
1	333.00	PETROLEUM, CRUDE	0.2%	$445,745	16.2%
2	723.00	CIVIL ENGINEERING EQUIPMENT, ETC	1.1%	$129,883	4.7%
3	781.00	MOTOR CARS	0.1%	$72,253	2.6%
4	041.00	WHEAT, UNMILLED	0.7%	$67,839	2.5%
5	784.00	MOTOR VEHICLE PARTS, ACCESSORIES, N.E.S.	0.1%	$64,743	2.4%
6	874.00	MEASURING, CONTROLLING INSTRUMENTS	0.3%	$53,839	2.0%
7	423.20	SOYA BEAN OIL	2.3%	$52,132	1.9%
8	598.00	CHEMICAL PRODUCTS, N.E.S. (EXCL. ANTI-KNOCK PREPARATIONS)	0.4%	$34,559	1.3%
9	591.00	DISINFECTINTS, INSECTICIDES, ETC.	0.8%	$33,204	1.2%
10	713.90	PISTON ENGINE PARTS	0.5%	$32,427	1.2%
11	523.00	OTHER INORGANIC COMPOUNDS OF PRECIOUS METALS	0.6%	$31,846	1.2%
12	334.50	LUBRICATING OILS, PETROLEUM OILS, N.E.S.	0.6%	$30,135	1.1%
13	263.00	COTTON	0.5%	$25,274	0.9%
14	744.20	LIFTING, LOADING MACHINERY	0.6%	$23,345	0.9%
15	625.00	RUBBER TYRES, TUBES, ETC.	0.3%	$21,766	0.8%
16	651.00	TEXTILE YARN	0.2%	$21,731	0.8%
17	725.00	PAPER MILL MACHINERY	0.9%	$21,676	0.8%
18	745.00	NON-ELECTRIC MACHINERY, TOOLS, ETC.	0.3%	$21,094	0.8%
19	764.10	LINE TELEPHONE, ETC EQUIPMENT	0.4%	$19,641	0.7%
20	759.00	OFFICE, ADP MACHINE PARTS, ACCESSORIES	0.1%	$18,755	0.7%
21	582.00	CONDENSATION, POLYCONDENSATION AND POLYADDITION PRODUCTS	0.2%	$18,005	0.7%
22	515.60	HETERCYCLIC COMPOUNDS; NUCLEIC ACIDS	0.4%	$17,713	0.6%
23	267.11	REGENERATED FIBRES SUITABLE FOR SPINNING	3.7%	$16,519	0.6%
24	074.10	TEA	0.8%	$16,425	0.6%
25	562.16	UREA	1.3%	$15,933	0.6%
26	641.80	COATED PAPER, IN ROLLS OR SHEETS	0.4%	$15,896	0.6%
27	727.00	FOOD MACHINERY (NON-DOMESTIC)	0.8%	$15,117	0.6%
28	658.00	TEXTILE ARTICLES N.E.S.	0.3%	$14,603	0.5%
29	322.10	COAL, ANTHRACITE	1.0%	$13,957	0.5%
30	691.10	IRON/STEEL STRUCTURES, PARTS	0.3%	$13,823	0.5%
31	892.11	PRINTED BOOKS, PAMPHLETS	0.4%	$13,738	0.5%
32	882.20	FILM ROLLS (EXCL. DEVELOPED)	0.2%	$13,527	0.5%
33	792.90	AIRCRAFT PARTS N.E.S.	0.2%	$13,403	0.5%
34	288.00	NON-FERROUS BASE METAL, WASTE AND SCRAP	0.3%	$12,547	0.5%
35	533.00	PIGMENTS, PAINTS, ETC	0.3%	$12,424	0.5%
36	652.20	WOVEN COTTON, BLEACHED ETC.	0.2%	$11,959	0.4%
37	775.00	HOUSEHOLD APPLIANCES ETC.	0.1%	$11,908	0.4%
38	894.20	TOYS, INDOOR GAMES	0.2%	$11,861	0.4%
39	562.92	NITRO-PHOSPHOROUS FERTILISERS N.E.S.	1.0%	$11,646	0.4%
40	266.00	SYNTHETIC FIBRES SUITABLE FOR SPINNING	0.5%	$11,535	0.4%
41	334.30	GAS OILS	0.1%	$11,333	0.4%
42	274.00	SULPHUR	0.6%	$11,053	0.4%
43	678.20	IRON/STEEL SEAMLESS TUBES	0.3%	$11,042	0.4%
44	752.20	DIGITAL COMPUTERS	0.3%	$10,958	0.4%
45	872.00	MEDICAL INSTRUMENTS	0.3%	$10,644	0.4%
46	751.00	OFFICE MACHINES	0.2%	$10,603	0.4%
47	762.20	PORTABLE RADIO RECEIVERS	0.4%	$10,410	0.4%
48	678.30	IRON/STEEL TUBES, PIPES, N.E.S.	0.2%	$10,291	0.4%
49	071.11	COFFEE	0.1%	$10,288	0.4%
50	898.30	SOUND RECORDING TAPES, DISCS, (INCL. VIDEO TAPES)	0.2%	$10,217	0.4%

R = RESIDUAL

CHILE'S TOP 50 COMPETITIVE INDUSTRIES
IN TERMS OF WORLD IMPORT SHARE
1985

	COMMODITY	DESCRIPTION	WORLD IMPORT SHARE (%)	CHILE IMPORT VALUE ($US'000)	CHILE IMPORT SHARE (%)
1	267.11	REGENERATED FIBRES SUITABLE FOR SPINNING	3.7%	$16,519	0.6%
2	423.20	SOYA BEAN OIL	2.3%	$52,132	1.9%
3	562.16	UREA	1.3%	$15,933	0.6%
4	723.00	CIVIL ENGINEERING EQUIPMENT, ETC	1.1%	$129,883	4.7%
5	322.10	COAL, ANTHRACITE	1.0%	$13,957	0.5%
6	621.05	UNHARDENED VULCANISED RUBBER TUBES	1.0%	$7,654	0.3%
7	562.92	NITRO–PHOSPHOROUS FERTILISERS N.E.S.	1.0%	$11,646	0.4%
8	278.40	ASBESTOS	1.0%	$5,127	0.2%
9	771.11	LIQUID DIELECTRIC TRANSFORMERS	0.9%	$6,336	0.2%
10	725.00	PAPER MILL MACHINERY	0.9%	$21,676	0.8%
11	591.00	DISINFECTINTS, INSECTICIDES, ETC.	0.8%	$33,204	1.2%
12	727.00	FOOD MACHINERY (NON–DOMESTIC)	0.8%	$15,117	0.6%
13	684.23	ALUMINIUM FOIL	0.8%	$9,186	0.3%
14	074.10	TEA	0.8%	$16,425	0.6%
15	653.50	CONTINUOUS SYNTHETIC FABRICS (REGENERATED)	0.8%	$4,324	0.2%
16	778.11	PRIMARY BATTERIES, CELLS	0.7%	$6,715	0.2%
17	041.00	WHEAT, UNMILLED	0.7%	$67,839	2.5%
18	662.32	REFRACTORY BRICKS, ETC	0.7%	$5,203	0.2%
19	523.00	OTHER INORGANIC COMPOUNDS OF PRECIOUS METALS	0.6%	$31,846	1.2%
20	572.00	EXPLOSIVES, ETC	0.6%	$5,580	0.2%
21	274.00	SULPHUR	0.6%	$11,053	0.4%
22	334.50	LUBRICATING OILS, PETROLEUM OILS, N.E.S.	0.6%	$30,135	1.1%
23	744.20	LIFTING, LOADING MACHINERY	0.6%	$23,345	0.9%
24	663.80	MANUFACTURING ASBESTOS	0.6%	$2,383	0.1%
25	699.20	IRON/STEEL CHAINS AND PARTS	0.5%	$3,289	0.1%
26	778.12	ELECTRIC ACCUMULATORS	0.5%	$4,920	0.2%
27	895.00	PENS, PENCILS, FOUNTAIN PENS	0.5%	$5,599	0.2%
28	642.10	PAPER, ETC CONTAINERS	0.5%	$8,006	0.3%
29	266.00	SYNTHETIC FIBRES SUITABLE FOR SPINNING	0.5%	$11,535	0.4%
30	657.70	TEXTILES FOR MACHINERY	0.5%	$4,308	0.2%
31	263.00	COTTON	0.5%	$25,274	0.9%
32	551.00	ESSENTIAL OILS, PERFUMES, ETC	0.5%	$8,290	0.3%
33	713.90	PISTON ENGINE PARTS	0.5%	$32,427	1.2%
34	657.32	PLASTIC COATED TEXTILES	0.5%	$4,484	0.2%
35	323.20	COKE AND SEMI–COKE	0.5%	$5,945	0.2%
36	762.20	PORTABLE RADIO RECEIVERS	0.4%	$10,410	0.4%
37	584.00	CELLULOSE DERIVATIVES, ETC.	0.4%	$6,436	0.2%
38	641.80	COATED PAPER, IN ROLLS OR SHEETS	0.4%	$15,896	0.6%
39	696.00	CUTLERY	0.4%	$5,958	0.2%
40	592.20	ALBUMINOIDAL SUBSTANCES, GLUES	0.4%	$6,383	0.2%
41	598.00	CHEMICAL PRODUCTS, N.E.S. (EXCL. ANTI–KNOCK PREPARATIONS)	0.4%	$34,559	1.3%
42	598.20	ANTI–KNOCK PREPARATIONS	0.4%	$7,834	0.3%
43	764.10	LINE TELEPHONE, ETC EQUIPMENT	0.4%	$19,641	0.7%
44	892.11	PRINTED BOOKS, PAMPHLETS	0.4%	$13,738	0.5%
45	744.10	FORKLIFT TRUCKS, ETC PARTS	0.4%	$8,480	0.3%
46	693.11	IRON/STEEL CABLE, ROPE, ETC	0.4%	$3,699	0.1%
47	554.20	WASHING PREPARATIONS, ETC	0.4%	$7,419	0.3%
48	515.60	HETERCYCLIC COMPOUNDS; NUCLEIC ACIDS	0.4%	$17,713	0.6%
49	678.20	IRON/STEEL SEAMLESS TUBES	0.3%	$11,042	0.4%
50	233.10	SYNTHETIC RUBBER LATEX	0.3%	$9,426	0.3%

Top Fifty Swiss Industries in Terms of World Export Share, 1985

Industry	Share of Total World Exports	Export Value ($ millions)	Import Value ($ millions)	Share of Total Swiss Exports
Rough, unsorted diamonds	89.3	303,694	15,548	1.10
Nongold, noncurrent coins	46.3	140,561	24,491	0.51
Weaving machines (looms)	45.1	361,864	11,671	1.32
Platen printing presses	37.2	15,586	537	0.06
Watches	34.1	1,413,763	47,464	5.14
Vegetable alkaloids and derivatives	32.0	152,366	8,588	0.55
Amide compounds excluding urea	26.6	321,689	34,613	1.17
Textured yarn, containing polyamide	25.9	212,011	36,925	0.77
Synthetic organic dyestuffs	25.3	664,318	211,208	2.42
Looms, knitting machines and parts	24.1	181,030	38,107	0.66
Precious metals, jewelry, pearls	23.9	230,464	65,241	0.84
Provitamins and vitamins	21.9	191,703	74,055	0.70
Herbicides	20.6	275,488	24,629	1.00
Fans, blowers, and parts	19.2	180,650	87,975	0.66
Electromechanical hand tools	17.6	228,209	48,674	0.83
Clocks with watch movements	17.3	151,578	89,838	0.55
Mixed perfume substances	17.2	194,333	22,396	0.71
Surveying instruments	16.2	79,018	13,637	0.29
Parts of textile processing machines	16.0	115,147	21,044	0.42
Hearing, orthopedic aids	15.9	151,006	37,710	0.55
Metalcutting machine tools	15.3	424,457	55,467	1.54
Precious, semiprecious stones	15.2	168,344	210,450	0.61
Paper product manufacturing machines	14.1	120,311	16,221	0.44
Heterocyclic compounds	14.0	696,186	245,601	2.53
Textile extruding, processing machines	13.9	79,438	4,542	0.29
Rolled platinum, platinum metals	13.6	158,800	90,900	0.58
Lace, ribbons, tulle	13.2	138,244	22,026	0.50
Clocks, clock and watch parts	13.0	210,745	83,206	0.77
Medicaments containing hormones	12.3	961,084	246,227	3.50
Metal reaming, etc., machines	12.3	109,340	30,852	0.40

Industry	Share of Total World Exports	Export Value ($ millions)	Import Value ($ millions)	Share of Total Swiss Exports
Textiles for machinery	11.4	98,334	26,257	0.36
Meters and counters	11.1	52,761	9,145	0.19
Oxygen-function amino compounds	10.8	212,415	69,353	0.77
Typesetting, bookbinding machinery, parts	10.5	215,268	59,212	0.78
Hand paintings	10.3	169,447	121,838	0.62
Optical instruments	9.9	169,289	65,462	0.62
Oxygen-function acids, derivatives	9.6	84,020	25,579	0.31
Spinning, reeling, etc., machines	9.6	80,521	12,182	0.29
Cut, unset nonindustrial diamonds	9.6	585,833	909,277	2.13
Other metalworking machine tools	9.5	314,943	85,821	1.15
Steel, copper nails and nuts	9.4	66,542	12,083	0.24
Aluminum foil	9.3	115,170	26,552	0.42
Steam engines, turbines	9.1	117,114	12,752	0.43
Other organic, inorganic compounds	8.8	68,273	36,218	0.25
Refined petroleum products	8.7	58,789	5,533	0.21
Office supplies	8.6	65,019	25,245	0.24
Non-outboard marine piston engines	8.5	60,860	2,364	0.22
Glycosides, glands, sera	8.2	93,610	47,984	0.34
Precious metal jewelry	8.1	372,719	531,262	1.36
Pearls worked and unworked	8.0	27,662	256,697	0.10
TOTAL				42.44

NOTE: No import data are reported if import value is less than 0.3 percent of the total trade for 1985.

Percentage of Swiss Exports of Competitive Industries by Broad Cluster

UPSTREAM INDUSTRIES

Materials / Metals
Share of Country Exports: 3.8 (0.1)
Share of World Cluster Exports: 0.7 (-0.0)

Forest Products
Share of Country Exports: 1.0 (0.3)
Share of World Cluster Exports: 0.6 (0.1)

Petroleum / Chemicals
Share of Country Exports: 8.0 (1.2)
Share of World Cluster Exports: 0.6 (0.2)

Semiconductors / Computers
Share of Country Exports: 0 (0.1)
Share of World Cluster Exports: 0 (-0.1)

Share of Country Exports: 12.8 (1.8)
Share of World Cluster Exports: 0.6 (-0.1)

INDUSTRIAL AND SUPPORTING FUNCTIONS

Multiple Business
Share of Country Exports: 28.1 (1.6)
Share of World Cluster Exports: 6.4 (-1.4)

Transportation
Share of Country Exports: 2.1 (-0.4)
Share of World Cluster Exports: 0.5 (-0.1)

Power Generation & Distribution
Share of Country Exports: 4.4 (-0.6)
Share of World Cluster Exports: 2.9 (0.1)

Office
Share of Country Exports: 2.3 (0.1)
Share of World Cluster Exports: 3.8 (-0.8)

Telecommunications
Share of Country Exports: 0 (-0.1)
Share of World Cluster Exports: 0 (-1.0)

Defense
Share of Country Exports: 0 (-0.7)
Share of World Cluster Exports: 0 (-4.3)

Share of Country Exports: 36.9 (0.1)
Share of World Cluster Exports: 2.1 (-0.6)

FINAL CONSUMPTION GOODS AND SERVICES

Food / Beverage
Share of Country Exports: 4.7 (0.1)
Share of World Cluster Exports: 0.6 (-0.0)

Textiles / Apparel
Share of Country Exports: 11.0 (-1.0)
Share of World Cluster Exports: 2.4 (-0.7)

Housing / Household
Share of Country Exports: 0.9 (0.1)
Share of World Cluster Exports: 0.6 (0.1)

Health Care
Share of Country Exports: 7.0 (0.2)
Share of World Cluster Exports: 7.2 (-3.4)

Personal
Share of Country Exports: 8.0 (-2.2)
Share of World Cluster Exports: 4.4 (-1.9)

Entertainment / Leisure
Share of Country Exports: 0.5 (0.1)
Share of World Cluster Exports: 0.2 (0.1)

Share of Country Exports: 32.0 (-2.7)
Share of World Cluster Exports: 1.7 (-0.4)

■ Identifies broad sectors in which the nation's international competitive positions are related.
▨ Identifies broad sectors in which the nation's international competitive positions are related.

Note: Numbers in parentheses are changes between 1978 and 1985.
Exports are those of competitive industries, not all industries.

Top Fifty Swedish Industries in Terms of World Export Share, 1985

Industry	Share of Total World Exports	Export Value ($ millions)	Import Value ($ millions)	Share of Total Swedish Exports
Kraft paper, paperboard	41.7	545,304	13,676	1.79
Kraft liner	31.7	378,772	—	1.24
Sawn conifer lumber	26.4	888,112	10,168	2.92
Iron, steel powders	24.1	52.549	4,991	0.17
High carbon steel heavy plate	22.9	147,522	7,066	0.48
Unmilled cereals	20.8	63,369	—	0.21
Nonelectric power handtools	20.8	166,970	14,088	0.55
Unbleached soda, sulphate woodpulp	18.7	53,711	624	0.18
Bleached sulphite woodpulp	17.6	101,983	14,984	0.34
Centrifuges	17.2	230,085	33,056	0.76
Unbleached chemical sulphite woodpulp	16.4	14,457	846	0.05
Bleached soda, sulphate woodpulp	15.5	818,021	16,369	2.69
Plastic coated paper	15.0	159,384	35,919	0.52
Power hand tool parts	14.6	44,111	8,323	0.14
Aircraft 2,000–15,000 kg	14.3	155,499	14,949	0.51
Iron, steel wire	14.2	100,133	9,712	0.33
Prefabricated builders woodwork	14.0	155,515	17,074	0.51
Iron, steel hoop, strip	13.5	134,529	17,135	0.44
High carbon steel medium plate	13.3	40,917	4,689	0.13
Nonoutboard marine engines	13.1	93,544	22.132	0.31
Other coated paper in bulk	12.6	328,646	64,447	1.08
Unrefined coppers	12.2	97,945	—	0.32
Motor vehicle chassis	11.1	113,780	—	0.37
Iron, steel wire rod	10.7	86,053	13,703	0.28
Dairy, other agricultural machinery	10.6	86,659	10,450	0.28
Zinc ores concentrates	10.0	97,415	4	0.32
Blades, tips for tools	9.9	337,832	89,082	1.11
Other pulp and waste paper	9.8	123,529	23,136	0.41
Line telephone equipment	9.3	515,615	41,080	1.69
Rubber articles	9.3	68,522	16.095	0.23
Worked copper alloys	9.1	72,569	27,544	0.24
Newsprint	8.9	514,813	—	1.69
Other furniture, parts	8.8	73,466	33,311	0.24
Other paper and paperboard	8.7	318,969	47,718	1.05

Industry	Share of Total World Exports	Export Value ($ millions)	Import Value ($ millions)	Share of Total Swedish Exports
Uncombed discontinuous regenerated fiber	8.6	37,507	2.926	0.12
Raw mink skins	8.5	58,567	17,560	0.19
ADP equipment	8.4	565,341	655,235	1.86
High carbon steel bars	7.7	211.841	53,283	0.70
Iron ore agglomerates	7.7	142,702	74	0.47
Rough or split pulpwood	7.6	17,483	124,373	0.06
Paper mill machinery	7.6	124,793	116,673	0.41
Precious, semiprecious stones, pearls	7.4	25,826	4,706	0.08
Mineral crushing machinery	7.1	19,002	2,810	0.06
Uncoated writing paper	7.1	229,894	13,158	0.76
Centrifugal pumps	6.7	69,156	23,658	0.23
Ship derricks, cranes	6.6	70,167	32,784	0.23
Bread, biscuits, bakery products	6.4	13,186	6,859	0.04
Sinks, wash basins, bidets	6.2	24,759	4,260	0.08
Tankers	6.1	148,092	1,287	0.49
Textiles for machinery	6.1	52,440	47,841	0.17
TOTAL				29.53

NOTE: No import data are reported if import value is less than 0.3 percent of the total trade for 1985.

Percentage of Swedish Exports of Competitive Industries by Broad Cluster

UPSTREAM INDUSTRIES

Share of Country Exports: 35.1 (-1.9)
Share of World Cluster Exports: 1.7 (-0.4)

Materials / Metals
Share of Country Exports: 12.5 (-1.7)
Share of World Cluster Exports: 2.4 (-0.1)

Forest Products
Share of Country Exports: 17.9 (-2.5)
Share of World Cluster Exports: 10.5 (-1.3)

Petroleum / Chemicals
Share of Country Exports: 2.6 (0.5)
Share of World Cluster Exports: 0.2 (+0.0)

Semiconductors / Computers
Share of Country Exports: 2.1 (0.9)
Share of World Cluster Exports: 0.9 (-0.4)

INDUSTRIAL AND SUPPORTING FUNCTIONS

Share of Country Exports: 30.7 (-0.6)
Share of World Cluster Exports: 2.0 (-0.2)

Multiple Business
Share of Country Exports: 4.2 (+0.0)
Share of World Cluster Exports: 1.1 (-0.1)

Transportation
Share of Country Exports: 20.5 (-0.4)
Share of World Cluster Exports: 2.3 (-0.2)

Power Generation & Distribution
Share of Country Exports: 1.0 (-0.7)
Share of World Cluster Exports: 1.1 (-0.5)

Office
Share of Country Exports: 0.7 (-0.1)
Share of World Cluster Exports: 1.0 (-0.2)

Telecommunications
Share of Country Exports: 3.7 (0.6)
Share of World Cluster Exports: 5.5 (-1.5)

Defense
Share of Country Exports: 0.7 (-0.0)
Share of World Cluster Exports: 3.6 (-0.6)

FINAL CONSUMPTION GOODS AND SERVICES

Share of Country Exports: 10.6 (0.5)
Share of World Cluster Exports: 0.6 (0.1)

Food / Beverage
Share of Country Exports: 2.5 (0.1)
Share of World Cluster Exports: 0.4 (0.1)

Textiles / Apparel
Share of Country Exports: 1.1 (+0.0)
Share of World Cluster Exports: 0.3 (0)

Housing / Household
Share of Country Exports: 3.9 (+0.0)
Share of World Cluster Exports: 2.4 (0.2)

Health Care
Share of Country Exports: 2.5 (0.6)
Share of World Cluster Exports: 2.8 (0.1)

Personal
Share of Country Exports: 0.1 (+0.0)
Share of World Cluster Exports: 0.1 (+0.0)

Entertainment / Leisure
Share of Country Exports: 0.5 (-0.2)
Share of World Cluster Exports: 0.3 (-0.2)

Note: Numbers in parentheses are changes between 1978 and 1985. Exports are those of competitive industries, not all industries.

▨ Identifies broad sectors in which the nation's international competitive positions are related.

TOP 50 NEW ZEALAND INDUSTRIES IN TERMS OF
EXPORT VALUE
1987

	COMMODITY	DESCRIPTION	WORLD EXPORT SHARE (%)	R	NZ EXPORTS ($US'000)	NZ IMPORTS ($US'000)	TRADE BALANCE ($US'000)	NZ EXPORT SHARE (%)
1	011.20	SHEEP MEAT, FRESH, CHILLED OR FROZEN	42.8%		$578,643	$0	$578,643	8.1%
2	268.20	SHEEP/ LAMBS WOOL SCOURED NOT CARDED,	36.4%		$571,262	$798	$570,464	8.0%
3	011.12	BEEF, FRESH, CHILLED OR FROZEN, BONELESS	10.6%		$559,181	$366	$558,816	7.8%
4	268.10	SHEEP/LAMBS WOOL, GREASY	10.5%		$339,996	$548	$339,448	4.7%
5	684.10	ALUMINIUM AND ALUMINIUM ALLOYS, UNWROUGHT	3.3%		$311,797	$5,581	$306,216	4.3%
6	023.00	BUTTER	10.4%		$306,361	$15	$306,346	4.3%
7	057.98	KIWIFRUIT, FRESH	50.0%		$291,092	$0	$291,092	4.1%
8	211.70	LAMB AND SHEEP PELTS (WITHOUT WOOL)	14.3%	*	$277,802	$7,857	$269,945	3.9%
9	022.43	BUTTERMILK, WHOLE MILK IN GRANULES OR POWDER	11.6%		$203,155	$551	$202,605	2.8%
10	024.00	CHEESE	2.8%		$166,424	$3,280	$163,144	2.3%
11	592.22	ALBUMINOIDAL SUBSTANCES (CASEIN)	7.2%	*	$164,013	$4,804	$159,209	2.3%
12	036.00	SHELLFISH, NOT PRESERVED OR PREPARED	1.7%		$140,217	$4,908	$135,309	2.0%
13	034.40	FISH FILLETS, FROZEN	4.9%		$121,200	$921	$120,279	1.7%
14	022.42	SKIMMED MILK IN GRANULES OR POWDER	6.0%		$120,199	$27	$120,172	1.7%
15	034.20	FISH, FROZEN	3.2%		$89,522	$423	$89,099	1.2%
16	001.50	LIVE HORSES (RACING)	4.1%		$83,543	$50,771	$32,772	1.2%
17	251.20	MECHANICAL WOOD PULP, WASTE PAPER	4.5%	*	$82,293	$2	$82,291	1.1%
18	057.40	FRESH APPLES	4.6%		$73,460	$1,367	$72,093	1.0%
19	251.71	CHEMICAL WOOD PULP, SODA OR SULPHATE, UNBLEACHED	14.4%		$67,112	$0	$67,112	0.9%
20	641.10	NEWSPRINT	0.8%		$61,837	$14,356	$47,481	0.9%
21	611.40	BOVINE AND EQUINE LEATHER	1.6%		$59,983	$3,899	$56,084	0.8%
22	291.93	SAUSAGE CASINGS	8.6%		$59,067	$2,440	$56,627	0.8%
23	651.26	TEXTILE YARN, OTHER THAN SILK OR COTTON (WOOLLEN)	3.2%	*	$56,895	$2,223	$54,672	0.8%
24	054.51	OTHER VEGETABLES, FRESH OR PRESERVED (ONIONS, PEAS, CORN)	0.8%	*	$55,667	$10,735	$44,932	0.8%
25	211.10	BOVINE AND EQUINE HIDES	1.8%		$55,664	$0	$55,664	0.8%
26	011.60	EDIBLE OFFALS	6.3%		$52,509	$104	$52,405	0.7%
27	641.61	HARDBOARD, PAPER AND PAPERBOARD NES	0.9%		$51,441	$13,800	$37,641	0.7%
28	659.42	WOOL CARPETS AND LINOLEUMS	2.5%		$51,346	$9,866	$41,480	0.7%
29	611.50	CALF, SHEEP AND OTHER LEATHER (LAMB SKIN)	1.5%	*	$43,348	$3,623	$39,725	0.6%
30	411.32	TALLOW	5.9%		$39,113	$245	$38,868	0.5%
31	634.92	LAMINATED OR SIMPLY SHAPED WOOD PRODUCTS	3.5%	*	$35,706	$858	$34,848	0.5%
32	251.72	CHEMICAL WOOD PULP, SODA OR SULPHATE, BLEACHED	0.4%		$35,292	$2,295	$32,997	0.5%
33	512.11	ACYCLIC HYDROCARBONS (METHANOL)	0.8%	*	$33,419	$9,132	$24,287	0.5%
34	011.11	BEEF, FRESH, CHILLED OR FROZEN, WITH BONE IN	0.7%		$32,784	$28	$32,755	0.5%
35	247.11	SAWLOGS AND VENEER LOGS OF CONIFERS, ROUGH	1.6%		$32,732	$0	$32,732	0.5%
36	248.21	WOOD OF CONIFERS, SAWN LENGTHWISE, SLICED OR PEELED	0.6%		$30,544	$11,356	$19,188	0.4%
37	699.79	BASE METAL MANUFACTURES NES (ROOF-TILES ETC)	0.3%	*	$28,248	$36,527	($8,279)	0.4%
38	892.89	POSTCARDS, PRINTED MATTER, NES	0.9%	*	$27,587	$14,265	$13,322	0.4%
39	081.41	ANIMAL MEALS OF MEAT OR OFFAL	12.6%		$27,523	$8	$27,515	0.4%
40	248.22	WOOD OF CONFERS, PLANED, TONGUED, GROOVED ETC	0.6%		$27,247	$315	$26,932	0.4%
41	034.10	FISH, LIVE OR DEAD, FRESH OR CHILLED	1.0%		$26,528	$143	$26,385	0.4%
42	054.20	DRIED BEANS, PEAS, LENTILS, OTHER LEGUMES	1.5%		$25,618	$2,330	$23,288	0.4%
43	848.31	ARTICLES OF FURSKIN (SHEEPSKIN RUGS, JACKETS)	1.2%		$24,892	$312	$24,580	0.3%
44	553.00	PERFUMERY, COSMETICS, TOILET PREPARATIONS	0.4%		$24,082	$24,666	($584)	0.3%
45	058.99	FRUIT AND NUTS, PREPARED OR PRESERVED, NES	0.7%	*	$22,147	$13,375	$8,772	0.3%
46	057.94	OTHER FRUIT, FRESH OR DRIED (NOT INC. KIWIFRUIT)	0.6%	*	$20,509	$10,594	$9,915	0.3%
47	292.50	SEEDS, FRUIT & SPORES, NES, FOR SOWING	1.6%		$19,703	$5,122	$14,581	0.3%
-48	672.51	IRON OR STEEL BLOOMS, BILLETS, STEEL BARS, PIECES	0.8%		$19,322	$35	$19,287	0.3%
49	641.32	SACK KRAFT PAPER, KRAFT PAPER AND PAPERBOARD	1.0%	*	$19,236	$569	$18,667	0.3%
50	073.00	CHOCOLATE AND OTHER PREPARATIONS CONTAINING COCOA	0.6%		$18,064	$8,549	$9,515	0.3%

# SOURCE : NEW ZEALAND KIWIFRUIT MARKETING BOARD
R = RESIDUAL

NEW ZEALAND'S TOP 50 COMPETITIVE INDUSTRIES
IN TERMS OF WORLD EXPORT SHARE
1987

	COMMODITY	DESCRIPTION	WORLD EXPORT SHARE (%)	R	NZ EXPORTS ($US'000)	NZ IMPORTS ($US'000)	TRADE BALANCE ($US'000)	NZ EXPORT SHARE (%)
1	057.98	KIWIFRUIT, FRESH	#50.0%		$291,092	$0	$291,092	4.1%
2	011.20	SHEEP MEAT, FRESH, CHILLED OR FROZEN	42.8%		$579,643	$0	$578,643	8.1%
3	268.20	SHEEP/LAMBS WOOL SCOURED NOT CARDED.	36.4%		$571,262	$798	$570,464	8.0%
4	251.71	CHEMICAL WOOD PULP, SODA OR SULPHATE, UNBLEACHED	14.4%		$67,112	$0	$67,112	0.9%
5	211.70	LAMB AND SHEEP PELTS (WITHOUT WOOL)	14.3%	*	$277,802	$7,857	$269,945	3.9%
6	081.41	ANIMAL MEALS OF MEAT OR OFFAL	12.6%		$27,523	$8	$27,515	0.4%
7	022.43	BUTTERMILK, WHOLE MILK IN GRANULES OR POWDER	11.6%		$203,155	$551	$202,605	2.8%
8	011.12	BEEF, FRESH, CHILLED OR FROZEN, BONELESS	10.6%		$559,181	$366	$558,816	7.8%
9	268.10	SHEEP/LAMBS WOOL, GREASY	10.5%		$339,996	$548	$339,448	4.7%
10	023.00	BUTTER	10.4%		$306,361	$15	$306,346	4.3%
11	291.93	SAUSAGE CASINGS	8.6%		$59,067	$2,440	$56,627	0.8%
12	592.22	ALBUMINOIDAL SUBSTANCES (CASEIN)	7.2%	*	$164,013	$4,804	$159,209	2.3%
13	011.60	EDIBLE OFFALS	6.3%		$52,509	$104	$52,405	0.7%
14	022.42	SKIMMED MILK IN GRANULES OR POWDER	6.0%		$120,199	$27	$120,172	1.7%
15	411.32	TALLOW	5.9%		$39,113	$245	$38,868	0.5%
16	034.40	FISH FILLETS, FROZEN	4.9%		$121,200	$921	$120,279	1.7%
17	057.40	FRESH APPLES	4.6%		$73,460	$1,367	$72,093	1.0%
18	251.20	MECHANICAL WOOD PULP, WASTE PAPER	4.5%	*	$82,293	$2	$82,291	1.1%
19	001.50	LIVE HORSES (RACING)	4.1%		$83,543	$50,771	$32,772	1.2%
20	634.92	LAMINATED OR SIMPLY SHAPED WOOD PRODUCTS	3.5%	*	$35,706	$858	$34,848	0.5%
21	684.10	ALUMINIUM AND ALUMINIUM ALLOYS, UNWROUGHT	3.3%		$311,797	$5,581	$306,216	4.3%
22	651.26	TEXTILE YARN, OTHER THAN SILK OR COTTON (WOOLLEN)	3.2%	*	$56,895	$2,223	$54,672	0.8%
23	034.20	FISH, FROZEN	3.2%		$89,522	$423	$89,099	1.2%
24	011.89	MEAT AND EDIBLE OFFALS (VENISON)	3.0%	*	$16,252	$70	$16,182	0.2%
25	024.00	CHEESE	2.8%		$166,424	$3,280	$163,144	2.3%
26	659.42	WOOL CARPETS AND LINOLEUMS	2.5%	*	$51,346	$9,866	$41,480	0.7%
27	091.49	MARGARINE, IMITATION LARD AND OTHER EDIBLE FATS	2.4%		$11,610	$489	$11,121	0.2%
28	001.11	BREEDING CATTLE (DAIRY)	2.4%		$8,300	$301	$7,998	0.1%
29	292.72	FRESH/DRIED FOLIAGE	2.0%		$4,384	$83	$4,301	0.1%
30	211.10	BOVINE AND EQUINE HIDES	1.8%		$55,664	$0	$55,664	0.8%
31	036.00	SHELLFISH, NOT PRESERVED OR PREPARED	1.7%		$140,217	$4,908	$135,309	2.0%
32	292.50	SEEDS, FRUIT & SPORES, NES, FOR SOWING	1.6%		$19,703	$5,122	$14,581	0.3%
33	291.16	CRUDE ANIMAL MATERIALS, NOT SAUSAGE CASINGS (HORNS, ANTLERS)	1.6%	*	$17,226	$3,960	$13,266	0.2%
34	247.11	SAWLOGS AND VENEER LOGS OF CONIFERS, ROUGH	1.6%		$32,732	$0	$32,732	0.5%
35	611.40	BOVINE AND EQUINE LEATHER	1.6%		$59,983	$3,899	$56,084	0.8%
36	611.50	CALF, SHEEP AND OTHER LEATHER (LAMB SKIN)	1.5%	*	$43,348	$3,623	$39,725	0.6%
37	054.20	DRIED BEANS, PEAS, LENTILS, OTHER LEGUMES	1.5%		$25,618	$2,330	$23,288	0.4%
38	212.09	FURSKINS, RAW, NOT MINK (OPUSSUM)	1.4%		$13,594	$424	$13,171	0.2%
39	775.22	DEEP FREEZERS OF HOUSEHOLD TYPE	1.4%		$6,669	$974	$5,696	0.1%
40	562.16	UREA	1.4%		$9,476	$39	$9,438	0.1%
41	848.31	ARTICLES OF FURSKIN (SHEEPSKIN RUGS, JACKETS)	1.2%		$24,892	$312	$24,580	0.3%
42	112.49	SPIRITS & DISTILLED ALCOHOLIC BEVERAGES.	1.1%		$14,239	$12,892	$1,347	0.2%
43	034.10	FISH, LIVE OR DEAD, FRESH OR CHILLED	1.0%		$26,528	$143	$26,385	0.4%
44	721.39	DAIRY AND OTHER AGRICULTURAL MACHINERY	1.0%	*	$11,226	$5,254	$5,972	0.2%
45	641.32	SACK KRAFT PAPER, KRAFT PAPER AND PAPERBOARD	1.0%		$19,236	$569	$18,667	0.3%
46	892.89	POSTCARDS, PRINTED MATTER, NES	0.9%	*	$27,587	$14,265	$13,322	0.4%
47	697.32	DOMESTIC HEATING, COOKING APPLIANCES (WOOD BURNERS)	0.9%	*	$11,985	$7,331	$4,654	0.2%
48	541.62	GLYCOSIDES, GLANDS AND EXTRACTS	0.9%	*	$14,410	$5,487	$8,923	0.2%
49	641.61	HARDBOARD, PAPER AND PAPERBOARD NES	0.9%	*	$51,441	$13,800	$37,641	0.7%
50	058.57	FRUIT OR VEGETABLE JUICE, NOT ORANGE (APPLE JUICE)	0.9%	*	$11,317	$6,202	$5,115	0.2%

# SOURCE : NEW ZEALAND KIWIFRUIT MARKETING BOARD
R = RESIDUAL

AGGREGATION OF COMPETITIVE INDUSTRIES - 1987

CODE INDUSTRY	WORLD EXPORT SHARE %	R	NZ EXPORT VALUE $US'000	NZ IMPORT VALUE $US'000	TRADE BALANCE $US'000	NZ EXPORT SHARE %	TOTAL NZ EXPORTS $US'000	WORLD EXPORT VALUE $US'000
001.11 PURE-BRED BOVINE ANIMALS FOR BREEDING	2.4%	◆	8300	301	7998	0.1%	7179408	346697
001.50 RACE HORSES AND LIVE SHEEP	4.1%	◆	83543	50771	32772	1.2%	7179408	2038760
TOTAL LIVE ANIMALS	3.9%		91843	51073	40770	1.3%	7179408	2385457
011.11 BEEF, FRESH, CHILLED OR FROZEN, WITH BONE IN	0.7%		32784	28	32755	0.5%	7179408	4493548
011.12 BEEF, FRESH, CHILLED OR FROZEN, BONELESS	10.6%		559181	366	558816	7.8%	7179408	5292771
011.20 MEAT OF SHEEP	42.8%		578643	0	578643	8.1%	7179408	1352365
011.60 EDIBLE OFFALS	6.3%		52509	104	52405	0.7%	7179408	837391
011.89 VENISON	3.0%	◆	16252	70	16182	0.2%	7179408	538680
TOTAL MEAT	9.9%		1239368	568	1238800	17.3%	7179408	12514755
014.90 CANNED MEAT	0.4%	◆	10725	2344	8381	0.1%	7179408	2753284
022.30 FRESH MILK, CREAM, YOGHURT, SKIMMED MILK, ETC	0.6%		8053	0	8053	0.1%	7179408	1296632
022.42 SKIMMED MILK IN GRANULES OR POWDER	6.0%		120199	27	120172	1.7%	7179408	2010925
022.43 BUTTERMILK, WHOLE MILK IN GRANULES OR POWDER	11.6%		203155	551	202605	2.8%	7179408	1746984
023.00 BUTTER	10.4%		306361	15	306346	4.3%	7179408	2946582
024.00 CHEESE	2.8%		166424	3280	163144	2.3%	7179408	5856272
592.22 CASEIN, ALBUMINS ETC	7.2%	◆	164013	4804	159209	2.3%	7179408	2270638
TOTAL DAIRY PRODUCTS AND CASEIN	6.0%		968205	8676	959529	13.5%	7179408	16128033
034.10 FISH, FRESH (LIVE OR DEAD) OR CHILLED	1.0%		26528	143	26385	0.4%	7179408	2699464
034.20 FISH, FROZEN	3.2%		89522	423	89099	1.2%	7179408	2826150
034.30 FISH FILLETS, FRESH OR CHILLED	0.4%		5716	22	5695	0.1%	7179408	1511538
034.40 FISH FILLETS, FROZEN	4.9%		121200	921	120279	1.7%	7179408	2480718
036.00 SHELLFISH, NOT PRESERVED OR PREPARED	1.7%		140217	4908	135309	2.0%	7179408	8177890
037.10 FISH FINGERS, FISH DINNERS	0.4%		9441	17964	-8523	0.1%	7179408	2689278
037.20 SHELLFISH, PREPARED OR PRESERVED	0.5%		7969	5044	2925	0.1%	7179408	1556516
TOTAL FISH	1.8%		400594	29425	371169	5.6%	7179408	21941554
043.00 BARLEY, UNMILLED	0.5%		10399	53	10347	0.1%	7179408	2224379
048.42 PASTRY, BISCUITS, CAKES & OTHER FINE	0.8%		17837	5206	12631	0.2%	7179408	2278607
054.20 DRIED PEAS	1.5%		25618	2330	23288	0.4%	7179408	1684761
054.51 ONIONS, PEAS, CORN, SQUASH	0.8%	◆	55667	10735	44932	0.8%	7179408	6589931
056.59 ASPARAGUS, CORN, PRESERVED	0.3%	◆	11584	7007	4577	0.2%	7179408	3745143
TOTAL VEGETABLES	0.8%		92869	20072	72797	1.3%	7179408	12019835

AGGREGATION OF COMPETITIVE INDUSTRIES - 1987

057.98 KIWIFRUIT	50.0%	E	291092	10594	280497	4.1%	7179408	
057.40 APPLES, FRESH, WHOLE OR PROCESSED	4.6%		73460	1367	72093	1.0%	7179408	1590623
057.94 FRESH STONEFRUIT, BERRYFRUIT, KIWIFRUIT	8.0%	*	311601	10594	301007	4.3%	7179408	3895441
058.57 JUICE OF ANY OTHER FRUIT OR VEGETABLE	0.9%	*	11317	6202	5115	0.2%	7179408	1304766
058.99 FRUIT AND NUTS, PREPARED OR PRESERVED, NES	0.7%	*	22147	13375	8772	0.3%	7179408	3224396
TOTAL FRUIT, INCL. JUICE	4.2%		418525	31539	386987	5.8%	7179408	10015226
073.00 CHOCOLATE AND OTHER PREPARATIONS CONTAINING COCOA	0.6%		18064	8549	9515	0.3%	7179408	2968115
081.41 ANIMAL MEALS OF MEAT OR OFFAL	12.6%		27523	8	27515	0.4%	7179408	218777
081.99 ANIMAL FOOD PREPARATIONS	0.3%	*	14831	7174	7657	0.2%	7179408	5142592
TOTAL ANIMAL FEED	0.8%		42354	7182	35172	0.6%	7179408	5361369
091.49 MARGARINE, IMITATION LARD AND OTHER EDIBLE FATS	2.4%	*	11610	489	11121	0.2%	7179408	477094
112.30 BEER MADE FROM MALT	0.3%		6570	6712	-142	0.1%	7179408	1937585
112.49 SPIRITS & DISTILLED ALCOHOLIC BEVERAGES,	1.1%		14239	12892	1347	0.2%	7179408	1344832
TOTAL ALCOHOLIC BEVERAGES	0.6%		20809	19604	1205	0.3%	7179408	3282417
211.10 BOVINE AND EQUINE HIDES	1.8%		55664	0	55664	0.8%	7179408	3039570
211.70 LAMB AND SHEEP PELTS (WITHOUT WOOL)	14.3%	*	277802	7857	269945	3.9%	7179408	1936895
212.09 OPOSSUM SKINS	1.4%		13594	424	13171	0.2%	7179408	941937
TOTAL HIDES AND SKINS	5.9%		347061	8281	338779	4.8%	7179408	5918402
247.11 SAWLOGS AND VENEER LOGS OF CONIFERS, ROUGH	1.6%		32732	0	32732	0.5%	7179408	2096460
248.21 WOOD OF CONIFERS, SAWN LENGTHWISE, SLICED OR PEELED	0.6%		30544	11356	19188	0.4%	7179408	5143926
248.22 WOOD OF CONFERS, PLANED, TONGUED, GROOVED ETC	0.6%		27247	315	26932	0.4%	7179408	4209912
TOTAL WOOD	0.8%		90523	11671	78852	1.3%	7179408	11450298
251.20 MECHANICAL WOOD PULP, WASTE PAPER	4.5%	*	82293	2	82291	1.1%	7179408	1827738
251.71 CHEMICAL WOOD PULP, SODA OR SULPHATE, UNBLEACHED	14.4%		67112	0	67112	0.9%	7179408	466381
251.72 CHEMICAL WOOD PULP, SODA OR SULPHATE, BLEACHED	0.4%		35292	2295	32997	0.5%	7179408	9039584
TOTAL PULP AND WASTEPAPER	1.6%		184697	2297	182400	2.6%	7179408	11333703
268.10 SHEEP/LAMBS WOOL, GREASY	10.5%		339996	548	339448	4.7%	7179408	3231336
268.20 SHEEP/ LAMBS WOOL SCOURED NOT CARDED,	36.4%		571262	798	570464	8.0%	7179408	1570169
268.30 FINE ANIMAL HAIR	0.8%	*	7784		7784	0.1%	7179408	925679
TOTAL WOOL	16.0%		919042	1346	917696	12.8%	7179408	5727184
278.21 POTTERY CLAY	0.7%		5881	3850	2031	0.1%	7179408	880069
281.50 IRON ORE AND CONCENTRATES, NOT AGGLOMERATED	0.3%		15329	0	15329	0.2%	7179408	4437251
288.23 ALUMINIUM WASTE AND SCRAP	0.6%	*	9000	1083	7917	0.1%	7179408	1632759
TOTAL ORES AND SCRAP	0.4%		24329	1083	23246	0.3%	7179408	6070010

AGGREGATION OF COMPETITIVE INDUSTRIES - 1987

291.16 ANIMAL MATERIALS (HORNS, ANTLERS, VELVET, ETC)	1.6%	*	17226	3960	13266	0.2%	7179408	1091262
291.93 SAUSAGE CASINGS	8.6%		59067	2440	56627	0.8%	7179408	687511
TOTAL CRUDE ANIMAL MATERIALS	4.3%		76293	6400	69893	1.1%	7179408	1778773
292.50 SEEDS, FRUIT & SPORES, NES, FOR SOWING	1.6%		19703	5122	14581	0.3%	7179408	1201268
292.71 CUT FLOWERS & FLOWER BUDS FOR BOUQUETS	0.4%		7913	386	7527	0.1%	7179408	2097779
292.72 FRESH/DRIED-FOLIAGE	2.0%		4384	83	4301	0.1%	7179408	215876
TOTAL SEEDS, FLOWERS AND FOLIAGE	0.9%		32000	5591	26409	0.4%	7179408	3514923
322.20 COAL, BITUMINOUS NOT AGGLOMERATED	0.3%	*	14696	25	14671	0.2%	7179408	5493120
411.32 TALLOW	5.9%		39113	245	38868	0.5%	7179408	663374
512.11 METHYL ALCOHOL (METHANOL)	0.8%	*	33419	9132	24287	0.5%	7179408	4110320
541.62 GLYCOSIDES, GLANDS AND EXTRACTS	0.9%	*	14410	5487	8923	0.2%	7179408	1586879
553.00 PERFUMERY, COSMETICS, TOILET PREPARATIONS	0.4%		24082	24666	-584	0.3%	7179408	5542158
554.10 CLEANSING SOAPS, POLISHES AND CREAMS	0.5%		4790	2413	2377	0.1%	7179408	950581
562.16 UREA	1.4%		9476	39	9438	0.1%	7179408	699371
611.40 BOVINE LEATHER	1.6%		59983	3899	56084	. 0.8%	7179408	3856392
611.50 LAMB SKIN LEATHER	1.5%	*	43348	3623	39725	0.6%	7179408	2813382
613.00 FURSKINS, TANNED OR DRESSED	0.4%		7691	1901	5790	0.1%	7179408	1770751
TOTAL LEATHER	1.3%		111021	9423	101599	1.5%	7179408	8440525
634.32 RECONSTITUTED WOOD	0.6%		8557	263	8294	0.1%	7179408	1458140
634.92 WOOD, SIMPLY SHAPED (HOOPWOOD ETC)	3.5%	*	35706	858	34848	0.5%	7179408	1023944
635.30 BUILDERS' WOODWORK, PREFABRICATED	0.3%		5941	1109	4832	0.1%	7179408	1939145
TOTAL WOOD MANUFACTURES	1.1%		50204	2230	47975	0.7%	7179408	4421229
641.10 NEWSPRINT	0.8%		61837	14356	47481	0.9%	7179408	7458804
641.31 KRAFT LINER, IN ROLLS OR SHEETS	0.6%		12182	3153	9028	0.2%	7179408	2002159
641.32 SACK KRAFT PAPER, PAPERBOARD	1.0%	*	19236	569	18667	0.3%	7179408	2024421
641.61 HARDBOARD, PAPER AND PAPERBOARD NES	0.9%		51441	13800	37641	0.7%	7179408	5833350
642.10 PAPER BAGS, CONTAINERS	0.3%		8583	5803	2780	0.1%	7179408	2759059
TOTAL PAPER AND PAPERBOARD	0.8%		153279	37683	115596	2.1%	7179408	20077793
651.26 WOOLLEN YARN	3.2%	*	56895	2223	54672	0.8%	7179408	1766001
658.99 TEXTILE ARTICLES NES (EXCLUDING HOUSEHOLD LINEN)	0.4%		9442	10621	-1179	0.1%	7179408	2224647
659.42 WOOLLEN CARPETS	2.5%	*	51346	9866	41480	0.7%	7179408	2016387
TOTAL TEXTILES AND PRODUCTS	2.0%		117683	22710	94973	1.6%	7179408	6007035
663.32 ARTIFICIAL STONE	0.3%		1961		1961	0.0%	7179408	623220
665.11 GLASS BOTTLES	0.3%		3665		3665	0.1%	7179408	1243929
672.51 IRON OR STEEL BLOOMS, BILLETS, STEEL BARS, PIECES	0.8%		19322	35	19287	0.3%	7179408	2509516
684.10 ALUMINIUM AND ALUMINIUM ALLOYS, UNWROUGHT	3.3%		311797	5581	306216	4.3%	7179408	9555863

AGGREGATION OF COMPETITIVE INDUSTRIES - 1987

684.21 ALUMINIUM AND ALUMINIUM ALLOYS,BARS, RODS, ETC	0.3%	6461	9291	-2830	0.1%	7179408	2293989
684.23 ALUMINIUM FOIL OF A THICKNESS NOT EXCEEDING 0.002mm	0.5%	11256	10431	825	0.2%	7179408	2060030
691.20 STRUCTURES, PARTS OF ALUMINIUM	0.3%	3779		3779	0.1%	7179408	1357598
TOTAL ALUMINIUM	2.2%	333293	25303	307990	4.6%	7179408	15267480
697.32 DOMESTIC HEATING, COOKING APPARATUS	0.9% •	11985	7331	4654	0.2%	7179408	1273451
699.79 BASE METAL MANUFACTURES NES (ROOFTILES ETC)	0.3% •	28248	36527	-8279	0.4%	7179408	10622064
721.21 LAWN MOWERS	0.4%	7129		7129	0.1%	7179408	1847747
721.39 DAIRY MACHINERY PARTS	1.0% •	11226	5254	5972	0.2%	7179408	1174925
724.42 WOOL SCOURING MACHINERY	0.8% •	9486	522	8964	0.1%	7179408	1219064
TOTAL AGRICULTURAL MACHINERY	0.7%	27841	5776	22065	0.4%	7179408	4241736
744.22 SHIPS' DERRICKS, CRANES	0.7%	8212	11969	-3757	0.1%	7179408	1258001
775.21 REFRIGERATORS WITH/OUT FREEZERS OF HOUSEHOLD TYPE	0.7%	14103	4038	10065	0.2%	7179408	1967481
775.22 DEEP FREEZERS OF HOUSEHOLD TYPE	1.4%	6669	974	5696	0.1%	7179408	474041
TOTAL DOMESTIC REFRIGERATORS AND FREEZERS	0.9%	20772	5011	15760	0.3%	7179408	2441522
778.32 ELECTRIC LIGHTING,SIGNALLING EQUIPMENT,	0.4%	6510	10536	-4026	0.1%	7179408	1811662
793.21 YACHTS	0.5%	8664	11122	-2458	0.1%	7179408	1851945
821.92 FURNITURE OF WOOD	0.3%	16528	3930	12598	0.2%	7179408	6358848
848.31 SHEEPSKIN RUGS, JACKETS AND COATS	1.2%	24892	312	24580	0.3%	7179408	2024878
892.89 POSTCARDS, PRINTED MATTER, NES	0.9% •	27587	14265	13322	0.4%	7179408	2904087
893.10 PLASTIC BAGS, SACHETS	0.3%	11029	7776	3253	0.2%	7179408	3580507

CLUSTERS OF INTERNATIONALLY COMPETITIVE NZ INDUSTRIES 1987

	FOOD/BEVERAGES		**TEXTILES/APPAREL**	**HOUSING/HOUSEHOLD**	**HEALTH CARE**
Primary Goods:	*Basic Food:* **BOVINE SPECIES, LIVE,** **BREEDING*** BEEF WITH BONE IN **BEEF, BONELESS** **SHEEP MEAT** **EDIBLE OFFAL** **VENISON*** FRESH MILK & CREAM FISH, FRESH, CHILLED, excl FILLET **FISH, FROZEN, excl Fillet** Fish Fillet, fresh, chilled **FISH FILLET, FROZEN** **SHELLFISH, FROZEN** **DRIED PEAS** ONIONS, PEAS, CORN & SQUASH* **APPLES** **KIWIFRUIT** **FRESH STONE & BERRY** **FRUITS**	*Processed Food:* Canned Meat **SKIMMED MILK POWDER** **<1.5% FAT** **BUTTERMILK >1.5% FAT** **BUTTER** **CHEESE** Shellfish, Prepared Fish Fingers, Fish Dinners PASTRY, CAKES, ETC Asparagus, Corn (Preserved)* PRESERVED FRUIT, JAM* CHOCOLATE & PRODUCTS *Beverages:* FRUIT OR VEGETABLE JUICE* Beer ALCOHOLIC SPIRITS *Edible Oils:* MARGARINE TALLOW	**SHEEP & LAMB LEATHER*** Furskins, tanned or dressed Textile Articles NES* **SHEEPSKIN RUGS, JACKETS,** **COATS**	*Furniture:* **CARPETS, LINOLEUMS*** Wood Furniture NES *Appliances:* DOMESTIC HEATING, COOKING APP* REFRIGERATORS, DOMESTIC **DEEP FREEZERS** *Other Household Products:* Soaps, Polishes & Creams Lawn Mowers* *Builders Woodwork:* Builders' Woodwork, Prefabricated	*Pharmaceuticals:* GLYCOSIDES, GLANDS & EXTRACTS*
Machinery:	DAIRY MACHINERY PARTS*		WOOL SCOURING MACHINERY*		
Specialty Inputs:	Unmilled Barley **MEAT MEAL FODDER** **Animal Food Preparations** **ANIMAL MATERIALS** **(HORNS, ANTLERS, VELVET,** **ETC)*** **SAUSAGE-CASINGS** **SEEDS FOR PLANTING** **UREA** **CASEIN, ALBUMINS, ETC** Glass Bottles Paper Containers, Bags		**BOVINE EQUINE HIDES, RAW** **LAMB, SHEEP PELTS** **OPPOSUM SKINS** **GREASY WOOL** **WOOL, SCOURED** **EQUINE, BOVINE, LEATHER** **WOOLLEN YARN*** FINE ANIMAL HAIR*	POTTERY CLAY Artificial Stone	
Services	AGRICULTURAL CONTRACTING† ANIMAL CONTROL SYSTEMS† GENETIC MANAGEMENT SYSTEMS†				

CLUSTERS OF INTERNATIONALLY COMPETITIVE NZ INDUSTRIES 1987

	TRANSPORTATION	**POWER GENERATION** **& DISTRIBUTION**	**OFFICE PRODUCTS** POSTCARDS, PRINTED MATTER NES*	**TELECOMMUNICATION**	**DEFENCE**
Primary Goods:	*Vehicle Equipment:* **MOBILE CRANES** Electric Lighting Signalling Equipment				
Machinery:					
Specialty Inputs:					
Services					

KEY:	BOLD CAPS:	1.2% world export share or above	†	Added due to in-country
	CAPS	0.6% world export share or higher, but less than 1.2%		research
	Mixed Caps	0.3% world export share or higher, but less than 0.6% share		
	*	Calculated Residuals		

CLUSTERS OF INTERNATIONALLY COMPETITIVE NZ INDUSTRIES 1987

	MATERIALS/ METALS	FOREST PRODUCTS	PETROLEUM/ CHEMICALS	SEMICONDUCTORS/ COMPUTERS	MULTIPLE BUSINESS
Primary Goods:	*Iron & Steel:* IRON, STEEL BLOOMS	*Wood Products:* SAWLOGS, CONIFER, ROUGH SAWN CONIFER TIMBER	*Organic:* METHANOL		
	Fabricated Iron & Steel:	SHAPED CONIFER TIMBER RECONSTITUTED WOOD WOODEN BEADINGS, MOULDINGS*	*Polymers:* Plastic Bags, Sachets		
	Non-Ferrous Metals: UNWROUGHT ALUMINIUM ALLOYS Aluminium Bars, Rods Aluminium Foil	*Pulp:* MECHANICAL WOOD PULP, WASTEPAPER* CHEMICAL WOOD PULP, UNBLEACHED Chemical Wood Pulp, Bleached			
	ALUMINIUM WASTE AND SCRAP*				
	Metal Manufacturers: Structures, Parts Of Aluminium Base Metal Mnfrs NES (Rooftiles)*	*Paper:* KRAFTLINER, BULK SACK KRAFT PAPER, PAPERBOARD* HARDBOARD, PAPER & PAPERBOARD NES*			
Machinery					
Specialty Inputs	Iron Ores, Concentrates, Not Aggl. Coal				
Services				INSURANCE SOFTWARE † PROGRAMMER PRODUCTIVITY TOOLS†	CONSTRUCTION TOURISM† ENGINEERING CONSULTING† INVESTMENT MANAGEMENT† EDUCATION SERVICES†

CLUSTERS OF INTERNATIONALLY COMPETITIVE NZ INDUSTRIES 1987

	PERSONAL	ENTERTAINMENT/LEISURE
Primary Goods:	Perfumery, Cosmetics	Cut Flowers FOLIAGE Yachts RACEHORSES/LIVE SHEEP*
Machinery:		
Specialty Inputs:		NEWSPRINT

KEY:	BOLD CAPS:	1.2% world export share or above	† Added due to in-country research
	CAPS	0.6% world export share or higher, but less than 1.2%	
	Mixed Caps	0.3% world export share or higher, but less than 0.6% share	
	*	Calculated Residuals	

COMPETITIVE NEW ZEALAND INDUSTRIES WITH GAINS OR LOSSES OF WORLD EXPORT SHARE OF 15 PERCENT OR MORE BETWEEN 1979 AND 1987

UPSTREAM INDUSTRIES

	Materials/Metals			Forest Products			Petroleum/Chemicals			Semiconductors/Computers			UPSTREAM INDUSTRIES		
	Total Competitive Industries	Gains	Losses	Total Competitive Industries	Gains	Losses	Total Competitive Industries	Gains	Losses	Total Competitive Industries	Gains	Losses	Total Competitive Indus.	Gains	Losses
Primary Goods	7	5	1	11	5	5	2	2	0	0	0	0	20	12	6
Machinery	0	0	0	0	0	0	0	0	0	0	0	0	0	0	0
Specialty Inputs	2	1	1	0	0	0	0	0	0	0	0	0	2	1	1
Total	9	6	2	11	5	5	2	2	0	0	0	0	22	13	7

INDUSTRIAL AND SUPPORTING FUNCTIONS

	Multiple Business			Transportation			Power Generation & Distribution			Office			Telecommunications			Defence			INDUSTRIAL AND SUPPORTING FUNCTIONS		
	Total Competitive Indus.	Gains	Losses	Total Competitive Indus.	Gains	Losses	Total Competitive Indus.	Gains	Losses	Total Competitive Indus.	Gains	Losses	Total Competitive Indus.	Gains	Losses	Total Competitive Indus.	Gains	Losses	Total Competitive Indus.	Gains	Losses
Primary Goods	0	0	0	2	2	0	0	0	0	1	1	0	0	0	0	0	0	0	3	3	0
Machinery	0	0	0	0	0	0	0	0	0	0	0	0	0	0	0	0	0	0	0	0	0
Specialty Inputs	0	0	0	0	0	0	0	0	0	0	0	0	0	0	0	0	0	0	0	0	0
Total	0	0	0	2	2	0	0	0	0	1	1	0	0	0	0	0	0	0	3	3	0

FINAL CONSUMPTION GOODS AND SERVICES

	Food/Beverages			Housing/Household			Textiles/Apparel			Health Care			Personal			Entertainment/Leisure			FINAL CONSUMPTION GOODS AND SERVICES		
	Total Competitive Indus.	Gains	Losses	Total Competitive Indus.	Gains	Losses	Total Competitive Indus.	Gains	Losses	Total Competitive Indus.	Gains	Losses	Total Competitive Indus.	Gains	Losses	Total Competitive Indus.	Gains	Losses	Total Competitive Indus.	Gains	Losses
Primary Goods	33	23	3	8	5	2	4	2	1	1	1	0	1	1	0	4	4	0	51	36	6
Machinery	1	0	0	0	0	0	1	1	0	0	0	0	0	0	0	0	0	0	2	1	0
Specialty Inputs	10	3	4	2	2	0	8	3	4	0	0	0	0	0	0	1	0	1	21	8	9
Total	44	26	7	10	7	2	13	6	5	1	1	0	1	1	0	5	4	1	74	45	15

* Included were industries exceeding the cutoff in 1987, or that had first achieved sufficient share to exceed the cutoff in 1987.

PERCENTAGE OF NEW ZEALAND EXPORTS OF COMPETITIVE INDUSTRIES BY BROAD CLUSTER 1987

UPSTREAM INDUSTRIES

Materials/Metals	Forest Products	Petroleum/Chemicals	Semiconductors/Computers	UPSTREAM INDUSTRIES
Share of Country Exports: 5.8 (1.4)	Share of Country Exports: 5.6 (-0.3)	Share of Country Exports: 0.6 (0.5)	Share of Country Exports: -	Share of Country Exports: 12.1 (1.6)
Share of World Cluster Exports:	Share of World Cluster Exports:	Share of World Cluster Exports:	Share of World Cluster Exports:	Share of World Cluster Exports:

INDUSTRIAL & SUPPORTING FUNCTIONS

Multiple Business	Transportation	Power Generation & Distribution	Office	Telecommunications	Defence	INDUSTRIAL & SUPPORTING FUNCTIONS
Share of Country Exports: -	Share of Country Exports: 0.2- (0.2)	Share of Country Exports: -	Share of Country Exports: 0.4 (0.2)	Share of Country Exports: -	Share of Country Exports: -	Share of Country Exports: 0.6 (0.4)
Share of World Cluster Exports:	Share of World Cluster Exports:	Share of World Cluster Exports:	Share of World Cluster Exports:	Share of World Cluster Exports:	Share of World Cluster Exports:	Share of World Cluster Exports:

FINAL CONSUMPTION GOODS & SERVICES

Food/Beverages	Textiles/Apparel	Housing/Household	Health Care	Personal	Entertainment/Leisure	FINAL CONSUMPTION GOODS & SERVICES
Share of Country Exports: 47.7 (-0.5)	Share of Country Exports: 20.6 (-3.8)	Share of Country Exports: 1.8 (0.3)	Share of Country Exports: 0.2 (0.1)	Share of Country Exports: 0.3 (0.2)	Share of Country Exports: 2.3 (0.2)	Share of Country Exports: 72.9 (-3.4)
Share of World Cluster Exports:	Share of World Cluster Exports:	Share of World Cluster Exports:	Share of World Cluster Exports:	Share of World Cluster Exports:	Share of World Cluster Exports:	Share of World Cluster Exports:

NOTE: Numbers in parentheses are changes between 1979 and 1987.
Exports are those of competitive industries, not all industries.

PERCENTAGE OF EXPORTS BY CLUSTER AND VERTICAL STAGE
NEW ZEALAND 1987

Upstream Industries

| | Materials/Metals | | | | Forest Products | | | | Petroleum/Chemicals | | | | Semiconductors/Computers | | | | Upstream Industries |
	SCE	Δ SCE	SWCE	Δ SWCE	SCE	Δ SCE	SWCE	Δ SWCE	SCE	Δ SCE	SWCE	Δ SWCE	SCE	Δ SCE	SWCE	Δ SWCE	SCE
Pri. Gds.	5.4	1.6			5.6	-0.3			0.6	0.5			.	.	.	.	11.7
Mach.	0.4	-0.2			.	.			.	.			.	.	.	.	0.4
Spec. Inp.																	
Total	5.8	1.4			5.6	-0.3			0.6	0.5			.	.	.	.	12.1

Industrial & Supporting Functions

| | Multiple Business | | | | Transportation | | | | Power Generation & Distribution | | | | Office | | | | Telecommunications | | | | Defence | | | | Industrial & Supporting Functions |
	SCE	Δ SCE	SWCE	Δ SWCE	SCE	Δ SCE	SWCE	Δ SWCE	SCE	Δ SCE	SWCE	Δ SWCE	SCE	Δ SCE	SWCE	Δ SWCE	SCE	Δ SCE	SWCE	Δ SWCE	SCE	Δ SCE	SWCE	Δ SWCE	SCE
Pri. Gds.	.	.			0.2	0.2			.	.			0.4	0.2			.	.			.	.			0.6
Mach.	.	.			.	.			.	.			.	.			.	.			.	.			.
Spec. Inp.																									
Total	.	.			0.2	0.2			.	.			0.4	0.2			.	.			.	.			0.6

Final Consumption Goods & Services

| | Food/Beverages | | | | Textiles/Apparel | | | | Housing/Household | | | | Health Care | | | | Personal | | | | Entertainment/Leisure | | | | Final Consumption Goods & Services | |
	SCE	Δ SCE	SWCE	Δ SWCE	SCE	Δ SCE	SWCE	Δ SWCE	SCE	Δ SCE	SWCE	Δ SWCE	SCE	Δ SCE	SWCE	Δ SWCE	SCE	Δ SCE	SWCE	Δ SWCE	SCE	Δ SCE	SWCE	Δ SWCE	SCE	SWCE
Pri. Gds.	42.9	-0.4			1.2	0.2			1.7	0.2			0.2	0.1			0.3	0.2			1.5	0.8			47.8	0.3
Mach.	0.2	-0.1			0.1	0.1			.	.			.	.			.	.			.	.			0.3	.
Spec. Inp.	4.7	0.0			19.3	-4.0			0.1	0.1			.	.			.	.			0.9	-0.6			24.9	
Total	47.7	-0.5			20.6	-3.8			1.8	0.3			0.2	0.1			0.3	0.2			2.3	0.2			72.9	
																									85.6	

Note: Totals may not add due to rounding.

Key

Pri. Gds.	Primary Goods	SCE	Share of country's total exports 1987
Mach.	Machinery	Δ SCE	Change in share of country's exports 1979–1987
Spec. Inp.	Specialty Inputs	SWCE	Share of world cluster exports 1985
		Δ SWCE	Change in share of world cluster exports 1979–1985

TOP 200 INDUSTRIES
NEW ZEALAND EXPORTS 1987

Percentage of Exports to Australia

CODE	DESCRIPTION	EXPORTS TO AUSTRALIA ($US'000)	TOTAL NEW ZEALAND EXPORTS ($US'000)	EXPORTS TO AUSTRALIA AS % TOTAL
26820	SHEEP, LAMBS WOOL, SCOURED, NOT CARDED, COMBED	$42,135	$571,262	7.38%
01112	MEAT OF BOVINE ANIMALS, FRESH, CHILLED OR FROZEN, BONELESS	$2,277	$559,181	0.41%
01121	MEAT OF LAMBS, FRESH, CHILLED OR FROZEN	$654	$493,952	0.13%
26810	SHEEP, LAMBS WOOL, GREASY, FLEECE WASHED	$1,362	$339,996	0.40%
68410	ALUMINIUM AND ALUMINIUM ALLOYS, UNWROUGHT	$27	$311,797	0.01%
02300	BUTTER	$21	$306,361	0.01%
05798	OTHER FRESH FRUIT	$7,002	$295,331	2.37%
21170	SHEEP AND LAMB SKINS WITHOUT WOOL	$215	$254,716	0.08%
02243	MILK AND CREAM IN POWDER/GRANULES, MORE THAN 1.5 PERCENT WEIGHT OF FAT	$1,303	$203,155	0.64%
02400	CHEESE AND CURD	$14,125	$166,424	8.49%
59221	CASEIN, CASEINATES AND OTHER CASEIN DERIVATIVES; CASEIN GLUES	$1,716	$148,202	1.16%
03600	CRUSTACEANS AND MOLLUSCS	$12,659	$140,217	9.03%
03440	FISH FILLETS, FROZEN	$11,610	$121,200	9.58%
02242	MILK IN POWDER/GRANULES, NOT MORE,THAN 1.5 PERCENT WEIGHT OF FAT	$280	$120,199	0.23%
93101	BUNKERING SHIPS OR AIRCRAFT	$0	$92,376	0.00%
03420	FISH, FROZEN (EXCLUDING FILLETS)	$5,753	$89,522	6.43%
01122	HOGGET AND MUTTON CARCASSES, CUTS, FRESH, CHILLED OR FROZEN	$384	$84,035	0.46%
25120	MECHANICAL WOOD PULP	$2,361	$78,771	3.00%
05740	APPLES, FRESH	$192	$73,460	0.26%
00150	HORSES, ASSES, MULES AND HINNIES, LIVE	$64,860	$70,671	91.78%
25171	WOOD PULP, CHEMICAL, SODA OR SULPHATE, UNBLEACHED	$12,353	$67,112	18.41%
64110	NEWSPRINT	$39,564	$61,837	63.98%
61140	LEATHER OF OTHER BOVINE CATTLE AND EQUINE LEATHER, (INCLUDING BUFFALO)	$21,453	$59,983	35.77%
29193	GUTS, BLADDERS AND STOMACHS OF ANIMALS (O/T OF FISH), WHOLE & PIECES THEREOF	$2,164	$59,067	3.66%
21110	BOVINE AND EQUINE HIDES	$2,512	$55,664	4.51%
01160	EDIBLE OFFALS OF ANIMALS IN HDGS 001.1 00013 & 001.5,FRESH, CHILLED OF FROZEN	$262	$52,509	0.50%
61150	SHEEP AND LAMB SKIN LEATHER (OTHER THAN 611.8)	$7,593	$43,058	17.64%
41132	BOVINE,SHEEP AND GOAT FATS, UNRENDERED, RENDERED/SOLVENT EXTRACTED FATS OF SAME	$83	$39,113	0.21%
65941	CARPETS, CARPETING,RUGS,MATS & MATTING OF WOOL/F.ANIMAL HAIR, TUFTED	$31,777	$38,525	82.48%
64161	HARDBOARD	$8,203	$35,502	23.10%
25172	CHEMICAL WOOD PULP, SODA OR SULPHATE, BLEACHED OR SEMI-BLEACHED O/T DISSOLV.	$24,422	$35,292	69.20%
65122	YARN CONT. MORE/T 85 % BY WEIGHT OF CARDED SHEEP'S/LAMBS' WOOL, NOT RETAIL	$26,639	$34,342	77.57%
51211	METHYL ALCOHOL (METHANOL)	$3,629	$33,012	10.99%
01111	MEAT OF BOVINE ANIMALS, FRESH, CHILLED OR FROZEN WITH BONE IN	$867	$32,784	2.64%
24711	SAWLOGS, VENEER LOGS, CONIFER, IN THE ROUGH	$2	$32,732	0.01%
33411	MOTOR SPIRIT (GASOLINE), INCLUDING AVIATION SPIRIT	$10,569	$30,849	34.26%
24821	WOOD OF CONIFEROUS SPECIES, SAWN LENGTH-WISE, SLICED/PEELED, EXCEEDING 5MM THICK	$14,636	$30,544	47.92%
08141	FLOURS, MEALS OF MEAT OR OFFALS,INEDIBLE	$185	$27,523	0.67%
24822	WOOD OF CONIFER, PLANED,TONGUED,GROOVED,V-JOINTED, ETC.	$24,663	$27,247	90.51%

Code	Description			
03410	FISH, FRESH (LIVE OR DEAD) OR CHILLED (EXCLUDING FILLETS)	$3,264	$26,528	12.30%
63491	HOOPWOOD; SPLIT POLES; PILES; CHIPWOOD; WOOD SHAVINGS; DRAWN WOOD; ETC	$0	$25,743	0.00%
05420	BEANS, PEAS, LENTILS & O/LEGUMINOUS VEGEDRIED. SHELLED, W/NOT SKINNED OR SPLIT	$5,865	$25,618	22.90%
84831	ARTICLES OF FURSKIN, NES	$3,584	$24,892	14.40%
89399	OTHER ARTICLES, NES OF MATERIALS FALLINGWITHIN DIVISION 58	$10,223	$24,660	41.46%
78490	OTHER PARTS & ACCESORIES, NES OF MOTOR VEHICLES WITHIN 722, 781, 782 OR 783	$7,447	$24,637	30.23%
05459	VEGETABLES, FRESH OR CHILLED, NES	$1,597	$24,569	6.50%
55300	PERFUMERY, COSMETICS, ETC; AQUEOUS DISTILLATES & SOLUTIONS OF ESS.OILS	$20,404	$24,082	84.73%
05461	VEGETABLES (WHETHER OR NOT COOKED). PRESERVED BY FREEZING	$7,874	$22,681	34.72%
93102	PASSENGERS DUTY FREE GOODS	$0	$22,417	0.00%
99920	GOODS ON LOAN OR LEASED	$14,825	$22,235	66.67%
67461	SHEETS & PLATES, ROLLED, UNDER 3 MM, OF OTHER THAN HIGH CARBON OR ALLOY STEEL	$8,417	$21,702	38.78%
69979	OTHER ARTICLES OF IRON, STEEL,NES, EXCL.CASTINGS, FORGINGS, STAMPINGS; IN ROUGH	$3,488	$20,871	16.71%
29250	SEEDS, FRUIT & SPORES, NES, FOR SOWING	$3,860	$19,703	19.59%
67251	BLOOMS, BILLETS ETC OF O/THAN HIGH CARBON OR ALLOY STEEL	$0	$19,322	0.00%
07300	CHOCOLATE AND OTHER FOOD PREPARATIONS CONTAINING COCOA, NES	$3,553	$18,064	19.67%
04842	PASTRY, BISCUITS, CAKES & OTHER FINE BAKERS' WARES, W/NOT CONTAINING COCOA	$12,917	$17,837	72.42%
77210	ELECTRICAL APPARATUS FOR MAKING AND BREAKING ELECTRICAL CIRCUITS, ETC; PARTS	$12,973	$17,517	74.06%
82192	FURNITURE, NES, OF WOOD	$4,186	$16,528	25.33%
01189	MEAT OR EDIBLE OFFALS,OTHER KINDS	$673	$16,252	4.14%
93103	SHIPS' STORES	$0	$15,783	0.00%
28150	IRON ORE AND CONCENTRATES, NOT AGGLOMERATED	$0	$15,329	0.00%
09149	IMITATION LARD AND OTHER PREPARED EDIBLEFATS,NES.	$23	$15,306	0.15%
08199	SWEETENED FORAGE; O/PREPARATIONS OF KINDUSED IN ANIMAL FEEDING, N.E.S.	$953	$14,743	6.47%
05861	FRUIT (W/NOT COOKED), PRESERVED BY FREEZING, NOT CONTAINING ADDED SUGAR	$2,508	$14,643	17.13%
89283	UNUSED POSTAGE REVENUE & SIM. STAMPS; BANKNOTES, CERTIFICATES, DOCUMENTS ETC	$518	$14,476	3.58%
11249	SPIRITS & DISTILLED ALCOHOLIC BEVERAGES,N.E.S; COMPOUND ALCOHOLIC PREPARATIONS	$13,234	$14,239	92.94%
77521	REFRIGERATORS AND DEEP-FREEZERS OF HOUSEHOLD TYPE ELECTRICAL AND OTHER	$11,296	$14,103	80.10%
32220	COAL,OTHER, NOT AGGLOMERATED	$0	$14,059	0.00%
64132	SACK KRAFT PAPER, IN ROLLS OR SHEETS	$12,068	$13,969	86.40%
59222	ALBUMINS AND DERIVATIVES	$539	$13,964	3.86%
89731	ARTICLES OF JEWELLERY & PARTS THEREOF,OFPRECIOUS METAL OR ROLLED PRECIOUS METAL	$12,386	$13,845	89.46%
79240	AIRCRAFT,NOT HELICOPTERS;MECH PROP OF UNLADEN WEIGHT EXCEEDING 15000KG	$0	$13,608	0.00%
21209	OTHER FURSKINS, RAW	$57	$13,594	0.42%
21120	CALF SKINS	$0	$12,928	0.00%
64131	KRAFT LINER, IN ROLLS OR SHEETS	$732	$12,182	6.01%
54179	MEDICAMENTS CONTAINING OTHER SUBSTANCES	$5,903	$11,938	49.44%
00121	SHEEP	$71	$11,905	0.60%
68423	ALUMINIUM FOIL OF A THICKNESS NOT EXCEEDING 0.20 MM	$4,016	$11,256	35.68%
65127	YARN CONT. LESS/T 85% BY WEIGHT OF CARDED SHEEP'S/LAMBS' WOOL, NOT RETAIL	$8,900	$11,154	79.79%
65942	CARPETS, CARPETING,RUGS,MATS & MATTING OF WOOL/F.ANIMAL HAIR, WOVEN	$8,749	$11,048	79.19%
89310	ARTICLES CONVEYANCE OR PACKING OF GOODS;STOPPERS; LIDS, CAPS & OTHER CLOSURES	$7,866	$11,029	71.32%
64159	OTHER PAPER AND PAPERBOARD (INCLUDING CELLULOSE WADDING); IN ROLLS/SHEETS, NES	$6,999	$10,943	63.96%
05857	JUICE OF ANY OTHER FRUIT OR VEGETABLE	$2,822	$10,922	25.83%

Code	Description			
77886	OTHER ELECTRICAL APPLIANCES & APPARATUS,HAVING INDIVIDUAL FUNCTIONS, NES	$2,970	$10,730	27.67%
04300	BARLEY, UNMILLED	$1	$10,399	0.01%
76481	RADIOTELEPHONIC OR RADIOTELEGRAPHIC RECEIVERS	$3,899	$10,052	38.79%
74920	TAPS, COCKS, VALVES & SIM. APPLIANCES FOR PIPES, BOILER SHELLS, TANKS,VATS ETC	$6,226	$9,929	62.70%
69732	STOVES,GRATES,SPACE HEATERS NES,OF IRON OR STEEL NOT ELECTRICALLY OPERATED	$7,476	$9,880	75.66%
01490	OTHER PREPARED OR PRESERVED MEAT OR MEATOFFALS	$511	$9,790	5.22%
87483	ELECTRONIC MEASURING CHECKING ANALYSING OR AUTOMATICALLY CONTROLLING INSTRUMENTS	$4,337	$9,733	44.56%
05659	VEGETABLES PREPARED OR PRESERVED O/THAN IN VINEGAR OR ACETIC ACID, N.E.S.	$7,365	$9,649	76.33%
56216	UREA	$3,001	$9,476	31.66%
72442	MACHINES OF A KIND USED FOR PROCESSING NATURAL OR MAN-MADE TEXTILE FIBRES, NES	$5,878	$9,475	62.04%
03710	FISH, PREPARED OR PRESERVED, N.E.S.(INCLCAVIAR AND CAVIAR SUBSTITUTES)	$4,684	$9,441	49.62%
79290	AIRCRAFT PARTS NES	$2,123	$9,403	22.57%
63492	WOODEN BEADINGS AND MOULDINGS	$7,458	$9,280	80.36%
62510	RUBBER TYRES, PNEUMATIC, NEW, USED ON MOTOR CARS	$8,393	$9,263	90.61%
69531	SAWS (NON-MECHANICAL) & BLADES FOR HAND OR MACHINE SAWS	$3,161	$9,262	34.13%
77586	ELECTRO-THERMIC DOMESTIC APPLIANCES, NES	$8,775	$9,097	96.46%
97101	GOLD,NON-MONETARY,UNWROUGHT OR SEMI-MANUFACTURED	$8,004	$9,068	88.26%
21160	SHEEP AND LAMB SKINS WITH WOOL ON (NOT ASTRAKHAN,CARACUL, ETC.)	$29	$8,884	0.32%
29199	ANIMAL PRODUCTS, NES; DEAD ANIMALS UNFITFOR HUMAN CONSUMPTION	$1,740	$8,878	19.60%
79321	YACHTS AND OTHER VESSELS FOR PLEASURE ORSPORTS	$2,607	$8,664	30.08%
64210	BOXES, BAGS, OTHER CONTAINERS,BOX FILES,LETTER TRAYS ETC OF PAPER OR PAPERBOARD	$3,361	$8,583	39.16%
63432	RECONSTITUTED WOOD, IN SHEETS,BLOCKS, SIMILAR	$559	$8,557	6.53%
06190	OTHER SUGARS; SUGAR SYRUPS; ART. HONEY (W/NOT MIXED WITH NAT. HONEY); CARAMEL	$2,970	$8,373	35.47%
00111	BOVINE, PURE BRED BREEDING ANIMALS	$340	$8,300	4.10%
72139	PARTS, N.E.S. OF MACHINERY FALLING WITHIN HEADING 721.3	$2,183	$8,282	26.36%
74422	SHIPS' DERRICKS; CRANES (OTHER THAN CABLE CRANES); MOBILE LIFTING FRAMES	$7,235	$8,212	88.10%
05451	ONIONS, SHALLOTS, GARLIC, LEEKS & OTHER ALLIACEOUS VEGES, FRESH OR CHILLED	$217	$8,131	2.67%
02230	MILK AND CREAM, FRESH (INCL. SKIMMED MILK ETC.) NOT CONCENTRATED OR SWEETENED	$260	$8,053	3.23%
03720	CRUSTACEANS AND MOLLUSCS, PREPARED OR PRESERVED N.E.S.	$351	$7,969	4.41%
29271	CUT FLOWERS & FLOWER BUDS FOR BOUQUETS ETC, FRESH, DRIED, DYED, BLEACHED ETC	$160	$7,913	2.02%
68271	BARS, RODS, ANGLES, SHAPES AND SECTIONS,WROUGHT, OF COPPER; COPPER WIRE	$4,226	$7,836	53.93%
61300	FURSKINS, TANNED OR DRESSED: PIECES OR CUTINGS OF FURSKIN,TANNED OR DRESSED	$1,065	$7,691	13.85%
28823	ALUMINIUM WASTE AND SCRAP	$595	$7,597	7.83%
75990	MACHINE PARTS AND ACCESSORIES FOR GROUP 752 OR 7512 NES	$2,151	$7,181	29.96%
54164	ANTISERA AND MICROBIAL VACCINES	$3,722	$6,986	53.28%

Code	Description			
74160	MACHINERY,PLANT & SIM. LAB. EQUIPMENT, PROCESS WITH CHANGE OF TEMP.; PARTS NES	$5,321	$6,974	76.29%
63420	PLYWOOD	$6,120	$6,948	88.08%
09809	FOOD PREPARATIONS, N.E.S.	$2,040	$6,904	29.54%
33300	PETROLEUM OILS, CRUDE, CRUDE OILS OBTAINED FROM BITUMINOUS MINERALS	$6,884	$6,884	100.00%
29116	IVORY,_TORTOISE-SHELL, HORNS, ANTLERS ETC UNWORKED; WHALEBONE UNWORKED; WASTE	$0	$6,728	0.00%
77522	DOMESTIC DEEP-FREEZERS	$2,221	$6,669	33.31%
05794	BERRIES, FRESH	$88	$6,573	1.34%
11230	BEER MADE FROM MALT (INCL ALE, STOUT ANDPORTER)	$1,223	$6,570	18.61%
77832	ELECTRIC LIGHTING,SIGNALLING EQUIPMENT,WINDSCREEN WIPERS,DEFROSTERS,ETC AND PTS	$721	$6,510	11.07%
68421	BARS, RODS, ANGLES, SHAPES & SECTIONS, WROUGHT,OF ALUMINIUM; ALUMINIUM WIRE	$4,547	$6,461	70.37%
05899	FRUIT AND NUTS, PREPARED OR PRESERVED, N.E.S.	$1,838	$6,412	28.67%
89211	PRINTED BOOKS, BOOKLETS, BROCHURES, PAMPHLETS AND LEAFLETS	$3,416	$6,323	54.03%
54162	ORGANO-THERAPEUTIC GLANDS ETC DRIED, EXTRACTS AND OTHER ANIMAL SUBSTANCES	$145	$6,141	2.36%
75280	DATA PROCESSING OFF-LINE EQUIPMENT NES	$1,658	$6,021	27.54%
69110	STRUCTURES & PARTS, OF IRON OR STEEL ANDSECTIONS ETC PREP. FOR USE IN STRUCTURES	$3,187	$5,950	53.57%
87430	INSTRUMENTS FOR MEASURING CHECKING CONTROLLING,FLOW,DEPTH ETC OF LIQUID,GAS	$5,228	$5,947	87.92%
63530	BUILDERS' CARPENTRY AND JOINERY (INCL. PRE-FAB. & SECTIONAL BUILDINGS & FLOORS)	$4,513	$5,941	75.96%
27821	CLAY, ANDALUSITE, KYANITE & SILLIMANITE,W/NOT CALCINED EXCL CLAYS IN 663.5; ETC	$76	$5,881	1.29%
69913	BASE METAL FITTINGS FOR FURNITURE,DOORS,ETC; BASE METAL HAT-RACKS AND THE LIKE	$2,246	$5,861	38.33%
33430	GAS OILS	$1	$5,778	0.01%
03430	FISH FILLETS, FRESH OR CHILLED	$757	$5,716	13.24%
51122	BENZENE, CHEMICALLY OR COMMERCIALLY PURE	$5,610	$5,610	100.00%
72848	OTHER MACHINERY & MECHANICAL APPLIANCES,HAVING INDIVIDUAL FUNCTIONS, N.E.S.	$3,725	$5,587	66.67%
74522	MACHINERY FOR CLEANING, FILLING,SEALING,LABELING BOTTLES & OTHER CONTAINERS;ETC	$1,518	$5,578	27.21%
77310	INSULATED ELECTRIC WIRE, CABLE, BARS ETCWHETHER OR NOT FITTED WITH CONNECTORS	$4,576	$5,394	84.85%
05793	STONE FRUIT, N.E.S., FRESH	$3,957	$5,372	73.66%
65831	TRAVELLING RUGS,BLANKETS (NOT ELECTRIC, KNITTED ETC) OF WOOL, FINE ANIMAL HAIR	$2,456	$5,358	45.83%
64139	KRAFT PAPER AND PAPERBOARD, IN ROLLS OR SHEETS, N.E.S.	$2,293	$5,267	43.54%
58313	POLYETHYLENE IN PLATES, SHEETS, FILM, FOIL OR STRIP	$2,212	$5,175	42.75%
77582	ELECTRIC SOIL HEATING APPARATUS AND ELECTRIC SPACE HEATING APPARATUS	$5,087	$5,130	99.17%
65126	YARN CONT. MORE/1 85% BY WEIGHT OF SHEEP/LAMBS' WOOL/FINE ANIMAL HAIR,RETAIL	$4,740	$4,802	98.72%
89424	EQUIPMENT FOR PARLOUR, TABLE AND FUNFAIRGAMES FOR ADULTS OR CHILDREN	$4,200	$4,746	88.49%
89289	OTHER PRINTED MATTER (INCLUDING PRINTED PICTURES AND PHOTOGRAPHS)	$1,232	$4,667	26.40%
11212	WINE OF FRESH GRAPES; GRAPE MUST WITH FERMENTATION ARRESTED BY ADDN OF ALCOHOL	$1,201	$4,568	26.30%
51691	ENZYMES	$602	$4,539	13.26%

Code	Description	Value	Percent
29272	FOLIAGE ETC., EXCEPT FLOWERS, MOSSES, LICHENS,GRASSES FOR BOUQUETS OR ORNAMENT	$23	0.52%
55410	SOAP: ORGANIC SURFACE-ACTIVE PRODUCTS & PREP FOR USE AS SOAP, IN BARS, CAKES ETC	$2,142	48.94%
06201	SUGAR CONFECTIONERY, NOT CONTAINING COCOA	$3,561	82.84%
74930	TRANSMISSION SHAFTS, CRANKS, GEARS, FLYWHEELS, PULLEYS, CLUTCHES ETC.	$2,005	46.71%
75250	PERIPHERAL UNITS INCL CONTROL AND ADAPT-ING UNITS DIRECTLY OR INDIRECTLY TO MAIN	$2,236	52.59%
74428	OTHER LIFTING, HANDLING, LOADING AND UNLOADING MACHINERY, N.E.S.	$1,474	34.75%
82191	FURNITURE, N.E.S. OF METAL	$3,593	84.97%
72121	LAWN MOWERS	$3,502	82.87%
33421	KEROSENE (INCLUDING KEROSENE TYPE JET FUEL)	$4	0.11%
87202	MEDICAL,SURGICAL AND VETERINARY INSTRUMENTS AND APPLIANCES	$1,222	30.36%
85102	FOOTWEAR WITH OUTER SOLES OF LEATHER, COMPOSITION LEATHER, RUBBER OR PLASTIC	$3,000	74.60%
65510	KNITTED OR CROCHEED FABRICS,NOT ELASTICNOR RUBBERISED, OF SYNTHETIC FIBRES	$3,910	98.06%
89320	SANITARY AND TOILET ARTICLES, OF THE MATERIALS FALLING WITHIN DIVISION 58	$3,378	84.80%
65174	YARN OF FINE ANIMAL HAIR, NOT FOR RETAIL SALE	$2,124	53.44%
74141	REFRIGERATORS AND EQUIPMENT OTHER THAN HOUSEHOLD TYPE REFRIGERATORS AND FREEZER	$2,193	55.84%
64230	PAPER AND PAPERBOARD REGISTERS,EXERCISE BOOKS,ALBUMS,DIARIES,FILE COVERS ETC.	$2,129	54.35%
72722	MACHINERY, NES USED IN CERTAIN FOOD AND DRINK INDUSTRIES E.G. BAKERY, BREWING ETC	$2,323	59.59%
84512	JERSEYS,PULL-OVERS,BEDJACKETS ETC OF COTTON	$114	2.94%
69120	STRUCTURES & PARTS, OF ALUMINIUM AND SECTIONS ETC PREP. FOR USE IN STRUCTURES	$1,114	29.48%
66511	GLASS CARBOYS, BOTTLES ETC FOR CONVEY ORPACKING GOODS; STOPPERS & O/CLOSURES	$2,017	55.04%
99910	GOODS BEING RETURNED AFTER REPAIR OR PROCESSING IN NEW ZEALAND	$1,027	28.02%
67830	OTHER TUBES & PIPES, OF IRON (O/T CAST) OR STEEL	$978	26.82%
89281	LABELS OF PAPER,PAPERBOARD, WHETHER OR NOT PRINTED OR GUMMED	$3,034	83.33%
65751	TWINE, CORDAGE, ROPES AND CABLES PLAITED OR NOT	$3,023	83.15%
68225	COPPER TUBES,PIPES AND BLANKS THEREFOR, HOLLOW BARS OF COPPER	$3,251	89.77%
29269	PLANTS,TREES,SHRUBS,BUSHES,ROOTS,SLIPS, CUTTINGS, OTHER ,LIVE	$57	1.59%
26830	FINE ANIMAL HAIR, NOT CARDED OR COMBED	$11	0.31%
64197	WALLPAPER AND LINECRUSTA; WINDOW TRANSPARENCIES OF PAPER	$1,422	40.17%
25110	WASTE AND SCRAP OF PAPER AND PAPERBOARD FOR USE IN PAPER-MAKING	$149	4.23%
02241	WHEY, PRESERVED, CONCENTRATED OR SWEETENED	$233	6.71%
59899	OTHER CHEMICAL PRODUCTS AND PREPARATIONS NES	$2,278	67.63%
7849	PARTS, NES OF MACHINES & MECHANICAL APP,OF HEADINGS 723.48,727.21,728.42 TO .48	$1,812	53.97%
77889	MACHINERY AND APPARATUS,ELECTRICAL PARTSNES CARBON ARTICLES FOR ELEC.PURPOSES	$677	20.42%
66430	DRAWN OR BLOWN GLASS, INCL FLASHED GLASSUNWORKED,IN RECTANGLES	$1,577	48.47%
84810	ARTICLES OF APPAREL & CLOTHING ACCESS- ORIES OF LEATHER OR COMPOSITION LEATHER	$2,884	89.68%

Page 6

89733	PEARL,PRECIOUS OR SEMI-PRECIOUS STONE ARTICLES,NES	$1,993	$3,177	62.72%
58322	POLYPROPYLENE PLATES,SHEETS,FILM,FOIL ORSTRIP	$2,564	$3,163	81.09%
63302	AGGLOMERATED CORK AND ARTICLES OF AGGLOMERATED CORK	$1,946	$3,161	61.54%
26870	WOOL, SHEEP,LAMB,OTHER ANIMAL HAIR, CARDED OR COMBED, NOT WOOL TOPS	$632	$3,125	20.22%
06160	NATURAL HONEY	$142	$3,095	4.60%
06120	REFINED SUGARS AND OTHER PRODUCTS OF REFINING BEET & CANE SUGAR, SOLID	$0	$3,045	0.00%
72839	PARTS, N.E.S. OF MACHINERY FALLING WITHIN HEADING 728.3	$773	$2,974	26.00%
74523	PARTS, NES OF THE MACHINERY FALLING WITHIN HEADINGS 745.22 AND 775.3	$102	$2,973	3.43%
74421	PULLEY TACKLE AND HOISTS (OTHER THAN SKIP HOISTS); WINCHES AND CAPSTANS	$895	$2,970	30.15%
67850	TUBE AND PIPE FITTINGS OF IRON OR STEEL	$1,775	$2,956	60.05%
66120	PORTLAND CEMENT, CIMENT FONDU, SLAG CEMENT, & SIMILAR HYDRAULIC CEMENTS	$10	$2,946	0.33%
59898	COMPOUND CATALYSTS	$190	$2,885	6.59%
99999	GRAND TOTAL	$1,143,904	$7,214,493	15.86%

TOP 50 NEW ZEALAND INDUSTRIES IN TERMS OF
IMPORT VALUE
1987

	COMMODITY	DESCRIPTION	WORLD IMPORT SHARE (%)	R	NZ IMPORTS ($US'000)	NZ EXPORTS ($US'000)	TRADE BALANCE ($US'000)	NZ IMPORT SHARE (%)
1	781.00	MOTOR CARS (ASSEMBLED & UNASSEMBLED)	0.5%		$598,817	$1,438	$597,379	8.3%
2	333.00	CRUDE PETROLEUM	0.2%		$288,030	$6,885	$281,145	4.0%
3	541.79	MEDICAMENTS, NOT INCLUDING ANTIBIOTICS	0.9%	•	$115,228	$12,424	$102,804	1.6%
4	764.10	TELEPHONE EQUIPMENT	1.4%		$115,136	$1,972	$113,164	1.6%
5	782.10	TRUCKS AND VANS	0.4%		$114,010	$12	$113,998	1.6%
6	752.50	EDP PERIPHERAL UNITS	0.6%		$110,275	$4,251	$106,024	1.5%
7	287.32	ALUMINIUM OXIDE	4.6%		$103,593	$32	$103,561	1.4%
8	334.11	GASOLINE	1.1%		$99,944	$30,849	$69,095	1.4%
9	759.90	DATA PROCESSING MACHINE PARTS	0.3%	•	$89,946	$7,928	$82,018	1.2%
10	674.61	IRON & STEEL SHEETS & PLATES (LESS THAN 3 MM)	1.4%		$80,804	$21,702	$59,102	1.1%
11	784.91	MOTOR VEHICLE PARTS	0.1%	•	$77,327	$24,816	$52,511	1.1%
12	652.24	WOVEN FABRIC (MAINLY COTTON)	1.0%		$76,296	$192	$76,104	1.1%
13	951.07	WAR FIREARMS, AMMUNITION	1.7%	•	$75,737	$508	$75,229	1.1%
14	792.40	AIRCRAFT EXCEEDING 15000 KGS	1.0%		$74,936	$13,609	$61,327	1.0%
15	874.83	MEASURING AND CONTROLLING INSTRUMENTS	0.3%	•	$74,167	$17,240	$56,927	1.0%
16	892.11	BOOKS	1.4%		$72,025	$6,323	$65,702	1.0%
17	775.86	DOMESTIC APPLIANCES (MAINLY MICROWAVE OVENS)	0.6%		$70,958	$22,896	$48,062	1.0%
18	641.22	WRITING PAPER (MAINLY CLAY-COATED)	1.2%		$70,437	$733	$69,704	1.0%
19	772.10	ELECTRICAL CIRCUIT APPARATUS	0.4%		$67,627	$17,517	$50,110	0.9%
20	752.20	DIGITAL DATA PROCESSING MACHINES	1.3%		$61,002	$841	$60,161	0.8%
21	653.41	FABRICS, WOVEN, SYNTH. FIBRES (DISCONTINUOUS)	0.8%	•	$59,945	$1,212	$58,733	0.8%
22	726.71	PRINTING MACHINERY (NOT PRINTING PRESSES)	1.3%		$56,668	$2,866	$53,802	0.8%
23	583.11	POLYETHYLENE	1.1%		$56,354	$795	$55,559	0.8%
24	598.99	WOOD, RESIN-BASED AND ORGANIC CHEMICAL PRODUCTS	0.4%	•	$51,173	$12,227	$38,946	0.7%
25	001.50	LIVE ANIMALS, NOT BOVINE (RACE HORSES)	2.2%	•	$51,136	$83,543	($32,407)	0.7%
26	893.99	MISC. SANITARY, ORNAMENTAL AND LIGHTING ARTICLES	0.4%	•	$49,906	$29,799	$20,107	0.7%
27	763.81	TELEVISION SETS	0.5%		$48,971	$632	$48,339	0.7%
28	723.90	PARTS AND MACHINERY FOR CIVIL ENGINEERING	0.3%		$46,636	$6,710	$39,926	0.6%
29	792.30	AIRCRAFT NOT EXCEEDING 15000 KGS	2.5%		$43,718	$1,368	$42,350	0.6%
30	764.93	TELECOMMUNICATION EQUIPMENT N.E.S.	0.2%		$43,496	$15,077	$28,419	0.6%
31	728.49	MACHINERY FOR SPECIALISED INDUSTRIES N.E.S.	0.3%	•	$41,525	$9,805	$31,720	0.6%
32	582.91	CONDENSATION AND POLYADDITION PRODUCTS	0.5%		$37,128	$3,724	$33,404	0.5%
33	699.79	IRON AND STEEL PRODUCTS (NOT CHAINS AND LOCKS)	0.3%	•	$36,531	$28,248	$8,283	0.5%
34	583.91	OTHER POLYMERIZATION & COPOLYMERIZATION PRODUCTS	0.5%		$36,022	$1,829	$34,193	0.5%
35	562.29	FERTILISERS, PHOSPHATIC, OTHER N.E.S.	1.0%		$35,115	$366	$34,749	0.5%
36	749.20	TAPS, COCKS, VALVES AND SIMILAR APPLIANCES	0.4%		$34,049	$9,929	$24,120	0.5%
37	894.23	TOYS (WORKING MODELS)	0.4%		$33,830	$1,546	$32,284	0.5%
38	892.20	NEWSPAPERS, JOURNALS AND PERIODICALS	1.2%		$32,723	$1,980	$30,743	0.5%
39	714.99	PARTS OF ENGINES AND MOTORS (NON-ELECTRIC)	0.2%	•	$32,540	$650	$31,890	0.5%
40	583.41	POLYVINYL CHLORIDE	1.2%		$31,607	$242	$31,365	0.4%
41	674.91	OTHER SHEETS & PLATES OF IRON AND STEEL	0.4%		$28,638	$146	$28,492	0.4%
42	792.90	AIRCRAFT PARTS	0.3%		$28,526	$9,403	$19,123	0.4%
43	751.82	PHOTO-COPYING MACHINES	0.7%		$27,269	$559	$26,710	0.4%
44	061.10	SUGARS, RAW	1.5%		$27,056	$0	$27,056	0.4%
45	741.60	MACHINERY, PLANT & SIMILAR LAB. EQUIPMENT	0.5%		$26,947	$7,421	$19,526	0.4%
46	098.09	OTHER FOOD PREPARATIONS	0.4%	•	$26,804	$12,699	$14,105	0.4%
47	541.71	ANTIBIOTICS	1.6%		$26,460	$1,351	$25,109	0.4%
48	664.40	GLASS (MAINLY PLATE AND BODY TINTED)	1.8%		$25,849	$156	$25,693	0.4%
49	271.32	NATURAL CALCIUM PHOSPHATES, ALUMINIUM	1.7%	•	$25,485	$0	$25,485	0.4%
50	785.10	MOTORCYCLES	1.1%		$25,258	$469	$24,789	0.4%

R = RESIDUAL

NEW ZEALAND'S TOP 50 COMPETITIVE INDUSTRIES
IN TERMS OF WORLD IMPORT SHARE
1987

	COMMODITY	DESCRIPTION	WORLD IMPORT SHARE (%)	R	NZ IMPORTS ($US'000)	NZ EXPORTS ($US'000)	TRADE BALANCE ($US'000)	NZ IMPORT SHARE (%)
1	287.32	ALUMINIUM OXIDE	4.6%		$103,593	$32	$103,561	1.4%
2	737.29	ROLLS AND PARTS OF ROLLING MILLS	2.6%		$22,600	$15	$22,585	0.3%
3	792.30	AIRCRAFT NOT EXCEEDING 15000 KGS	2.5%		$43,718	$1,368	$42,350	0.6%
4	713.31	MARINE OUTBOARD INTERNAL COMBUSTION	2.4%		$15,349	$65	$15,284	0.2%
5	057.52	GRAPES, DRIED	2.2%		$12,269	$25	$12,244	0.2%
6	001.50	LIVE ANIMALS, NOT BOVINE (RACE HORSES)	2.2%	*	$51,136	$83,543	($32,407)	0.7%
7	664.40	GLASS (MAINLY PLATE AND BODY TINTED)	1.8%		$25,849	$156	$25,693	0.4%
8	744.19	PARTS, NES OF THE TRUCKS AND TRACTORS	1.7%		$17,827	$806	$17,021	0.2%
9	951.07	WAR FIREARMS, AMMUNITION	1.7%		$75,737	$508	$75,229	1.1%
10	271.32	NATURAL CALCIUM PHOSPHATES,ALUMINIUM	1.7%	*	$25,485	$0	$25,485	0.4%
11	541.71	ANTIBIOTICS	1.6%		$26,460	$1,351	$25,109	0.4%
12	061.10	SUGARS, RAW	1.5%		$27,056	$0	$27,056	0.4%
13	764.10	TELEPHONE EQUIPMENT	1.4%		$115,136	$1,972	$113,164	1.6%
14	674.61	IRON & STEEL SHEETS & PLATES (LESS THAN 3 MM)	1.4%		$80,804	$21,702	$59,102	1.1%
15	892.11	BOOKS	1.4%		$72,025	$6,323	$65,702	1.0%
16	752.80	OFF LINE DATA PROCESSING EQUIPMENT	1.4%		$21,860	$6,021	$15,839	0.3%
17	726.71	PRINTING MACHINERY (NOT PRINTING PRESSES)	1.3%	*	$56,668	$2,866	$53,802	0.8%
18	791.10	RAIL VEHICLES & EQUIP. (NOT TRAM & RAIL PARTS, N.E.S.)	1.3%		$14,564	$188	$14,376	0.2%
19	271.31	NATURAL CALCIUM PHOSPHATES, ALUMINIUM	1.3%		$14,451	$0	$14,451	0.2%
20	752.20	DIGITAL DATA PROCESSING MACHINES	1.3%		$61,002	$841	$60,161	0.8%
21	651.66	YARN OF DISCONT. SYNTH. FIBRES, 85% BY WEIGHT OR LESS	1.3%	*	$19,045	$331	$18,714	0.3%
22	583.41	POLYVINYL CHLORIDE	1.2%		$31,607	$242	$31,365	0.4%
23	641.22	WRITING PAPER (MAINLY CLAY-COATED)	1.2%		$70,437	$733	$69,704	1.0%
24	892.20	NEWSPAPERS, JOURNALS AND PERIODICALS	1.2%		$32,723	$1,980	$30,743	0.5%
25	744.22	SHIPS' DERRICKS; CRANES (OTHER THAN CABLE CRANES)	1.1%		$11,967	$8,212	$3,755	0.2%
26	583.11	POLYETHYLENE	1.1%		$56,354	$795	$55,559	0.8%
27	334.11	GASOLINE	1.1%		$99,944	$30,849	$69,095	1.4%
28	674.70	TINNED SHEETS & PLATES OF STEEL	1.1%		$22,610	$0	$22,610	0.2%
29	785.10	MOTORCYCLES	1.1%		$25,258	$469	$24,789	0.4%
30	751.88	OFFICE MACHINES, N.E.S. (NOT PHOTO-COPYING APPARATUS)	1.1%	*	$13,531	$223	$13,308	0.2%
31	652.24	WOVEN FABRICS (MAINLY COTTON)	1.0%	*	$76,296	$192	$76,104	1.1%
32	686.10	ZINC & ZINC ALLOYS, UNWROUGHT	1.0%		$16,904	$0	$16,904	0.2%
33	562.29	FERTILISERS, PHOSPHATIC, OTHER N.E.S.	1.0%	*	$35,115	$366	$34,749	0.5%
34	792.40	AIRCRAFT EXCEEDING 15000 KGS	1.0%		$74,936	$13,609	$61,327	1.0%
35	657.32	TEXTILE FABRICS IMPREGNATED, COATED,	0.9%		$16,114	$1,203	$14,911	0.2%
36	751.11	ELECTRIC TYPEWRITERS	0.9%		$6,900	$394	$6,506	0.1%
37	674.63	STAINLESS STEEL SHEETS AND PLATES (UNDER 3MM)	0.9%		$13,482	$104	$13,378	0.2%
38	682.21	WIRE RODS OF COPPER	0.9%		$24,137	$7,836	$16,301	0.3%
39	335.42	PETROLEUM COKE	0.9%		$11,038	$0	$11,038	0.2%
40	657.73	WADDING, WICKS AND TEXTILE FABRICS FOR MACHINERY	0.9%	*	$12,530	$490	$12,040	0.2%
41	112.49	SPIRITS & DISTILLED ALCOHOLIC BEVERAGES,	0.9%		$12,893	$14,239	($1,346)	0.2%
42	541.79	MEDICAMENTS, NOT INCLUDING ANTIBIOTICS	0.9%	*	$115,228	$12,424	$102,804	1.6%
43	673.33	IRON & STEEL ANGLES, SHAPES, SECTIONS (80MM OR MORE)	0.9%		$10,833	$171	$10,662	0.2%
44	655.10	KNITTED OR CROCHETED FABRICS, NOT ELASTIC	0.8%		$16,098	$3,987	$12,111	0.2%
45	778.40	ELECTRIC HAND TOOLS	0.8%		$17,500	$1,890	$15,610	0.2%
46	653.41	FABRICS, WOVEN, SYNTH. FIBRES (DISCONTINUOUS)	0.8%	*	$55,899	$1,156	$54,743	0.8%
47	725.20	PAPER, PAPERBOARD CUTTING MACHINES	0.8%		$11,434	$440	$10,994	0.2%
48	583.43	POLYVINYL CHLORIDE IN PLATES, SHEETS, STRIPS, ETC	0.8%		$16,434	$1,295	$15,139	0.2%
49	894.24	EQUIPMENT FOR PARLOUR, TABLE AND FUNFAIR	0.8%		$12,603	$4,746	$7,857	0.2%
50	121.21	TOBACCO, WHOLLY OR PARTLY STRIPPED	0.7%		$11,845	$0	$11,845	0.2%

R = RESIDUAL

NEW ZEALAND

1950 EXPORTS - MAJOR COMMODITIES (December year)

COMMODITIES	($NZ)
Wool	149,306,014
Butter	71,133,986
Frozen and chilled meats	57,258,212
Cheese	29,071,514
Sheep skins and pelts	13,472,324
Milk, dried and condensed	6,643,766
Sausage casings	5,321,668
Seeds (grass and clover)	4,167,260
Cattle and horse hides	3,246,860
Inedible fats	3,037,246
Gold	2,593,220
Calf skins	1,989,606
Canned meats	1,769,570
Edible fats	1,560,740
Fresh apples	1,357,984
Casein	1,314,180
Fish	1,234,076
Peas	873,953
Timber, sawn and hewn	743,114
Rabbit skins	693,730
Butterfat, dry	612,762
Sugar of milk	446,818
Opossum skins	401,644
Inedible offals	261,098
Kauri gum	251,786
Fish and fish liver oils	249,234
Canned vegetables	242,034
Live horses	228,250
Potatoes	224,862
Other preserved meat	194,012
Meat meal	180,134
Barley	177,922
Seeds (various)	146,658
Deer skins	146,352
Soap and soap powder	131,234
Dairying machinery	120,006
Building board	103,306
Ale, stout and cider	102,856
Neatsfoot oil	89,242
Malted milk	87,810
Honey	83,916
Electrical apparatus	70,192
Whale oil	68,944
Onions	63,236
Live cattle and sheep	62,984
Meat extract	59,886
Books, papers, printed matter	57,786
Silver	51,790
Chinaware and earthenware	51,312
Metals, scrap (not precious)	46,446
Sugar, refined	43,258
Soup, soup powders	42,490
Manures	41,370
Cocoa	39,026

Commodity	($NZ)
Coal	36,890
Tobacco, manufactured	35,336
Biscuits	30,252
Scheelite	27,078
Leather	21,270
Pumice, sand and stone	18,374
Cement	18,346
Phormium fibre and tow	6,758
Linen-flax fibre and tow	6,176

Total Exports of New Zealand produce   364,664,302

NEW ZEALAND

1960 EXPORTS - MAJOR COMMODITIES (December year)

COMMODITIES	($NZ)
Wool	204,639,800
Meat, frozen and chilled	152,333,400
Butter	100,270,000
Cheese	37,115,400
Sheep skins and pelts	19,057,600
Milk, dried and condensed	11,064,600
Casein	8,428,000
Sausage casings	6,968,800
Newsprint	6,160,400
Wood pulp	5,617,800
Cattle hides	4,911,600
Apples	4,743,600
Inedible tallow	4,710,200
Seeds, grass and clover	3,358,800
Sawn timber	2,686,000
Meat, canned	2,530,800
Calf skins	1,824,600
Crayfish	1,767,200
Inedible offals (incl. dried blood)	1,703,600
Scarp metal	1,639,200
Edible tallow	1,132,000
Logs, radiata pine	1,117,400
Fish, fresh and frozen	1,099,200
Peas, seed	890,600
Live horses	860,600
Sugar of milk	795,000
Peas, food	662,600
Gold	622,800
Frozen vegetables	559,000
Whale oil	444,800
Other paper and paper board	397,000
timber, for cases in shooks	383,600
Oppossum skins	327,800
Textile waste	305,200
Other preserved meat	297,000
Cut tobacco	253,000
Eggs, not in shell	237,800
Meat, extract	206,400
Dairy machinery	198,400
Onions	186,600
Lard	175,800
Coal	158,000
Potatoes	155,000
Liver meal	126,200
Deer skins	122,400
Soaps	119,800
Edible Stearine	117,400
Infant and invalid food(cereal)	115,000
Honey	108,000
Canned vegetables	106,800
Neatsfoot oil	103,400
Fish oils and fish liver oils	68,000
Other seeds	67,200
Ale, beer, stout	63,500
Pears	62,200

Live sheep	59,200
Chamois leather	53,200
Biscuits	40,800
Fish, other	40,600

Total Exports of New Zealand produce   624,272,000

NEW ZEALAND

1970 EXPORTS - MAJOR COMMODITIES (June year)

COMMODITIES	($NZ)
Meat, frozen and chilled	364,774,000
Wool	204,465,000
Butter	109,695,000
Cheese	44,343,000
Milk, dried and condensed	31,357,000
Casein	25,753,000
Logs, radiata pine	23,459,000
Newsprint	15,846,000
Sausage casings	13,495,000
Crayfish	11,336,000
Cattle hides	10,326,000
Sawn timber	9,714,000
Apples	8,724,000
Inedible tallow	8,382,000
Wood pulp	7,229,000
Inedible offals (incl. dried blood)	6,665,000
Other agricultural products	5,597,000
Other paper and paper board	4,535,000
Live horses	3,820,000
Seeds, grass and clover	3,576,000
Meat, canned	3,224,000
Frozen vegetables	2,895,000
Calf skins	2,891,000
Fish, fresh or frozen	2,856,000
Other pastoral products	2,796,000
Drinking Chocolate	2,175,000
Sugar of milk	2,144,000
Scarp metal	1,911,000
Peas, food	1,714,000
Biscuits	1,627,000
Peas, seed	1,470,000
Dairy machinery	1,209,000
Canned vegetables	1,090,000
Other preserved meat	990,000
fish, other	917,000
Other dairy produce	832,000
Onions	819,000
Live cattle	752,000
Edible tallow	630,000
Building board	587,000
Pears	509,000
Potatoes	493,000
Other seeds	474,000
Ale, beer, stout	449,000
Plywood	416,000
Soaps	312,000
Cigarettes	305,000
Timber, for cases in shooks	280,000
Meat extract	280,000
Honey	262,000
Textile waste	257,000
Deer skins	202,000
Cut tobacco	190,000
Chamois leather	175,000

Total Exports of New Zealand produce	1,064,466,000

1980 EXPORTS - MAJOR COMMODITIES (June year)

COMMODITIES	($NZ)
Wool, Scoured	516,665,000
Beef boneless	478,498,000
Lamb Carcasses	373,022,000
Wool, Greay	366,921,000
Butter	360,607,000
Aluminium, unwrought	151,115,000
Skimmed milk powder	119,199,000
Casein	112,522,000
Cheese	105,861,000
Mutton	97,704,000
Other Dried	91,153,000
Newsprint	80,988,000
Wood pulp, Sulphate, not dissolving grades	76,571,000
Other Meat and edible offals	71,285,000
Sawlogs and veneer logs, conifer	68,741,000
Lamb pelts	63,909,000
Fish, fresh, chilled or frozen	62,250,000
Wool, Slipe	47,174,000
Wood Pulp, Mechanical	43,265,000
Tallow, inedible	42,194,000
Carpets and carpeting (revised)	41,651,000
Petroleum products, Residual fuel oil	38,711,000
Yarn of wool or hair	36,200,000
Apples, fresh, whole fruit	35,752,000
Kiwifruit	34,526,000
Sheep pelts	34,302,000
Sausage casings, natural	33,481,000
Kraft paper and Kraft cardboard	32,277,000
Hides, skins & furskins, undressed, cattle	29,789,000
Timber, sawn, sliced or peeled, Pinus Radiata	29,239,000
Iron ore and conentrates	29,230,000
Crayfish, fresh and simply preserved	28,351,000
Petroleum products, Distillate fuel	26,800,000
Beef bone in	26,622,000
Opossum skins	23,422,000
Veal	23,307,000
Race Horses	23,298,000
Iron or steel, universal, plates, and sheets	17,822,000
Caseinates	17,560,000
Iron or steel, bars, rods, angles, etc.	17,244,000
Domestic electric refrigerators and freezes	16,703,000
Meal of meat, fish, etc	16,393,000
Sheep and Lamb skins in fleece	16,012,000
Marfarine and shortening	15,193,000
Clover and grass seeds	13,990,000
Calf and kip skins	11,757,000
Barley, unmilled	11,505,000
Lamb boneless	11,475,000
Peas, Dry incl. split	10,659,000
Other Kinds, feeding stuff for animals	10,468,000
Chocolate and preparations	7,901,000
Timber, sawn, sliced or peeled, Douglas Fir	7,821,000
Finished structural parts & structures, n.e.s, of metal	6,418,000
Onions, fresh	6,201,000
Peas, frozen	6,174,000
Vegetables, frozen, excl. peas	6,049,000
Other Kinds	5,142,000
Peas, for sowing	4,613,000
Maize, unmilled	3,875,000
Lucerne meal and pellats	3,063,000
Total Exports of New Zealand produce	5,012,453,000

NEW ZEALAND

1989 EXPORTS - MAJOR COMMODITIES (June year)

COMMODITIES	($NZ)
Beef, boneless	1,215,620,000
Wool, scoured	1,079,467,000
Aluminium, unwrought	775,214,000
Wool, greasy	651,764,000
Butter	609,214,000
Other dried milk powder	540,313,000
Lamb cuts, bone & boneless	492,030,000
Kiwifruit	455,110,000
Skimmed milk powder	368,651,000
Lamb carcasses	363,715,000
cheese	319,819,000
Lamb pelts	288,114,000
Casein	260,344,000
Wood pulp, chemical (not dissolving)	245,586,000
Fish, other	185,338,000
Fish, orange roughy	171,090,000
Iron & steel, plates, sheets etc.	165,038,000
Apples, fresh	154,940,000
Wood pulp, mechanical	153,237,000
Mutton	152,064,000
Newsprint	149,517,000
Horses	146,173,000
Other meat & edible offals	130,968,000
Sawlogs, veneer logs, conifer	128,109,000
Squid	124,176,000
Sausage casings, natural	122,467,000
Pinus radiata, sawn, sliced etc.	120,318,000
Sheep pelts	112,854,000
Yarn of wool or hair	106,524,000
Fibreboard	96,987,000
Caseinates	78,871,000
Fish, surimi	78,421,000
Crayfish	73,337,000
Tallow, inedible	69,658,000
Wool, slipe	64,658,000
Kraft paper, kraft cardboard	61,523,000
Meal of meat, fish	57,823,000
Chocolate & preparations	55,408,000
Fish, hoki	54,868,000
Crude petroleum	52,814,000
Fish, snapper	47,380,000
Domestic refrigerators, freezers	40,888,000
Veal	35,205,000
Wood chips	32,196,000
Asparagus	30,393,000
Beef, bone in	28,348,000
Squash & similar gourds	27,261,000
Mussels	26,604,000
Aluminium foil	25,604,000
Veges., frozen (excl. peas, asparagus)	25,023,000
Peas, dry (incl. split)	23,637,000
Metal structures, parts	23,302,000
Douglas fir, sawn, sliced etc.	23,031,000
Clover & grass seeds	21,625,000
Onions, fresh	21,138,000

Peas, frozen	20,761,000
Sheep and lamb skins in fleece	20,732,000
Urea	19,491,000
Barley, unmilled	19,044,000
Iron ore & concentrates	16,665,000

Total Exports of New Zealand produce 14,484,344,000

NEW ZEALAND

1950 IMPORTS - MAJOR COMMODITIES (December year)

COMMODITIES	($NZ)
Machinery	55,216,634
Textile piece-goods and drapery	48,899,188
Vehicles and rubber tires	27,606,502
Foodstuffs of vegetable origin	25,160,482
Metals	23,838,398
Oils, greases, waxes and inedible fats	23,478,480
Metal manufactures(other than machinery)	14,555,972
Manfactured fibres and misc. textile manufactures	12,622,116
Paper	8,207,880
Chemicals, drugs and druggists' wares	7,861,882
Apparel, footwear and minor articles therefor	7,431,436
Miscellaneous	7,210,592
Manures	6,136,870
Beverages (non-alcoholic), raw materials therefor	5,258,236
Stationery and paper manufactures	5,117,034
China- , earthen- , glass- and stone-wear	4,658,712
Optical, surgical, dental instruments, photographic goods	4,229,788
Vegetable substances and manufactured fibres	3,681,826
Tobacco and manufactures thereof	3,654,270
Rubber and rubber manufactures n.e.i	3,240,588
Fancy goods, jewellery, sporting requisites & timepieces	2,902,826
Spirits and alcoholic beverages	2,676,922
Timber	2,385,368
Foodstuffs of animal origin	2,147,424
Paints, colours and varnishes	1,896,634
Stone, earth, ores and non-metallic minerals	1,743,388
Animal substances, inedible	1,679,358
Leather and leather manufactures n.e.i	1,532,752
Wood, cave and wicker manufactures	519,182
Live animals, birds and fish	335,012
Total produce imported	315,885,752

NEW ZEALAND

1960 IMPORTS - MAJOR COMMODITIES (December year)

COMMODITIES	($NZ)
Base metals	60,690,010
Machinery other than electric	76,033,272
Textile yarn, fabrics, made-up articles and related products	73,427,754
Mineral fuel, lubricants, and materials	52,007,544
Transport equipment	45,031,602
Electric machinery, apparatus and appliances	31,981,806
Manufacture of metal	24,541,232
Miscellaneous manufactured articles n.e.i	21,418,390
Paper, paperboard and manufactures thereof	14,957,734
Explosives and miscellaneous chemical materials and products	14,295,814
Crude fertilisers and crude minerals excl. coal, petroleum and precious stone	13,719,160
Fruits and vegetables	11,680,714
Chemical elements and compunds	11,637,890
Coffee, tea, cocoa, spices and manufactures thereof	10,401,808
Prof., scientific & controlling instruments, photographic & optical goods watches, clocks	10,040,802
Non-metallic mineral manufactures n.e.i	9,486,262
Cereals and cereals preparations	8,627,968
Medicinal and pharmaceutical products	8,262,692
Sugar and sugar preparations	7,010,318
Wood, lumber and cork	6,224,388
Crude rubber, including synthetic and reclaimed	5,687,788
Beverages	4,963,440
Fertilisers, manufactured	4,188,372
Tobacco and tobacco manufactures	4,108,990
Dyeing, tanning and colouring materials	3,558,170
Rubber manufactures n.e.i	3,521,496
Textile fibres (not manufactured into yarns, thread of fabics) and waste	3,337,742
Clothing	2,836,436
Unclassified goods under $20 in value	2,776,730
Leather, leather manufactures n.e.i and dressed furs	2,258,730
Fish and fish preparations	1,982,820
Animal and vegetable crude materials n.e.i	1,920,640
Silver, platinum, gems and jewellery	1,552,928
Prefabricated buildings, sanitary, plumbing, heating and lighting fixtures and fittings	1,434,882
Wood and cork manufactures (excluding furniture)	1,338,128
Oil seeds, oil nuts and kernels	1,301,176
Pulp and waste paper	1,208,294
Animal and vegetalbe oils(not essential) fats,greases and derivatives	1,078,168
Footwear	977,984
Essential oils and perfume materials, toilet, polishing and cleansing preparations	964,884
Meat and meat preparations	463,434
Mineral tar and crude chemicals from coal, petroleum and natural gas	324,436
Live animals not for food	253,982
Furniture and fixtures	222,384
Miscellaneous food preparations	193,598
Returned goods and special transactions	184,022
Gold	159,752
HIdes, skins and fur skins undressed	129,566
Live animals chiefly for food	104,034
Metalliferous ores and scrap metal	46,694
Feeding stuff for animals (not including unmilled cereals)	37,550
Travel goods, handbags and similar articles	24,428
Dairy produce, eggs and honey	11,544
Total produce imported	509,170,000

NEW ZEALAND

1970 IMPORTS - MAJOR COMMODITIES (June year)

COMMODITIES	($NZ)
Transport equipment	137,260,000
Machinery other than electric	131,377,000
Textile yarn, fabrics, made-up articles and related products	93,313,000
Iron and Steel	79,751,000
Petroleum and petroleum products	75,253,000
Electric machinery, apparatus and appliances	55,660,000
Non-ferrous metals	41,894,000
Miscellaneous manufactured articles n.e.s	35,430,000
Crude fertilisers and crude minerals exc. coal, petroleum and precious stone	34,387,000
Chemical elements and compounds	33,455,000
Manfactures of metals	31,910,000
Prof., scientific & controlling instruments; photographic & optical goods watches, clocks	25,814,000
Plastic materials,regenerated cellulose, artificial	25,611,000
Medicinal and pharmaceutical products	20,752,000
Coffee, tea, cocoa, spices and manufactures thereof	17,749,000
Miscellaneous chemical materials and products	17,308,000
Fruit and vegetables	15,846,000
Non-metallic mineral manufactures, n.e.s	13,424,000
Paper, paperboard and manufactures thereof	11,984,000
Sugar and sugar preparations	11,899,000
Textile fibres (not manufactured into thread, yarn or fabrics) and waste	8,317,000
Crude rubber, including synthetic and reclaimed	8,207,000
Dyeing, tanning and colouring materials	7,578,000
Fertilisers, manufactured	7,487,000
Rubber manufactures, n.e.s	7,277,000
Wood and Cork	6,764,000
Beverages	4,920,000
Animal and vegetable crude materials n.e.s	4,657,000
Tobacco and tobacco manufactures	4,631,000
Arms of war and ammunition therefor	4,163,000
Essential oils and perfume materials, toilet, polishing and cleaning preparations	3,761,000
Clothing	3,206,000
Wood and cork manufactures (excluding furniture)	2,910,000
Live animals	2,850,000
Cereals and cereal preparation	2,784,000
Pulp and waste paper	2,164,000
Fish and fish preparations	2,152,000
Oil seeds, oil nuts and oil kernals	2,005,000
Explosives	1,792,000
Vegetable oils and fats, unprocessed	1,671,000
Vegetable oils and fats, unprocessed	1,671,000
Leather, leather manufactures, n.e.s and dressed furs	1,617,000
Footwear	1,574,000
Sanitary, plumbing, heating and lighting fixtures and fittings	982,000
Coin (except gold coin) not being legal tender	666,000
Hides, skins and fur skins undressed	597,000
Miscellanous food preparations	566,000
Mineral tar and crude chemicals from coal, petroleum and natural gas	521,000
Furniture and fixtures	280,000
Feeding stuff for animals (not including unmilled cereals)	262,000
Metalliferous ores and metal scrap	238,000
Animal and vegetable oils & fats processed, & waxes of animal or vegetable origin	228,000
Dairy products and eggs	153,000
Gas	150,000
Travel goods, handbags and similar articles	137.000
Animal oils and fats	68,000
Live animals n.e.s including zoo animals and animals of a kind commonly kept as pets	20,000
Coal, coke and briquettes	6,000
Total produce imported	1,007,198,000

NEW ZEALAND

1980 IMPORTS - MAJOR COMMODITIES (June year)

COMMODITIES	($NZ)
Crude petroleum	397,291,000
Motor cars, unassembled	210,115,000
Partly refined petroleum	184,670,000
Motor spirit	173,840,000
Iron or Steel, universals, plates and sheets	170,874,000
Distillate fuels	117,498,000
Kerosine and white spirit	101,161,000
Other plastic materials, regenated cellulose, artificial resins	74,008,000
Natural calcium phosphate	68,127,000
Tractors	64,392,000
Paper and paperboard manufactures	55,921,000
Textile yarn and thread	54,336,000
Aluminium oxide	48,299,000
Sugar, not refined	45,472,000
Crde rubber, including synthetic and reclaimed	35,026,000
Copper and copper alloys excl. foils, powders & flskes	34,973,000
Coffee, raw	29,528,000
Motor Cycles	28,438,000
Internal combustion engines, not aircraft	25,371,000
Iron or Steel, bars and rods	23,930,000
Iron or Steel, tubes, pipes and fittings	21,553,000
Textile fibres, unmanufactured and waste	21,091,000
Unwrought zinc	18,730,000
Iron or Steel, wire	18,004,000
Vegetable oils and fats unprocessed	17,868,000
Sulphar, other than sublimed, precipitated	17,829,000
Iron or Steel, angles, shapes and sections	16,828,000
Tobacco, unmanufactured	16,096,000
Tea	15,333,000
Rubber tyres and tubes, exclude bicycle	14,567,000
Cocoa beans, raw or roasted	14,220,000
Potassium chloride (fertiliser)	12,030,000
Polymerisation, copolymerisation products in bulk form	11,755,000
Bananas	9,564,000
Domestic sewing machines	9,088,000
Canned pineapples	8,766,000
Oranges	7,049,000
Motor cars, assembled	4,337,000
Rice	3,870,000
Bicycles	525,000
Total produce imported	5,172,607,000

NEW ZEALAND

1989 IMPORTS - MAJOR COMMODITIES (June Year)

COMMODITIES	($NZ)
Motor cars, assembled & unassembled	991,817,000
Crude petroleum	473,355,000
Paper & paperboard manufactures	224,001,000
Trucks, vans, assembled, unassembled	212,769,000
Aluminium oxide	206,159,000
Iron & steel plates, sheets etc.	177,010,000
Polyethelene	126,956,000
Copper & copper alloys	107,797,000
Textile yarn and thread	106,596,000
Motor spirit	78,524,000
Video recording apparatus	70,311,000
Internal combustion engines	54,762,000
Natural calcium phosphate	54,571,000
Knitted or crocheted fabrics	52,666,000
Iron & steel tubes, pipes, fittings	52,488,000
Unwrought zinc	51,449,000
Polyvinyl chloride	48,902,000
Sugar, not refined	48,006,000
Iron & steel bars and rods	41,214,000
Photocopying apparatus	40,158,000
Bananas, fresh	38,766,000
Crude rubber, synthetic & reclaimed	35,837,000
Microwave ovens	32,551,000
Fruit and vegetable juices	32,323,000
Typewriting, calculating machines	31,842,000
Petroleum coke	30,249,000
Motor cycles	29,864,000
Tractors	27,974,000
Rubber tyres, new, for buses & trucks	25,168,000
Polystyrene and co-polymers	25,052,000
Phosphatic fertilisers	23,903,000
Float glass	23,726,000
Tobacco, unmanufactured	22,884,000
Iron & steel wire	22,828,000
Polypropylene	22,757,000
Potassic fertilisers	22,219,000
Rubber tyres, new, for cars	22,011,000
Sulphur	21,780,000
Iron & steel angles, shapes etc.	21,481,000
Coffee, raw	17,845,000
Bicycles	17,738,000
Oranges, fresh or dried	16,290,000
Other fertilisers	15,866,000
Salmon, canned or in jars	15,234,000
Cocoa paste and cocoa butter	13,295,000
Tea	13,285,000
canned pineapples	13,165,000
Domestic sewing machines	12,227,000
Rice	11,263,000
Nitrogenous fertilisers	7,530,000
Distillate fuels	3,089,000
Rubber tyres, new, for motor cycles	2,857,000
Total produce imported	12,491,430,000

NEW ZEALAND

1950 EXPORTS - MAJOR TRADING PARTNERS (December year)

COUNTRY	($NZ)
United Kingdom	242,686,868
United States of America	36,737,458
France	16,122,634
Federal Republic of Germany	11,877,730
Australia	9,052,572
Canada	7,107,926
Netherlands	6,838,440
Belgium	5,903,274
Italy	3,794,144
Poland	3,127,156
Russia (U.S.S.R)	2,069,174
Czechoslovakia	2,008,540
Japan	1,997,656
Denmark	1,800,582
India	1,518,364
Yugoslavia	1,171,388
British West Indies	1,126,054
Greece	903,014
Sweden	781,276
Mexico	726,606
Malaya	674,908
Norway	567,780
Union of South Africa	559,696
Fiji	485,294
Netherlands Antilles	417,228
Pakistan	404,768
Western Samoa	375,382
Irish Republic	370,344
Austria	367,172
Egypt	306,234
Panama Republic	300,866
Iran	254,940
Society Islands	198,938
Hong Kong	182,292
Switzerland	154,856
Tutuila (American Samoa)	138,844
Tonga	128,822
Saudi Arabia	124,632
Thailand	124,124
Philippine Islands	121,686
Gilbert and Ellice Islands	84,158
Tuamotu Archipelago	79,548
Turkey	74,720
Finland	73,036
British Guiana	61,018
Panama Canal Zone	58,892
Burma	53,888
Nauru	47,930
British West Africa	47,334
Norfolk Islands	14,632
Total exports of New Zealand produce	364,664,302

NEW ZEALAND

1960 EXPORTS - MAJOR TRADING PARTNERS (December year)

COUNTRY	($NZ)
United Kingdom	319,787,438
United States of America	76,505,924
France and Monaco	40,570,096
Australia	24,991,702
German Federal Republic	21,230,190
Japan	17,775,600
Belgium and Luxemburg	15,346,498
Italy and San Marino	15,134,096
Philippines	12,296,105
Netherlands	8,307,412
Canada	7,270,852
Union of Soviet Socialist Republics	5,021,374
Poland	4,752,770
China	4,670,434
Czechoslovakia	3,500,552
Jamaica	3,121,220
Hawaii	2,148,348
Trinidad and Tobago	2,133,934
India	2,060,700
Sweden	1,619,116
South Africa	1,610,214
Western Samoa	1,434,952
Peru	1,256,190
Portugal	1,067,198
Venezuela	1,039,732
Denmark	1,031,298
Singapore	975,374
Hong Kong	952,142
Ceylon	922,306
Fiji	879,906
Malaya	855,448
Greece	745,842
Panama Republic	581,598
Ireland Republic of	546,734
Netherlands Antilles	522,484
Tonga	515,972
Egypt	514,182
Barbados	452,974
Yugoslavia	439,280
Bulgaria	391,394
Finland	388,582
Bermuda	385,556
Burma	276,640
American Samoa	272,160
German Democratic Republic	263,370
Society Islands	244,738
Kenya and Uganda	241,698
Mexico	231,826
Norway	217,692
Federation of Rhodesias and Nyasaland	197,270

Total exports of New Zealand produce   624,272,000

NEW ZEALAND

1970 EXPORTS - MAJOR TRADING PARTNERS (June year)

COUNTRY	($NZ)
United Kingdom	383,395,882
U.S.A	164,747,221
Japan	104,921,231
Australia	80,896,431
Canada	45,230,559
Germany, Federal Rep.	29,363,652
France	28,662,954
Italy	23,667,826
Belgium	21,226,200
U.S.S.R	16,934,493
Netherlands	15,987,946
Singapore	8,551,135
Greece	8,467,159
Fiji	7,672,847
Malaysia	7,238,928
Philippines	6,085,733
Hong Kong	4,517,644
Spain	4,474,530
Jamaica	4,436,019
Trinidad and Tobago	4,435,650
China, Peoples Republic	4,076,836
French Polynesia	3,841,331
Yugoslavia	3,720,466
Thailand	3,148,952
Poland	3,128,536
South Africa	3,123,464
Taiwan	3,067,232
New Caledonia	3,028,780
Czechoslovakia	2,756,182
Samoa	2,713,849
Papua New Guinea	2,641,119
Sweden	2,566,869
Denmark	2,438,253
American Samoa	2,190,598
Switzerland	2,091,607
Sri Lanka	2,048,405
Ireland	1,987,381
Pakistan	1,831,865
Portugal	1,797,669
Barbados	1,750,343
Korea, Republic of	1,606,040
Tonga	1,486,775
Bermuda	1,412,060
Iran (Islamic rep.)	1,318,493
India	1,315,916
Guam	1,302,638
Mexico	1,254,813
Kenya	1,222,878
Bangladesh	1,202,027
Norway	1,198,118
Total Exports of N.Z. produce	1,064,466,000

NEW ZEALAND

1980 EXPORTS - MAJOR TRADING PARTNERS (June year)

COUNTRY	($NZ)
United Kingdom	709,755,833
U.S.A	691,297,853
Japan	633,966,615
Australia	604,941,957
U.S.S.R	250,919,008
Iran (Islamic Rep.)	129,586,078
Italy	128,225,597
France	126,423,251
China, Peoples Republic	117,366,772
Germany, Federal Rep.	115,610,277
Canada	97,411,362
Netherlands	83,446,800
Hong Kong	78,275,195
Singapore	69,911,702
Philippines	67,811,858
Fiji	64,144,422
Korea, Republic of	64,031,123
Indonesia	60,306,887
Malaysia	57,667,478
Greece	55,244,017
Belgium	51,756,959
Taiwan	47,204,767
Iraq	38,269,855
Saudi Arabia	35,803,585
Papua New Guinea	34,189,071
Thailand	27,393,693
Peru	26,172,207
Spain	23,286,000
Mexico	21,703,735
French Polynesia	21,667,853
Samoa	17,356,404
Pakistan	16,266,557
Czechoslovakia	15,940,321
Dest. unknown E.C.	15,547,204
Yugoslavia	14,087,804
New Caledonia	14,034,194
Egypt	13,367,764
American Samoa	12,929,619
Mauritius	12,407,316
Poland	12,381,119
United Arab Emirates	12,227,039
Switzerland	11,857,176
Venezuela	11,848,258
Ireland	11,285,795
India	10,967,748
Argentina	10,261,547
South Africa	10,259,782
Trinidad and Tobago	9,778,258
Tonga	9,762,459
Nigeria	8,730,070
Total Exports of N.Z. produce	5,012,453,000

NEW ZEALAND

1989 EXPORTS - MAJOR TRADING PARTNERS (June year)

COUNTRY	($NZ)
Japan	2,655,637,872
Australia	2,424,079,416
U.S.A	1,912,856,773
United Kingdom	1,009,738,775
China, Peoples Rep.	537,736,345
Korea, Republic of	466,682,839
U.S.S.R.	351,342,894
Italy	316,331,735
Germany, Federal Rep.	302,677,365
Belgium	302,418,665
Taiwan	279,980,311
Canada	256,380,814
Malaysia	245,613,332
Hong Kong	241,236,137
France	202,425,134
Netherlands	167,291,179
Singapore	160,199,611
Philippines	158,724,214
Destination Unknown E.C.	152,080,379
Indonesia	147,251,153
Mexico	139,652,784
Iran	130,542,408
Fiji	119,632,735
Saudi Arabia	115,012,008
Venezuela	114,229,471
Thailand	106,220,409
Spain	95,259,446
India	83,683,045
Papua New Guinea	76,091,364
Greece	58,253,391
French Polynesia	49,188,123
Pakistan	47,242,194
Switzerland	44,726,757
United Arab Emirates	33,438,272
New Caledonia	30,998,489
Sweden	29,941,161
Denmark	29,740,065
South Africa	29,674,434
Egypt	29,562,190
Sri Lanka	29,354,401
Turkey	26,957,797
Samoa	26,523,138
Jamaica	25,981,528
Jordan	23,389,125
Cook Islands	23,221,653
Mauritius	22,985,488
Peru	22,944,301
Ireland	22,293,015
Dominican Republic	21,452,702
Czechoslovakia	21,140,066
Total Exports of N.Z. produce	14,484,344,000

GP PRINT LTD 1991